ROBERT MOSS

The Collapse of Democracy

TEMPLE SMITH · LONDON

First published in Great Britain 1975
by Maurice Temple Smith Ltd
37 Great Russell Street, London WC1
© Copyright 1975 ROBERT MOSS
ISBN 0 8511 7088 9
Printed photolitho in Great Britain by
Ebenezer Baylis & Son Ltd
The Trinity Press, Worcester, and London

CONTENTS

Introduction   *page*   7

1   Letter from London, 1985   21

2   From Liberal to Mass Democracy   36

3   The Nature of Subversion   56

4   The Disease of Money   77

5   In Fear of Strikes   97

6   The Necessity of Property   118

7   Pseudo-Legality and Revolution   137

8   The Prague Model   162

9   Lessons from Chile   175

10   The Portuguese Way   192

11   The Limits of Tolerance   213

12   Violence and the State   225

13   The Need for the 'People's Veto'   236

14   In Defence of Liberty   248

15   The Logic of Breakdown   262

Acknowledgments   280

Notes   281

Index   293

Introduction

The first chapter of this book is fantasy: a picture of what Britain might become ten years from now (or sooner?) transformed from a free society into the drab Utopia of a minor civil servant, a country Communist in all but name. Much of the remainder of the book is theory: an attempt to determine the conditions for a free society and the way that liberal democracy can evolve into mass democracy, to end up, perhaps, as no sort of democracy at all. But I have included enough facts—the thumb-prints of our own times as well as the memory of how other democratic societies have succumbed to totalitarian or authoritarian solutions—to show that the theory is relevant to the condition of Britain today, and that the fantasy is more than mere fantasy.

Only a very bushy-tailed optimist or someone who has been living in Majorca for the past ten years without access to the world press would say that there is *no chance at all* of my fantasy turning into reality. Not precisely, of course, in the way that I have imagined, but along recognisably similar lines. We can debate whether there is only a ten per cent probability that the breakdown will take place, or whether the odds have narrowed to say, four to one or three to one against. But surely the danger is real enough, even in this motherland of Parliaments, to make it essential for those who do not share the goals of the Minister of Equality in my fictional quasi-Communist government to look to their defences.

My argument proceeds from a number of assumptions that are likely to prove highly controversial, so it may be as well to state the more important ones briefly at the very beginning. The first is that democracy is not a particular form of society, and still less an ideology. It is a mechanism for appointing and removing governments through majority decision. It is, of course, a mechanism that is subject to constant redesign and alteration. It is also, as a distinguished British social democrat put it, 'a *method* of taking political decisions, of compromising and reconciling conflicting interests'.[1] It is possibly the best method that has so far been devised for reducing political violence and for creating a broad social consensus within which conflict can be contained.

Now the mechanistic analogy is hardly a satisfactory one and should not be swallowed whole in a country like Britain, where political institutions were not invented in a flash, but evolved over a very long period.[2] The point I wish to make is that those institutions—the democratic mechanism—can be exploited by the advocates of many contending ideologies and of many different forms of society. No one can afford to remain ignorant of the fact that *democracy can be destroyed through its own institutions.* In 411 BC, during the hardships of the Peloponnesian war, the Athenian assembly was won over to the argument of the oligarch Pisander that 'what we have to think about is survival, not the form of our constitution'.[3] The freemen of Athens voted to abolish democracy. The oligarchy that was then set up was quickly overthrown, but this classic example of how the enemies of democracy were able to use the opportunities provided by the system in order to destroy it has been repeated on several notable occasions in modern times—by the Nazis in Germany, for example, and by the communists in Czechoslovakia and Chile. The enemies of democracy understand very well that in an advanced and highly politicised society, they can win only if they preserve some of the democratic appearances. But we should also take note that we have supplied them with more opportunities than we can afford to keep open.

This leads on to my second assumption: that what is really at stake is the survival of the kind of society and the kind of public philosophy that make democratic institutions meaningful The apparatus of elections and referenda is retained in many dictatorships. But only a few fellow-travellers of the most hypocritical kind would make out, for example, that the April 1975 elections in North Vietnam (in which most of the successful candidates won over ninety-five per cent of the votes recorded) were democratic. It is perfectly obvious to (almost) everyone that the existence of a political opposition is basic to democracy.

But the survival of democracy depends on the dispersal of power in a much broader sense, and it is when people try to define just what that means that the real arguments begin. It seems to me perfectly clear that you cannot hope to enjoy political democracy for long if economic democracy—which, in its true sense, involves the maintenance of a strong private sector—is lost; if the press is gagged, or if a monopoly social pressure group is able to assert its own interests at the expense of the community at large. Nor can you hope to enjoy political democracy for long in the absence of a public philosophy, an underlying consensus about the values and purposes of society. As Walter Lippmann put it, 'liberal democracy is not an intelligent form of government and cannot be made to work except by men who possess the philosophy in which liberal democracy was conceived and founded'.[4] The public philosophy is not something that is written out on a bit of paper by an inspired thinker: it is founded on the cumulation of social conventions and moral beliefs over many generations. The community as a whole is the guardian of these conventions—or should be. The problem is that in Britain, as in other places, disciplined minorities moved by radical ideologies and an equally radical contempt for the past have successfully overruled the conventions of the great majority. This will be a recurring theme in my book, together with the argument that social health will depend on finding more ways to reassert the will of the majority.

The idea of a public philosophy involves the idea of a tacit agreement about the *limits* of politics. Another basic condition for a free society is that those who succeed in politics must accept the idea that there are a large number of things that are *beyond* politics: for example, that a democratic government cannot properly set out to abolish democracy, or ban religious beliefs, or destroy the family, or (and here the list becomes more controversial) deny the right to own and bequeath property or to exercise individual choice in crucial areas of social life such as health and education. A government that sets out to interfere in such areas is a totalitarian government that may preserve the democratic mechanism - at least for a time - but will certainly destroy what is left of the free society.

My third proposition is that the threat from totalitarian movements and ideologies (which are not always recognised for what they are) is rapidly increasing, and that subversion—which is defined in a later chapter—must be counted as one of the primary threats to democracy in Britain today. I would argue that the weapons used by those who set out to destroy the free society can also be used by those who wish to defend it—not only *can,* but in some cases *must* be used if the society under attack is to survive. Those who have passed through the inferno of revolution and totalitarian dictatorship understand this principle far better than those who have not. The Federal Republic of Germany, conscious of how Hitler came to power, made it a cardinal principle of its new constitution that there could be no freedom to oppose freedom. We shall have to explore what that concept means in a later section. It is enough for now to say that, while tolerance is one of the signal virtues of a free society, it can also prove to be a crippling weakness if it is not always remembered that totalitarian movements should be tolerated only *on sufferance*—that is, if they spread their wings too far, they will need to be clipped.

My final proposition is one on which I would ask the reader to reserve judgement until he has pieced his way through this book. It is that, in the event that a democratic society breaks down irretrievably, it has *two* alternatives to anarchy, not one: the choice is then between authoritarian or totalitarian rule. The semantic confusion characteristic of much public debate has often blurred the distinction between these two fundamentally different types of regime. The characteristic of authoritarian rule is that it substitutes the authority of a self-appointed (or hereditary) elite for the political process, without directly interfering in many areas of social, intellectual and economic life. Under an authoritarian regime, you are forbidden to engage in politics, but you may well be allowed to travel and marry as you please, to set up any kind of business, to live wherever you choose, and study courses in economics or political science indentical to what might be offered in a democratic country (except at Marxist-run universities like Bremen). A totalitarian regime also substitutes the authority of a self-appointed elite for the political process. But here, politics intrudes on everything: there is no escape, in ideas, economics or life-style, from the politico/bureaucratic conformity imposed by the ruling ideology. This is a distinction we shall need to examine in later pages.[5] It means that, if a society collapses, the subsequent choice of evils may genuinely be a choice between the greater and the lesser evil.

There may well be no return from the long dark night of a totalitarian dictatorship, short of defeat of that dictatorship in war. An authoritarian regime, in contrast, is likely to be less durable because of the liberties it leaves intact and may in some cases amount to no more than a holding operation: an attempt to pick up the pieces after a social explosion.

It is not a choice that will appeal to anyone who believes, as I do, that the only society worth living in is a society that values individual freedom. But it is hardly worth examining the causes of the collapse of democracy without also looking at the costs—and the prospects of building something from the rubble that would offer more to liberty and social creativity than the totalitarians have ever been willing to offer. A society confronted with disaster must spare a thought for workable 'post-disaster systems'—to use Brian Crozier's phrase. But the tremendous strength of the democratic tradition and the liberal cause is far from exhausted. Many of the fortresses that have been lost were simply abandoned; it will be necessary to do battle for those that remain.

It will be clear already that this book is not just about Britain, although a great part of it is addressed to Britain, and although Britain supplies a better contemporary example of some of its central propositions—about how democracies break down—than any other advanced western society with the sole exception of Italy. But I hope that readers elsewhere—despite differences in constitutions, party organisation, relative economic stability or the social power of groups such as the trade unions—will find that at least some of those propositions have a general application. My book ranges widely over time and space in the attempt to identify the conditions for the collapse of democratic societies. It is not suggested that there is any inevitability about such breakdowns; there are no general laws. But there are certainly general lessons to be drawn. It is clear that situations can develop—a hyper-inflation, a prolonged campaign of terrorism and subversion, or the rise of a totalitarian movement with a mass following, for example— which provide a severe test for democratic institutions. It is clear that a society that expends its energies in redistributing wealth instead of creating it will succumb to stagnation and eventually fail to satisfy the very expectations of wealth without work that it has encouraged. In such situations, the notorious tendency of routine politicians to flatter the electorate with the notion that there is always a soft option will damage a society's chances of survival. And there is a still more pervasive danger: that egalitarian socialism of the kind that has swayed recent governments in Britain can, if it goes unchecked, eventually knock away the bases for a free society. Bureaucratic conformity will take the place of originality and inventiveness; power will be concentrated in the hands of increasingly unrepresentative minorities. Britain today can indeed be seen as a singularly depressing example of the abuse of democratic institutions by the enemies of the free society.

Britain is remarkable among the advanced industrial democracies in at least two respects. The first involves the extraordinary power that is concentrated in the hands of a single social pressure group, the industrial trade unions. This is particularly marked because of the absence of effective organisations to defend the interests of other economic groups, although there have been recent efforts to create bodies to defend ratepayers and the self-employed, and suggestions that industry might show its 'muscle-power' through a tax strike. The situation is made worse by the disproportionate influence of communists and others who are openly dedicated to the overthrow of the free society within the British trade union movement—and by the special links between that movement and the Labour Party. It was hardly an exaggeration to say that, at the time of writing, every major economic decision made by British politicians was being taken *in fear of the trade unions.* The feeling that a confrontation with the unions must be avoided at any cost—especially in view of the way that the Heath government was said to have been 'defeated' by the miners in February 1974—induced otherwise rational men to acquiesce in decisions that distorted the whole structure of the British economy.

The other singular feature of British political life is the equally exceptional power that is vested in a single political assembly, the House of Commons. In practice, this is qualified only by the countervailing force of the trade unions. It seems to be possible to do almost anything by a simple majority vote in the House of Commons, in the absence of a strong upper house, a written constitution with an entrenched Bill of Rights, and a Supreme Court to rule on the constitutionality or otherwise of new legislation. Any serious programme to resolve the 'British problem' will therefore need to involve (i) an attempt to reassert the rule of law in industrial relations, to reform trade union election procedures and to return the trade unions to their original, and necessary, role in free collective bargaining, which is something different from the relationship between a highwayman and a stagecoach; and (ii) a new constitutional settlement, which should certainly involve an entrenched Bill of Rights. If both are 'politically impossible', as we are frequently told, then you can tell the bookies to lower the odds against the fantasy in Chapter 1 coming to pass.

John Middleton Murry published a book in 1932, in the midst of another great ideological upheaval in Europe, in which he argued the *necessity* of communism in Britain. It would not be the same as Russian Communism. 'Every country', he thought, 'gets the communism it has deserved.' In Britain, communism would not necessarily entail bloody revolution— unless (and he thought it unlikely) a relatively gentle and peace-abiding middle class decided to make armed resistance. It was perfectly plausible, as Engels had suggested, that the social revolution would come about in Britain by entirely peaceful and legal means, through the capture of parliament by a Socialist party that had resolved 'to be on the winning side'. It would proceed to destroy capitalism and the middle class by economic means, and above all by taxation. The short-term effects of its economic programme would appal the economists. 'That they will *appear* disastrous to "economists"—even to Labour "economists"—who cannot free their minds from the unconscious assumptions of economic individualism, is perfectly true. But the mind that cannot free itself from these assumptions is a mind from which we have nothing to expect, and ultimately, nothing to fear.'[6]

Middleton Murry was prescient about many things. Whether he was prescient in his final prediction—that, at the end of the day, the revolution had 'nothing to fear' from the liberal order—is something that the reader will have to decide for himself after weighing the arguments in this book. But surely even the most carefully-contrived democratic institutions are only as strong as the social consensus that underpins them and above all the willingness of those who believe in liberty to fight for it. Parliaments are only painted boards if a society loses its cohesion and its moral courage—and, indeed, the memory of Germany in 1933, of Czechoslovakia in 1948 and of Chile in 1970 is a sufficient reminder that the enemies of democracy can strut before those boards as well as its defenders.

We are in danger of witnessing the same kind of usurpation in Britain. This reflects a serious failure of political leadership. But, contrary to the conventional arguments of the elitist critics of democracy (see Chapter 2) the solution will entail more, not less, public involvement in political decision-making. It is the bureaucratic hold of unrepresentative minorities over much of the trade union apparatus and over the Labour movement as a whole that has exposed Britain to its present economic plight and constitutional danger. This has come about, to a large degree, because of the apathy or blank incomprehension of the great majority, and the failure of those who have their eyes half-open to devise an effective organisational weapon with which to resist. We require a new spirit of 'referendum-mindedness': a greater willingness on the part of ordinary citizens to take an interventionist attitude to the political process. John Stuart Mill's warning to those who elected to live under a representative government is more timely today than when he wrote:

> A people may prefer a free government, but if, from indolence, or carelessness, or cowardice, or want of public spirit, they are unequal to the exertions necessary for preserving it; if they will not fight for it when directly attacked; if they can be deluded by the articles used to cheat them out of it; if by momentary discouragement, or temporary panic, or fit of enthusiasm for an individual, they can be induced to lay their liberties at the feet even of a great man . . . in all these cases they are more or less unfit for liberty: and although it may be for their good to have had it even for a short time, they are unlikely long to enjoy it.[7]

It is a problem of ideas as well as organisation. One of the basic fault-lines in the current debate within Britain, and within the Western societies as a whole, is between individualism (which also involves the defence of the family) and collectivism. This is so obvious that it should scarcely need to be restated. And yet the conventional shorthand of politics, and above all the frequently bogus distinction between right and left, has served to obscure it. The ever-advancing frontiers of state intervention in the economy and in society generally give rise to genuine doubts about the future of pluralist democracy. The connection between economic pluralism and political pluralism is as familiar to Marxists as to classical liberals; it is a symptom of the debasement of much contemporary political discussion that socialists have so often been permitted to brush it aside as irrelevant. The danger is that if Britain carries on much further down the road it is now on, it could be left with a dismal choice between contending forms of socialism: the one that, carried to its logical extreme, can only be called communism and the other that tends towards corporatism (which is what a significant minority of Labour leaders in Britain, if they are honest with themselves, are moving towards).

The one area, ironically, where the power of the state has been dwindling instead of expanding is precisely where it should be strongest: in the realm of defence. And this at a moment when the Western sphere of influence in the world is shrinking fast, and the strategic threat to the European democracies is unparalleled since the rise of Nazi Germany.

'Fear and I were born twins', said Thomas Hobbes, who was born in the year that the Spanish Armada set sail for England, escaped into exile from a regicide civil war and survived to found a bleak but compelling philosophy of politics on his sense of the innate depravity and anarchic tendencies of man.[8] Our age is another of fear and uncertainty, after a quarter-century of peace and prosperity—at any rate for those lucky enough to live in the extreme north-western corner of the Eurasian land-mass or in the continents of Australia and North America. Now our horizons have been abruptly foreshortened. The retreat from empire by the European powers has been followed by a still more rapid retreat from world hegemony by the United States. Events over great swathes of the map—and the control of formerly secure sources of raw materials—have spun out of the control of the Western powers. The Soviet Union has achieved strategic parity with America, and is bent on more than parity. The appeal of pluralist forms of government has waned throughout the developing world, which has been quick to substitute politburos or juntas or down-at-heel one-party socialist systems for the models bequeathed by the departing colonial powers.*

Britain's problem cannot be detached from this shifting balance of power, even if Britain's leaders, growing more insular from day to day, choose to avert their eyes from it. At a polite dinner-party in London in the spring of 1975, a Vietnamese girl whose family had fled from Hanoi two decades before, only to be trapped as the Communist forces closed in on Saigon, turned on the guests and said: 'The question that all of you now have to face is whether the philosophy of the West can survive an enemy who is so much more ruthless and sure in his own beliefs than you.' The issues that were at stake in the Vietnam war, and the rights and wrongs of both the American involvement and the American withdrawal, will be endlessly disputed. The triumph of North Vietnam's war machine, supported by a society fully mobilised by leaders convinced that history was on their side, has encouraged some people to revert, in new phrases, to the old argument that might is right. The failure of South Vietnam's leaders, and the rout of its army, has produced the corresponding argument that the Americans were mad to attempt to try to prop up an alien conception of democracy with such unpromising material.

The spectacle of those sad columns of refugees, fleeing southward and eastward from Hué, Danang, Kontum and Pleiku in a hopeless bid to outpace the invader's army showed that, for the Vietnamese themselves, the issue looked rather different. Hanoi radio put out the story that they were being driven south by the South Vietnamese authorities, just as Hanoi's sympathisers had claimed, during past offensives, that the refugees were running away from the American bombers. But there were no bombers to run away from this time round, and no government authorities with the time or manpower to tell the refugees which way to go. At the end of a war that, in its several phases, had dragged on for nearly three decades, a large part of the population of South Vietnam was still voting with its feet for the possibility of a free society. It was a vote more impressive than any ballot or referendum that

*Although one should not underrate the western legacy. The de facto one-party states characteristic of east Africa and the Indian sub-continent have espoused a kind of redistributionist Socialism that Daniel Moynihan has identified, in a perceptive recent article[6], as characteristically British—the gift of Harold Laski and the London School of Economics of his day.

had taken place, but a vote that could in no way determine who was to govern South Vietnam.

The words of a Vietnamese exile, which strangely echo those of successive waves of refugees from the East—Russians, Czechs, Hungarians, Cubans—may be shrugged off as the unreliable evidence of 'professional anti-communists'. Who are they to discuss the 'philosophy of the West' anyway?

Well, there are lessons to be drawn from such 'far-off places', and some of them may help to determine the truth or otherwise of a remarkable prophecy that was made by one of the epigones of post-war British socialism, the late Richard Crossman. In an article written for a popular tabloid in 1965, Crossman suggested that 'the second half of the twentieth century will see the West go into a peaceful decline, while the world is united under communist leadership'.[10] With a quarter of the century still to run, it might be premature to dismiss Crossman's view of the future as a silly rhetorical extravagance. Over the decade since he wrote, the West has suffered a series of notable reverses. America's failure in Indochina and the initial inability of the Nato alliance to prevent one of its smaller members, Portugal, from being sucked into the Soviet sphere of influence are perhaps the ones that will have the most enduring effects. But, more generally, there has been a process of turning inwards, first perceptible in Western Europe after Suez, now equally apparent in the rebirth of isolationism in the United States.

The retreat of American power and the reluctance of West European governments to contemplate a world role and even to pay for their own defences cannot be explained by any supposed lack of resources, technology or manpower. The explanation must be sought in a creeping paralysis of the will. Despite its present difficulties, the West retains a permanent economic and technological lead over the communist world—which has only been narrowed by the suicidal transfer of technology to the Soviet Union. It has been shown convincingly, by Professor Anthony Sutton and others, that totalitarian systems, by their very nature, are not inventive and that the Russians, over the entire period since the Bolshevik revolution, have had to import ninety per cent of their technology from the West. The economic inefficiencies of the communist command system have also been abundantly demonstrated.

The communist dictatorships have succeeded in only one area: in harnessing huge populations and borrowed technologies to the requirements of a colossal war machine. Russia is a superpower in only one sense, the military one. The past expansion of Soviet influence has been related to the abdication of Western leadership and the continuing appeal of communist ideologies in countries that have not yet experienced the rigours of a communist system. The future expansion of Soviet power is likely to be bound up with the calculated threat of force—which may well involve gunboat diplomacy in a literal sense in oceans where the Russian navy has been allowed to gain supremacy. The Russians remain fully conscious of the fact that great power diplomacy is always bound up with the use, or threatened use of force, at a time when the Western powers appear to be in some doubt about just what issues they would be prepared to fight for. The continued Soviet military build-up, at the expense of the consumer and of normal economic priorities, cannot be supposed to be purely defensive. The aim is to achieve overall strategic superiority, or, failing that, to be able to stare down the Western powers in a future confrontation over an issue that may be felt, even in the jaded capitals of Western Europe, to be more vital than Portugal or that small country in Asia. The watershed may well be a move to pull Yugoslavia back into the Warsaw Pact after Tito's death.

The prospects for communist expansion in Europe appear to be more auspicious than at any moment since the immediate aftermath of Hitler's war, when the Red Army paved the way for the definitive 'liberation' of Eastern Europe. It is the relative lucidity and self-confidence of East and West, as well as the military balance between them, that has changed since then. The nature of the conflict has also been changing; its focal points are now *inside* Western societies, and inside the Atlantic Alliance as a whole. There are few signs, unhappily, that the challenge has elicited the necessary response. Portugal is the most immediate example. Like a man heavily drugged, Western opinion blinked under the naked light of a communist *fait accompli* in Lisbon, and crawled back into its dreary private nightmare of relative wage claims and household accounts.

Yet the attempt to transform Portugal into the Cuba of

Western Europe (which is analysed in a later chapter) is the most striking demonstration that the ideological battle in Europe is being fought exclusively on *our* side of the divide. The status quo in the communist dictatorships appears to be permanent, accepted by all and sundry, and our politicians are regularly invited to append their names to pieces of paper acknowledging that this is so. God help the democrats in Moscow, Prague or Budapest, because nobody else will. If a country comes under communist sway, that is that, and anyone who thinks otherwise must be a dangerous lunatic.

Things are ordered somewhat differently in our neck of the woods, in that poorly-attended but still pleasant club of countries that can reasonably be described as belonging to the 'free world'. (It is a sign of our semantic confusion that while some Western politicians regularly refer to the Soviet bloc as 'socialist', they are coy about mentioning the fact that some societies still stand for freedom.) There is no 'Brezhnev doctrine' for the West, stating that no member of Nato will be allowed to adopt communism. How could there be, while there are powerful Communist Parties in a number of Western countries that could perfectly legally come to power through the ballot-box? The battle-fields are all located on *our* territory.

It is within this framework that we must examine the crisis of structures and beliefs that now afflicts Britain, as well as other democratic societies. I have already suggested that the external threat, and the genuine challenge of communist subversion within Western societies, are not the only, or even the principal reasons for misgivings about the future. The communists are able to exploit our failings, but the origins of those failings must be sought in economic mismanagement, the way we have allowed some of our institutions to evolve, the absence of decisive leadership, and the apparent crisis of faith in the values and purposes of a liberal society. As in Constantine FitzGibbon's parable—*When the Kissing Had to Stop*—in order to be defeated, we must first disarm ourselves. FitzGibbon rightly perceived that moral decline and the pursuit of false idols are what start to lower the boom. We should hardly need reminding, as a recent Russian commentator put it, that 'the struggle between the bourgeois and communist ideologies is, in the last analysis, a fight for influence over the masses, a fight for men's minds'.[11] What can happen if that is lost is the theme of the fable that follows.

1

Letter from London 1985

Outside the Ministry of Equality (formerly Buckingham Palace; it was renamed when the Royal Family moved to New Zealand) a couple of sleazy-looking individuals had just caught sight of a likely touch. One of them sidled up to the solitary American tourist and addressed him with the inevitable, 'Pssst. Got any dollars?' The official exchange rate was frozen at £48 to the dollar when the Working People's Government was sworn in a year ago. Since then, the black market rate has crept up to nearly £500. The penalty for a British citizen found in possession of gold or foreign currency is ten years' imprisonment, but this no longer seems to deter anyone. There is a story of a woman pensioner who lived for six months on a $20 bill smuggled in by a nephew from Canada.

The Knightsbridge Barracks is now the headquarters of the Volunteer Constables, a new mobile police force. Its nucleus was drawn from the factory militias that appeared in the north of England during the General Strike a few years back. The defence chiefs objected strongly to its formation—one of them even offered his view to a now-defunct newspaper, that Britain would soon be ruled by 'communist thugs'.

However, it was difficult for the generals to respond. In successive budgets, the socialists had reduced the Army to 60,000 men, and cut back overall defence spending to a level comparable with Iceland. And then the armed forces had suffered the further humiliation of being deployed in the unsuccessful attempt to maintain vital services during the General Strike. The present Government's decision to issue the Volunteer Constables with automatic weapons was the last straw. The Chief of the Defence Staff resigned (together with the chiefs of all three services) and was replaced with a junior brigadier who was said to have been a member of the Anglo-Soviet Friendship Society in his university days.

The rundown of the armed forces made it impossible for the Government to respond with force when Scotland proclaimed its independence. Minesweepers from the British (ex-Royal) Navy, backed up, according to Scottish press reports, by Soviet submarines, were used, however, to maintain English control of the North Sea oil rigs. This action seems to have been undertaken largely for prestige reasons. The world glut of oil around 1980 that sent prices crashing, the collapse of three drilling platforms built by the Ministry of Power after the foreign corporations were driven away, and the soaring foreign exchange cost of imported materials had made extraction unprofitable. The British Government's official line towards Scottish independence was that the whole operation had been hatched by right-wing British exiles in Edinburgh in collusion with the Americans.

Foreign visitors are often surprised that the English continue to fly the Union Jack, although the official name of the country has of course been changed from the United Kingdom to the Republic of Britain. Scotland was not the first part of the union to break away. Protestant leaders in Northern Ireland issued a unilateral declaration of independence when the British Government withdrew its troops from Belfast and recognised the IRA as a legitimate police authority in Catholic areas. Britain now operates a total ban on all trade between Ulster and the mainland, under the terms of a resolution adopted by the Socialist United Nations (renamed after the exclusion of the United States). Only Wales is left. This, no doubt, has something to do with the presence of a number of well-known Welsh politicians in the Working People's Government, and the subsidies that are still being paid at their behest to keep antiquated Welsh coal mines and steel mills alive.

But few Englishmen seem to know much about what is happening in any part of the island these days. You need a special pass, as well as the identity card that must be carried at all times, in order to move between the six regions into which England and Wales have been divided. Some British economists, now in exile in Chicago, maintain that this is the logical conclusion of the immobilism that overcame the British workforce in the early 1970s. Low-rent council housing (and the near impossibility of finding a second council house) made people want to stay put in their own areas, regardless of the jobs that were locally available. The socialists soon solved the job problem anyway by making it plain that they would print money to keep men employed in whatever business they happened to be working, and at whatever wage they thought they should be paid.

For the sake of economy, the Government has reduced the number of newspapers to two dailies and one Sunday: *The British Times, The Morning Star* and *The People's Mirror*. This decision caused heavy redundancies and was bitterly attacked by the printers' unions and by the Trotskyist leaders of the National Union of Journalists, who had themselves been responsible in the late 1970s for the sacking of hundreds of 'reactionary' reporters and the bankrupting of several major Fleet Street dailies in the course of strikes to ensure that newspapers echoed union policy, or that two men were employed to do one man's job in the printing shops. There are also a number of theoretical journals representative of different strands of opinion within the Working People's Government, the British Assembly, and the Trades Union Congress (also known as the Upper House). These include communist, Trotskyist and socialist publications, as well as a monthly called *Corporate Britain* which is representative of an influential group of trade union leaders whose ideas—especially on government by 'economic interest groups'—appear to owe something to the Italian socialist, Benito Mussolini. Since China and Russia signed the non-aggression pact, the Maoist *People's News* has also reappeared; it was formerly banned, allegedly at the request of the Soviet Embassy.

It is difficult to gauge the mood of the times from these organs, although their editors are mostly people who were prominent in Fleet Street or the provincial press even before the General Strike. Television is, if anything,worse. The news documentary has disappeared completely—which is ironic in view of the fact that it was through this particular medium that the leaders of the present Government were able to present their version of events during the political storms of the late 1970s. Hours of prime time television were then occupied by Trotskyist directors and script-writers who depicted every strike as a blow against capitalist exploitation. Sport, old horror films, the Bolshoi ballet and historical sagas—many of them re-runs of serials popular in the 1970s—are now the order of the night. There are also the late night blue movies on BBC-2 which, rumour has it, were introduced to divert those insomniacs who might otherwise be thinking about politics.

The control of foreign newspapers is still far from complete. There is little concern, for example, about foreign-language publications; the abolition of most examinations, and the sacking of headmasters who believed in òld-style schooling led to a situation in which fewer and fewer Englishmen had the ability, let alone the desire, to read in any language, including their own. It is the English-language press, and above all the Scottish and American papers, that the Government really worries about. The fact that the people who get hold of them, if caught out, are dealt with much as drug-traffickers used to be is still not an effective deterrent; copies of the *Glasgow Herald*, and *Scottish Express* (which has been acquired by a junior member of the Beaverbrook family in exile) and the *International Herald Tribune* are smuggled over the border each day. However, things will get more difficult for the suppliers if the Government goes ahead with the scheme to build an electrified fence along the whole length of the border—a sort of new Hadrian's Wall. (This, of course, would be designed to stop the flight of refugees rather than the entry of newspapers.)

A recent issue of the *Scottish Express* which has been xeroxed and widely circulated in London contains what purports to be the text of a confidential memorandum prepared by the present Minister of Equality when he was serving in the former socialist government. I cannot vouch for the accuracy of this document, which appears to have been submitted to a certain foreign embassy. Prepared soon after the General Strike, it is now of course somewhat out of date, but it does throw a remarkable light on the events that created the present situation. The title appears to refer to the successful plan to remove the former Prime Minister after using him as a front man to 'legitimise' the seizure of total power. There is room here only for some of the more salient passages:

PROSPECTS FOR OPERATION BRUTUS

The satisfactory outcome of the recent events is well known to you. It has now been convincingly shown that neither a Conservative nor a Labour Government can resist the weapon of industrial power that is now firmly in our hands.

My real fear, two years ago, was that the Conservatives

would find the nerve—and the public backing—to pursue their two-point programme. As you will recall, this involved (i) the promise to restore the sovereignty of market forces so that if, for example, it was found necessary to give in to a large wage demand, it would immediately be translated into higher prices and unemployment; and (ii) the pledge to bring trade unions back within the law through a new Industrial Relations Act. Some Tory thinkers at the time thought that the device of the referendum could be used to provide a mandate for (ii). They were of course right. Any serious attempt to involve the community as a whole in a bid to reduce trade union power would have exposed our supporters' isolation and lack of mass support, due to the limited political education of the British working class at this stage. Fortunately, the referendum was not used for this purpose. Amazingly, one of the criticisms that the bourgeois ideologists used against it was that it would limit 'parliamentary sovereignty'. Nothing could have better illustrated the bankruptcy of their ideology: sovereignty already lay with us, in the factories and streets. Under these conditions, the extraordinary constitutional power of Parliament—which allows it to do almost *anything,* in theory, through a majority vote in a single house—was something only *we* could employ.

In the end, the Conservatives (caught up in a pathetic family feud) and the electorate shied away from confrontation with us on ground where they could win. We were left to face a confrontation on ground where, as it turned out, it was easier for us to win—the struggle against new wages controls.

A quite remarkable number of people thought that this time round, a wages freeze could work. The opportunist in No. 10 Downing Street* had tried it before (not very successfully), and this time, he had the bulk of the Conservative Opposition on his side. It is, indeed, extraordinary how many Tories were delighted to have the Socialists back in office again because of the naive belief (proof, if any more were needed, of how effete the British middle classes have become) that Labour men are 'better' at dealing with trade unions. When you remember that, even at this stage, 3-4 million trade unionists were still voting for the Conservatives, you will be fully conscious of just how defeatist these Tories had become. Compare their influence

*The home of the British Prime Minister before the move, for security reasons, to Windsor Castle.

in trade union structures with ours—and yet the Communist Party of Great Britain was still pulling in only 30,000 votes in the country!

So we went back to the wages freeze. The government propaganda was not bad. 'This is the answer to inflation', television audiences were told. Appeals were made to the self-sacrificing character of the British people, to the homespun heroism of the old girl sitting by a paraffin lamp during the blitz. And I must confess that I thought that the Prime Minister, who has as many lives as a cat, had escaped again when he picked his target: the rubbishmen. Their job is simple, and can easily be done by troops or blacklegs. No one is overjoyed with their performance, and they don't excite the same sympathy as miners. It looked like a very easy way to demonstrate that the Government could stand up to strikers.

Then, of course, things went awry. That picket who died trying to stop soldiers taking over his rubbish cart really got the ball rolling; I managed to hush up the inquest, showing that he died of natural causes. You know the rest: how we set in motion a wave of sympathy strikes, started occupying more factories in the North, and finally called a General Strike when troops were used again to hold the power stations. Then six cabinet ministers and twenty junior ministers resigned from the Government together. The old weasel's nerve was broken. He was urged to set up a National Government with the Tories, but he was scared of what he described as 'doing a Ramsay MacDonald'. He accepted our terms, and I believe that we are now in a position to dispense with him as soon as he has outlived his diminishing usefulness. . .

As this memorandum makes clear, however, the effect of the General Strike was only the culmination of a very long process. A later section concludes that

the bourgeoisie and the entrepreneurial class clearly never believed that we were for real. Occasionally some reactionary politician would get up (more often in the House of Lords than in the House of Commons) and raise the subject of communist infiltration—in the unions, the media, and Parliament itself. It was even suggested from time to time that there might be 'sleepers' in the senior ranks of the socialist government. We were able to brush this all aside, even when there was all that fuss about the revelations of those Czech defectors, with a well-orchestrated chorus of calumny. We were even able to 'frame' one or two of our best-informed opponents on charges of business fraud or contact with the Americans. Every time the activities of your embassy were brought up, we managed to manufacture a new exposé of the CIA involvement in Britain. . .

The mid-1970s, of course, saw the rise of a number of Poujadist movements among ratepayers, farmers, the self-employed, and a number of conspiracies involving retired officers, businessmen and right-wingers, some of them half-baked, others quite serious for us. I would like to thank you again for all the help your people gave us in keeping tabs on these organisations, and also for the invaluable assistance that Colonel Zhivkov later gave us in setting up the new security service to deal with them.

In my opinion, there were three reasons for the failure of the Poujadists and the 'private armies': (i) The middle class never managed to develop the strike weapon as a *credible* pressure on government; no doubt you remember that occasion when managers in the engineering industry went on strike and we organised workers' 'self-control' committees to take over from them. Production dropped and some plants were wrecked, but we had again showed who was the boss. Similarly, the taxpayers' strike fell apart when we jailed the ringleaders. If you aren't prepared to face going to jail for your beliefs, you will never be able to stand up to a disciplined revolutionary movement. (ii) We succeeded in infiltrating the so-called 'patriotic' movements, exposing what was going on and inventing, where necessary, the 'evidence' that enabled us to suppress the dangerous ones; by this means, we were also able to purge potentially unreliable elements from the police, the armed forces, and a certain department of the Home Office. (iii) The truth of Lenin's profound observation that the capitalist will sell you the rope with which he is hung.

You remember those people in the industrialists' association who supported our electoral campaign; I think they actually believed that they could domesticate us, turn us from predators into house-cats. It was the apathy and fatalism of the capitalist elite in this country—their willingness to compromise with the processes that were bound in the end to destroy them—that made our victory easier than any of us had ever dreamed. Look at the way the press barons meekly accepted the closed shop and did not lift a finger as our people took over the editorial policy of their papers. . .

The Minister was particularly caustic about those who had failed to comprehend what he describes as the 'battle on the economic front'. He observes that well into the 1970s (despite the example of the Allende regime's tactics in Chile, which he considers highly relevant) the consensus was still that Britain's vulnerable economic position, and particularly the need to control inflation, to restore foreign confidence and to maintain a competitive position for exports would somehow restore economic 'sanity'. He quotes the words of a Chilean communist—apparently one of the thousands of Marxist revolutionaries who were granted asylum in Britain in the 1970s—to the effect that 'what is an economic crisis for the exploiting class is not a crisis for us, but a tremendous opportunity'. Maybe that is why the Government rejected the IMF's terms for that emergency credit and seemed to have viewed the flight of foreign capital with relative equanimity. The Minister goes on to explain what foreign economists have since studied in detail:

> Inflation was used to destroy the middle class. The fact that inflation appeared to get out of hand was not an administrative blunder, but a conscious political strategy. We understood, and it is the very essence of Marxist-Leninist teaching, that economic power is the key to political power. You start by curtailing the private sector; you carry on with the redistribution of wealth by progressive income tax, then wealth tax, gift tax and so on; you proceed to confiscate land and encourage workers' occupations of firms on whatever pretext falls to hand; you make sure that the inflation that you unleash damages your social enemies and not your own supporters, and you end up with *control through the stomach*. We are already approaching the stage when, as Trotsky said, opposition will be a form of slow star-vation . . .

Rationing, in the framework of a siege economy, was already in force at the time the Minister drew up this document—rationing, and all that goes with it. Today, when friends visit each other for dinner, they bring their own food. With a thousand per cent surcharge on most alcoholic drinks, these are out of the question (apart from home-brewed spirits or bootleg Scotch smuggled in at great risk). The issue of ration coupons is in the hands of local 'supply committees' which are, in effect, a political arm of the Working People's Government. If you fall out of favour with your local committee, you could, indeed, go hungry, unless you have enough money (or barter goods) stashed away to buy on the black market.

The final passage in the Minister of Equality's memorandum is by far the most interesting. By now it has only an academic interest, but it does serve to remind us of the curious complacency with which most people continued to view 'the British question' in the 1970s. If Britain's symptoms had been ascribed to, say, Italy, the pundits would all have predicted either a right-wing coup (which is what actually happened in Rome) or a communist takeover. But the same people stubbornly regarded Britain as 'different'. Britain was, after all, the mother of parliaments. Juntas and politburos were peculiar to places where people ate funny food and shouted at each other in strange languages.

The British people seemed to be engaged in an act of collective self-hypnosis, which some psychologists blamed on television. All the world's horrors came and went on the small screen in the front room, and left the British populace unmoved. Britain had become the model of a *demobilised* society, in which all the major decisions were left to more or less unrepresentative elites—and increasingly, to the men who were to create the Working People's Government. Pericles' famous summation of Athenian democracy—'We consider anyone who does not share in the life of the citizen not as minding his own business but as useless'—would have been greeted with blank incomprehension in this inert polity that had once declared itself to be the Athens of the modern world.

So many things were happening that should have aroused the British and yet did not seem to. After all, they were (until Northern Ireland was abandoned) fighting a major internal war and, in addition to that, traditions of non-violence were obviously breaking down throughout Britain as a whole with the upsurge of armed terrorism, race riots and criminal violence of all kinds. The strategic threat from the Soviet Union grew daily more immediate, and yet Britain's defences were run down to the point where one Tory critic (now in Canada) suggested that the Government might as well scrap everything and substitute a tape recording saying in Russian, 'Don't shoot, we're on the same side'. The balance of payments deficit yawned wider and wider—producing the inevitable flight of foreign capital—while governments continued to spend as if there was no tomorrow. The monopoly power of those social pressure groups that are so peculiarly English, the industrial trade unions, distorted the whole structure of the country's economy and ensured that anyone who was not protected by the strongest among them (the lower-paid, the entire middle class and pensioners) would suffer most in an incipient hyper-inflation. The inflation itself, advancing almost un-checked, swept away what was left of traditional attitudes of financial probity and fair play; honest men came to regard tax evasion almost as a public duty, and saving ceased altogether.

Yet the British and their resolute admirers elsewhere continued to maintain that 'it can't happen here'—in other words that the system could fail to solve all the problems and yet survive. There was a blind faith in the docile character of the British race which, since the seventeenth century, had not been given to smashing up political institutions and lopping of the heads of kings. Yet it was precisely this attitude, this determination to muddle through rather than tackle problems head-on that contributed (as the last part of the Minister's memorandum reminds us) to the collapse of democracy in Britain:

We must not move precipitately, or else we may lose control of the weapons that are now in our hands. I find that some of our friends in your country are not sufficiently aware of the desperate longing of the British people to maintain the semblance of respectability and constitutional order in everything they do. If we had seized the Government by force during the General Strike (and it is possible that we would have succeeded) we would have forfeited the immense advantage of appearing to be a democratically-constituted force. This might in turn have at last dragged our enemies out of their sloth and provided them with the rallying point from which they could move against us. Even now that the Government is basically in our hands, there is a need to move cautiously. We will call it a socialist government for a little longer—perhaps indefinitely. We will not break with Nato just yet. We will hold a referendum on our terms, when the time is right, on a new constitutional settlement. Above all, we will make use of Parliament. . .

I agree with you on the importance of creating another American scare. I have already suggested the names of the five people in the Socialist Party who should be implicated in the next CIA 'plot'. I think that this time round, we will be able to consider the banning of the Conservative Party. Certainly the American ambassador will have to be expelled.

I do not expect any effective resistance to Operation Brutus. The Prime Minister is vulnerable in ways that you know about, and I am sure that he will go quietly into retirement. The Chief of the General Staff is weak and confused, and lacks forces anyway. The potential leaders of a businessmen's backlash got out after the strike if they did not go before. Scotland is the one thing that worries me. . .

Above all, everything must be done with as much *decorum* as possible. We must never forget that this is a country of civil servants. They will do what they're told if they're given the proper forms. That's where Hitler was wrong. A country of shopkeepers is not all that easy to deal with. A country of deputy post-masters is.

Perhaps none of us was fully aware, even at this stage, of the colossal power that can be exercised through the House of Commons by a party with an effective majority. When Allende in Chile set out to do many of the things that the Minister of Equality and his friends succeeded in doing here, he had to contend with a real system of checks and balances: he could make use of the tremendous powers of the Chilean presidency, but still ran up against strong and, for a time, effective resistance from Congress and the Supreme Court. In Britain, once the Left had captured Parliament (by methods too multifarious to be remembered here, but often camouflaged by the badges and ensigns of something described at the time as 'social democracy') all things were possible. The executive and the legislature, in this situation, were one and the same, and there was no legal body to rule on the constitutionality or otherwise of the parliamentary votes. The House of Lords made a valiant attempt to impose some restraints—only to be silenced by a threat (which had been used before) to flood it with socialist peers. The British now realised the terrible vulnerability of their system, which lacked both a constitutional court and a strong upper house—in short, any effective separation of powers—once the social consensus had broken down and a group had come to power which was committed to none of the principles of a liberal democracy.

The parliamentary strength of this group was, I suppose, to be partly explained by steady Marxist infiltration into the Socialist Party over a prolonged period, as well as to that characteristically English phenomenon, public school socialism. (I am not aware of any other country where snobbery and egalitarianism have been so closely interlocked.) It had long been accepted that it was not sensible in Britain to join small parties or to form new ones. As one of the Minister of Equality's colleagues in King Street put it, 'We must work through the Labour movement, not in competition with it'. This strategy resulted in a bureaucratic triumph—the capture of the command levers in many major unions—which eventually brought with it the control of the key extra-parliamentary organs of the Socialist Party: the national executive and the annual conference, whose decisions were determined by union bloc votes, which in turn were decided by rigged ballots.

From here it was a short leap to the control of the nomination of most parliamentary candidates and the overriding of constituency parties. There were, it is true, efforts to resist the trend, but at the crucial watershed, when the party split in the midst of the General Strike, only a handful of socialist Members of Parliament left the party to join the new Social Democratic Movement. Party loyalty, or fear of the unknown (or the tested strength of the union left) held the others back. It was the same when the Prime Minister was finally pushed into retirement and an ex-communist who had not publicly identified himself with the party's Marxist faction for several years took over to apply an openly totalitarian programme. The stage was set for the eventual break with constitutional appearances—I hesitate to say with *legality*, because the Minister of Social Communications has repeatedly stressed that the Government always acted under statute law. The law lords living abroad have issued a detailed report refuting this view (which has been presented to the European Court) but I am not competent to judge its contents.

Of course, the Minister of Equality does not tell the whole story. There *was* resistance in the end. It is rumoured that the

Socialist Minister who was among those incriminated in the 'Grosvenor Square Plot' (which led to the expulsion of the American Ambassador) had actually asked for Nato assistance to prevent a communist *coup d'état*. Surprisingly, a number of trade union leaders who had participated in the General Strike opposed the Government's subsequent proposals for a new constitution abolishing the House of Lords and substituting the Trades Union Congress—expanded to include delegates of other economic interest groups. There was quite remarkable last-ditch resistance by farmers and small businessmen to the expropriation of their properties by inspectors from the Ministry of Equality sent out to enforce the collectivisation decrees. This resulted in a number of serious shooting incidents. There were also violent brawls when inspectors from the same Ministry went from house to house assessing, and often impounding, paintings, furniture, jewellery and other 'anti-egalitarian' possessions.

But by and large, the reorganisation of the country under the Working People's Government proceeded very smoothly. If there had been any residual thought of resisting the ban on the Conservative Party and other opposition groups, it was probably laid to rest by the arrival of a Russian fleet on a friendship visit the previous day and the display of spanking new armoured cars and automatic weapons by the Volunteer Constables and factory militias. And it is true that the Government was quite generous at the beginning about allowing citizens to emigrate: the problem was finding a country to go to, especially since nobody seems to believe that the British will do any work whatsoever. But more recently, passports have been withdrawn from most people and it is virtually impossible to obtain foreign exchange facilities legally.

I find that the only reliable sources of news, apart from the Scottish papers, which I see only infrequently, are Radio Free Britain, operating from somewhere in West Germany, and a number of underground news-sheets which are unlikely to survive much longer, given the vast improvement in surveillance techniques. (There have long been detailed files on every man, woman and child in Britain and the information has all been fed into a computer system that makes instant retrieval possible.) Some of the news-sheets emanate from libertarian communes that are holding out in remoter parts of the country; one of these is said to include two former Conservative cabinet ministers who are now reduced to growing their own food—for as long as the Government lets them.

There is also Radio New Order, the English-language propaganda station which broadcasts by satellite from Johannesburg and specialises in relaying the views of right-wing exiles. A typical excerpt from today's programme reads as follows:

The liberal capitalists in America and Germany should take note of how the Reds came to power in Britain. There is no clearer demonstration of the degeneracy of the philosophy of Manchester and of its latter-day exponents. The pursuit of material gain in the name of 'economic freedom' and of permissive and anti-patriotic life-styles in the name of 'individual liberty' is what handed Britain over to Muscovy. In the face of the ideological menace from the East, Western civilisation must return to the sterner, simpler values of National Order. The class-war is a fiction. We aim to unite all those who work with hand or brain in the great community of the Corporate State. Americans and Germans, take note: our philosophy offers you the *only* way to divert the inevitable Socialist revolution into a Nationalist course. The alternative is Britain today: the drab Utopia of a minor civil servant, ruled from Moscow, where nothing works except the labour camps.

Substitute 'nationalism' for 'class-war' (and vice-versa) throughout this passage, alter an inflection or two, and you have a statement that is not all that dissimilar from the speeches that are made by members of the Working People's Government.

It is clear to me now, with hindsight, that the struggle in Britain was not, as it then seemed, primarily a struggle between right and left, and certainly never a struggle between fascists and communists, but between individualists and collectivists, between the Party of Liberty and the Party of Equality, between those who believed in a liberal order in which men would be allowed to make their own choices, and those who wanted the total state, a state that would make all the choices—in the economy, in education, in literature and the arts—for us. But the liberals got themselves tied up in knots. They were too prudish to set about mobilising public opinion effectively, or to borrow weapons from their enemies' arsenal. They sat about like Victorian spinsters clucking at the mention of sex. It was not so much that they were defeated, but that they never really fought. They didn't understand that if the enemy is storming the battlements, you have to be prepared to pour boiling oil on his head. They were made of the wrong stuff: the fire that melts the butter tempers the steel . . .

Britain really isn't much of a country to live in any more. Anyone as old as I am is still shocked to be asked to pay £250 for a gin-and-tonic in a pub, although we know it's only paper. With the rationing and the import quotas, you're lucky to eat meat more than once or twice a week, although the Government says that that will improve when we enter Comecon. It's a relief not to have commercials on television, but that's because all the choices are made by little men in Whitehall, not the consumers. There are just three models of cars, for example, which are all out of date and which no one wants to buy, but we can't export them anywhere because real labour costs are three times as high as in Spain and North Africa, where Ford and Chrysler have moved all their plant.

I worry about the kids all the time. At school, English history seems to be all about peasant revolts, trade union martyrs and Marx's travails in the British Museum. The morning's work begins with an hour of 'social education'. Mind you, I suppose it was getting like that when you left ten years ago. Weren't they studying Marx and Mao Tse-tung, along with abortion and the pill, in religious education classes?

It is a cold world we have entered in the name of equality and peace, and I doubt whether there is any return from it, at least in our lifetimes.

2

From Liberal to Mass Democracy

> For two hundred years we had sawed and sawed and sawed at the branch we were sitting on. And in the end, much more suddenly than anyone had foreseen, our efforts were rewarded, and down we came. But unfortunately there had been a little mistake. The thing at the bottom was not a bed of roses after all, but a cesspool full of barbed wire.
>
> *George Orwell*[1]

You can go on heating water for a very long time before it turns into something else and becomes steam. It is perhaps the simplest possible example of how a series of quantitative changes, carried to a certain point, can produce a qualitative change, a change in kind as well as degree. If you happen to know the boiling-point of water, and happen to have measuring instruments available, you can predict exactly when it is going to take place. It is rather more difficult in politics: the boiling-points are unknown, and reliable thermometers are unobtainable. But the basic principle is much the same. Go on adding to the power of governments or trade unions and subtracting from individual liberty and consumer choice for long enough and you will find that you have achieved a qualitative change in a liberal democracy: it will certainly have ceased to be liberal; it may no longer be democratic, and it may even have ended up as Orwell's 'cesspool full of barbed wire'.

Britain has stumbled a long way down the road from liberal to mass democracy: from the kind of society that values individual freedom to a society of levellers that kills off private enterprise, penalises people who work harder than most or who are ready to accept personal sacrifice in order to choose their doctor or their children's school, and frowns upon most kinds of originality, above all in the realm of ideas. Until very recently, the debate about this downhill slide has been between those who thought it was happening too fast and those who thought it was not happening fast enough. Few people were prepared to look behind the pedestals of the hollow gods, Equality and Social Justice, before which a generation of politicans and communicators felt compelled to make obeisance. Fewer still were prepared to ask whether, in the name of those gods, Britain (the mother of modern democracy) was not in danger of confirming the fears of those classical Greek and nineteenth-century political philosophers who believed that majority rule would in time produce a new form of tyranny. Much political discussion succumbed to a curious kind of determinism; even supposedly liberal newspapers in London greeted new redistributionist demands and proposals to add to the monopoly power of the trade unions or extend the dead hand of bureaucracy over the economy with the timorous sighs that this was all 'inevitable'. The classical and contemporary champions of the free society were relegated to the libraries, or obscurer places. The works of Ludwig von Mises, Friedrich Hayek and, in Britain, of Lionel Robbins and (most recently) Samuel Brittan were so neglected or misunderstood that a writer in *The Observer* could seriously claim that socialism 'is the only systematic political thought we have'. Expediency, not principle, ruled the day, and many of those who knew better placed themselves in the position of the gypsy in Ortega y Gasset's story, who went to confession and was asked whether he knew the commandments of God. He replied, 'Well, Father, I was going to learn them, but I heard talk that they were going to do away with them.'[2]

You cannot, of course, do away with the commandments. You can fail to observe them and take the consequences—and you will be all the more inclined to do so if you believe that Hell is an invention of desert madmen. Equally, you can cheerfully set about scrapping the things that make a free society possible in the name of some superior code of values; the fact remains that if you do that, you are going to have an unfree society. The irony is that wherever the Party of Equality triumphs over the Party of Liberty (as seems to be happening in Britain today) it usually transpires that there is not only not much liberty, but not much equality either. What is left is the socialist 'new class', and slow starvation for those who think differently about how the country should be run.

This is the alluring horizon towards which Britain is steaming at full speed under a crew who, having squandered their fuel, have begun throwing the ship's timbers and the lifeboats into the furnaces. The problems created by egalitarian socialism will all be solved, we are told, by more of the same. State-run industries are inefficient, so we'll have more of them. Private investment has been strangled by rising taxation and Alice-in-Wonderland systems of subsidies and price controls, so we'll have more of those too—and if hopelessly unprofitable firms go bankrupt, why then, we'll haul those into the state sector so as not to lose jobs. Standards of state education are falling because of the spread of comprehensive schooling, so we'll kill off the good streamed or independent schools that are left. The National Health Service is short of funds, so we'll forbid patients to pay for beds. The restrictive practices of trade unions are some of the major obstacles to the rational deployment of economic resources, as well as a serious threat to a man's right to choose his employer—so we'll give the unions increased power by encouraging the spread of the closed shop and the right to intimidatory picketing. It will all be done in the name of Equality and the Rights of Man, but when we are honest about it we will admit, as a left-wing Labour MP was prepared to do in a recent article, that we are doing it because 'we are the masters now'.[3]

Mr Kilroy-Silk's article should really be quoted at length, because it is a typical statement of a certain state of mind. Politics is not, in his view, concerned with 'compromises and bargains' and the quest for 'a spurious consensus'. The function of government, and above all a socialist government, is 'to impose its values on society. Its role is creative: to cast, so far as it is able, society in its image'. Socialists should not be timid about this; they should not worry about charges that they want to exercise dictatorial powers; they must troop forward with 'a tint of arrogance' (I nearly found myself adding: with the confidence of a sleepwalker).

Now what is both remarkable and representative in this article is the view that a government in a democratic society is concerned with imposing *values*—with ramming them down the throats, if need be, of a bovine and recalcitrant public chewing the cud of its own material self-interest. It is clear that these values, whatever they happen to be, do not grow spontaneously out of the traditions of British society; you can forget about all that. They are to be written out on a bit of paper, made law, and executed, if necessary, by the police. I am drawn, irresistibly, to borrow Burke's splendid rejoinder to the Jacobins in France: 'I cannot conceive how any man can have brought himself to that pitch of presumption, to consider his country as nothing but *carte blanche,* upon which he may scribble whatever he pleases'.[4]

Mr Kilroy-Silk must at least be congratulated for putting up a road-sign that tells us a bit about where we are going. If you believe, as he does, that a socialist government can and should prescribe the values of a particular society, then you will impose few—if any—restrictions on what it can do. If pink is considered to be a virtuous colour, then the government could ensure that everyone cleaned his teeth with a pink toothbrush; that would have an added advantage for someone who also believes (as do many of Mr Kilroy-Silk's colleagues) that the consumer economy is inherently wasteful and immoral, since you could stop the production of dozens of different sorts of toothbrushes, including those electric ones that send some high-principled people into paroxysms of rage. If the government, because of its changed foreign policy, decided that schoolchildren should be issued with maps of the world that did not show North America, or with history books that did not mention the Marshall Aid programme, that would also be unexceptionable.

These, of course, are absurd examples, but they are logical extensions of what many socialists besides Mr Kilroy-Silk are saying—and, indeed, of what other sorts of collectivists, in the name of *raison d'état,* the prophet Muhammad, or the Thousand-Year Reich, have said in the past. The point to be observed is that latter-day collectivists in Britain and other Western societies maintain, for the most part, that their views are compatible with a democratic system. This is true, but only when one eliminates a confusion that has arisen in many people's minds, and introduces a time element that is rarely mentioned. Collectivists of different hues (socialists, communists, Nazis etc.) who want to impose values on society can achieve their aims through democratic *machinery* and have done in various places before now; but what they are doing amounts to the systematic destruction of *liberal* democracy, which is indeed close to expiring in Britain today. This destruction of pluralism in its social, economic and intellectual senses—which is what Mr Kilroy-Silk's totalitarian approach to politics implies—is likely in time, if unresisted, to bring about the collapse of political pluralism as well. The democratic machinery is then reduced (if it remains at all) to the rubber-stamping of rule by a new oligarchy. In other words, the transition from liberal to mass democracy is likely to end in no sort of democracy at all.

Time to define a few terms. Liberalism (in its classical sense, of course, and not as applied to *sub rosa* socialists in the United States) and democracy are clearly very different things. Ortega, one of the foremost critics of the trend towards 'hyper-democracy', maintained that 'liberalism and democracy happen to be two things which begin by having nothing to do with each other and end by having meanings that are mutually antagonistic.' If there is no necessary connection between liberalism and democracy, it is largely because they are answers to different sorts of questions. Democracy is a method for choosing (and removing) governments; liberalism is a doctrine for determining what governments should and should not do, and above all for defining the *limits* to governmental power. As Hayek puts it, 'Liberalism is a doctrine about what the law ought to be, democracy a doctrine about the manner of determining what will be law.'[5]

A great deal of confusion has arisen because people tend to talk loosely about democracy as if it were something more than a method for deciding who will exercise authority. Thus democracy has come to be talked about as an end in itself, as a whole way of life, and even as a special kind of civilisation. It is in fact none of these things. It is a mechanism (subject to a vast number of modifications in various situations) which, as Churchill once put it, would be the worst in the world—if it were not for all the others. Many of those who applaud democracy are in fact talking about *liberal* democracy or *social* democracy—two specific variants. They may, alternatively, be referring to such faddish concepts as 'economic' or 'industrial' democracy, which I shall turn to later. There has, of course, been a close historical connection between liberalism and democracy. This is largely to be explained by the fact that democracy has proved more likely than other systems to safeguard those individual liberties that genuine liberals consider to be all-important, while it would seem that only a liberal society can provide the social and economic conditions that will prevent democracy from fast deteriorating into some variant of tyranny. But it must be stressed again that there is no inevitability about this historical relationship. There have been authoritarian regimes which have allowed considerable scope for non-political freedoms, just as it is plausible to study the possibility of 'totalitarian democracy'.[6]

In normal discourse, the word 'democratic' has usually implied a value-judgement. In the writings of the ancient Greek philosophers, and in British society until relatively recently, it tended to mean 'bad'. Today, it tends to mean 'good' and the Communist dictatorships have borrowed it from us as a flattering euphemism for their own systems. When Wordsworth remarked, in the early years of the French revolution, that 'I am of that odious class of men called democrats', it is almost certain that he was not speaking tongue-in-cheek. His design was to *épater les bourgeois* with this dangerous and extremist profession of faith, just as a retired brigadier's son might bang his fist on the dinner-table today and pronounce his adherence to some group committed to blowing up Parliament.

Plato and Aristotle did not think much of democracy as a means of selecting governments. Plato, who believed that the perfect society would be ruled by an austere elite of those who were best at philosophy and war, viewed democracy as a system that would come about through class war—when a ruling oligarchy had grown soft and effete, when its 'young men live in luxury and idleness, physical and mental, become idle, and lose their ability to resist pain and pleasure'. Then the poor would seize power, kill or exile their opponents, and set up 'an agreeable anarchic form of society, with plenty of variety, which treats all men as equal, whether they are equal or not'. Democracy, in Plato's view, would be destroyed by its own innate logic. A democratic society would carry its thirst for license and equality to an extreme, tolerating social indiscipline and rewarding commonplace minds, reserving its approval, 'in private life as well as in public, for rulers who behave like subjects and subjects who behave like rulers'. At last some tribune of the people would exploit resentment at inequalities of wealth to establish himself as tyrant.[7]

Aristotle shared this class-oriented conception of democracy: 'where the poor rule, that is a democracy'. There was, indeed, a class element in the word itself. Democracy means rule by the *demos,* a word that, for the Greeks, could mean either rule by the people as a whole, or rule by the 'common people'.[8] Hence the fear of the ancient philosophers that democracy would degenerate into government in the interest of a single class that would place the property, and possibly the lives, of others at risk. Amongst the forms of class repression that the majority in a democracy might initiate, under demagogic leadership, Aristotle mentioned a 'forced capital-levy' on the rich, 'a levy on income for public services' and the bringing of 'slanderous accusations against the rich with a view to getting their money transferred to the public purse.'[9] He believed that the best hope of averting, or at any rate delaying, a gradual drift into that form of 'extreme democracy' in which 'all share equally in everything' and private associations of all kinds would be broken up, lay in predominantly agrarian societies—preferably with property qualifications for senior office. His main argument on this score was that it would be physically impossible in such a society for the majority of the citizenry to exercise their democratic rights to attend meetings of the assembly. Thus the business of government would be left to a qualified (or at any rate, propertied) ruling class which would not be swayed by the sudden passions and enthusiasms that had contributed to the collapse of many Greek polities.[10]

From here it is possible to trace the pedigree of what Professor Finley has recently assailed as the 'elitist theory of democracy'—that is, the argument that 'the principles on which democracy had traditionally been justified are not operating in practice; furthermore, that they cannot be allowed to operate if democracy is to survive'.[11] This theory pops up again and again in various guises. Thus it is argued that democracy works best if it is left to a class of professional politicians who will tend to grow more and more like each other, so that changes of government will cease to bring major social upheavals, political extremism will die away, and everyone will be able to celebrate the 'end of ideology' and get on with bargaining over 'differences in the division of the total product within the framework of a Keynesian welfare state'.[12]

This suspicion that democracy works best—or perhaps can

only work—when most people are in some way excluded from effective participation in politics has many variants. One common thread is the conviction (as expressed by Boling-broke) that 'reason has small effect upon numbers. A turn of imagination, often as violent and as sudden as a gust of wind, determines their conduct.' Proponents of this view frequently turn back to the experience of ancient Athens, or to Hitler's or Louis Napoleon's coming to power for examples of the inconstancy of citizens in a democracy. Under the strains of the Peloponnesian war, remember, the Athenian assembly agreed to an act of bloody genocide: the slaughter of the Melians. A few years later, the same assembly—the torch-bearer of democracy to the ancient world—voted democracy out of existence and gave way to the oligarchic Council of Four Hundred that plotted peace with Sparta before it was thrown out in turn in a flurry of street-fighting. Later still, we find these same enlightened Athenians voting to put Socrates to death for 'not believing in the gods in whom the city believes, introducing other new divinities' and 'corrupting the young' with his unheard-of ideas.[13] When this performance is compared with the use of the plebiscite by would-be dictators in modern times, and with the fact that electorates have given a plurality of the votes to anti-democratic parties in various modern situations (such as Weimar Germany or Chile in 1970) can we not agree that the elitist critics of democracy have a point? Before looking at their evidence more closely I want to turn to some variations on the classical theme of the 'inevitable' decay of democratic socities.

One of the most disturbing arguments is that a full democracy will succumb to envy: the rule of all will degenerate (as Plato and Aristotle feared) into a form of class rule in which the poor plunder the rich. Even ambitious attempts to alter the distribution of wealth and income in a democratic society will fail to prevent the politics of reason giving way to the politics of envy, since, as de Tocqueville observed with devastating accuracy, the smaller the social gap becomes, the more bitterly it is resented. 'The slightest dissimilarity is odious in the midst of general uniformity.'[14] The destruction of property will eliminate variety in society, substituting a drab conformity. It will remove the incentives for productive work, but still more for savings and investment. It will also remove the social basis for political opposition to snatch-and-grab government, which led Sir Henry Maine to assert, at the end of the last century, that 'nobody is at liberty to attack several property and to say at the same time that he values civilisation. The history of the two cannot be disentangled'.[15] Maine feared the corruption of mass democracy, which would result in 'legislating away the property of one class and transferring it to another.'[16] The whole movement of civilisation, which he associated with the progress from 'status' (collective or feudal tenure) to 'contract' (individual, or 'several' ownership) might thus be thrown into reverse, and a new form of barbarism would arise.

Envy will result not only in the destruction of property but in the levelling of ideas. Mass democracy will produce the 'mass man', whose attitude towards the society that gave him life will be parasitical, concerned with taking rather than giving, and anchored in no conception of his country's past. 'Those who demand nothing special of themselves', as Ortega put it, will triumph through mere arithmetic over those who do—and may even then proceed to punish them for their pains. There will be a corresponding loss of reverence for special ability and for excellence in any form. That farmyard crow, 'We are the masters now', will result in the exaltation of the commonplace. 'The characteristic of the hour is that the commonplace mind, knowing itself to be commonplace, has the assurance to proclaim the rights of the commonplace and impose them wherever it will.'[17]

James Fitzjames Stephen, a conservative Victorian critic of democracy who is too little studied today, put it even more strongly. Stephen believed (unlike contemporary socialists who want to *impose* values) that 'governments ought to persuade and instruct'; his deep religious conviction of original sin led him to call for government by the virtuous ('I think that wise and good men ought to rule those that are foolish and bad'). Those who would set out, bible in hand, to overcome the apparently insurmountable 'badness' and 'idleness' of the greater number would not, however, be filling in a blank page; they would be working against the background of those customs, and moral standards and established institutions that Stephen likened to a system of dams, sluices and watercourses through which the 'life of the great mass of men' would flow like a watercourse.[18] Blow up the dykes, break with conventional morality, substitute the pursuit of equality for the emulation of the best, and Stephen believed, like the ancients, that you would succeed only in devising new forms of tyranny. The strongest would always win but, in the context of a mass democracy, their strength would consist in the flattering beguilement of the elector. Stephen's greatest fear was again the moral one: that universal suffrage would create a system of government by mediocrity in which bread-and-circuses politicians under the banner of equality would encourage men to behave like the 'primeval apes of Mr Darwin's theory, with just enough sense to defeat the operations of natural selection. Their one maxim would be to single out every ape who had got a few rudiments of human qualities in him and, instead of making him their king, stone him to death.'[19]

But among the modern English doubters of democracy the one we can turn to with most profit today is W. H. Mallock—again a name that crops up in very few university reading lists and has long vanished from catalogues of books in print. Mallock took up the broader themes that have begun to emerge in these pages: the inevitable conflict between the pursuit of liberty and the pursuit of equality, the fickle character of the electorate in a mass democracy, the perilous tendency of its citizens to reject the necessary style of leadership (and, it might be added, the necessary tough choices), the potentially barbarous decline into the rejection of everything that makes individuality and excellence.

He was fully aware of the irony in the unremitting pursuit of equality—that it can succeed only, in the end, in establishing a new oligarchy. As his Swiss contemporary, Robert Michels, put it, 'every attempt to eliminate oligarchy is bound to end in a re-creation of it'.[20] As Michels saw it, even the most fanatically egalitarian movement would soon divide into a beer-and-telly majority which would slump into 'gregarious inertia', and a hard core of activists who would remain to monopolise the levers of government. The separation of leaders and followers in any form of social organisation was the iron law of oligarchy. All political power at last detaches itself from its source. Power that issues from the people will end by raising itself above the people—and Michels, as well as many others before and since, have been profoundly sceptical about whether institutions or paper constitutions can be devised to prevent this happening.

Surely it is better, Mallock argued, to accept the iron law of oligarchy as just that. If you abandon the Utopian dreams and realise that pure democracy, and a literally equal society, are impossibilities, you can begin to examine constructively what kind of marriage between democracy and oligarchy (the terms that Mallock persistently used) is likely to produce the greatest good of the greatest number. And to decide on that, you are going to have to recognise the inequality of man. Pure democracy 'is not, nor ever has been, nor ever can be' a system of government. 'It is simply one principle out of two, the other being that of oligarchy, which two may indeed be combined in various proportions, but neither of which alone will produce what is meant by a government, any more than saltpetre or charcoal will itself produce gunpowder.'[21] Those who fail to understand this will be condemned to temper democracy, not with the rule of the specially gifted, but with the usurpation of power by a sordid 'new class'. Mallock took issue with the modern orthodoxy that equality is the natural state of man: a proposition that of course is totally detached from genetics. Steady progress towards equality, in his view, was not progress at all, since the desire for *inequality* (in the form of wealth, power, fame or other satisfactions) was the dynamo of human efforts.

Michels' and Mallock's fears about the emergence of a mass democracy in which—in the name of equality—a parvenu oligarchy would emerge to practise unlimited government, were truly prophetic. The twin problems of modern democracy are, first, a constant expansion of the power of central government and, second, the manipulation of that power by disciplined ideological minorities that invoke the 'people's will' but are wholly impervious to the true wishes of the majority. The first inevitably leads to the second, and so (in the British context) to a stage of proto-communism. Both are justified by a ritualistic appeal to ideals that are rarely scrutinised, and are made possible by general ignorance of—or indifference to—the fact that liberty depends on limited government. The whole process of evolution lends a sinister weight to Hayek's pessimistic assertion that 'it would seem that the particular form of representative government which now prevails in the western world, and which so many feel they must defend because they mistakenly regard it as the only possible form of democracy, has an inherent tendency to lead away from the ideals which it was intended to serve.'[22]

The paradox is inescapable in Britain today. On the one hand, the British are burdened with 'big government' that gobbles up more and more of the taxpayer's money, takes more and more people onto its payroll, and promotes a fussy bureaucratic intrusion into the last remaining crevices of private life. On the other hand, the state appears to be invertebrate when the need arises to curb inflation, combat terrorism and subversion, restrain the power of labour monopolies and secure the country's external defences. Government is swollen, not strong. There has never been so much government, and yet people rightly fear that society is becoming ungovernable.

The explanation lies in a derangement of the functions of government. Its power has expanded beyond measure in areas it should never have entered, and contracted beyond reason in those areas where the state should be strongest. The government's resources (which are merely on loan from society as a whole: governments have no *real* money of their own) are squandered on public housing schemes which are notoriously less efficient than the market, or on buying up private companies, while the armed forces are systematically reduced at a time of immense strategic danger. The government has razor-edged teeth when it comes to attacking private 'privilege' and plundering the taxpayer, but it is a toothless invalid when it comes to controlling certain latter-day forms of private coercion—the restrictive practices of the trade unions are only the most egregious example. Government is highly proficient at encouraging—directly or indirectly—the belief that economic rewards go, not to those who work and invent, but to those who are good at organising protection rackets. But it fails to provide the moral leadership that is needed to promote the interests of the nation as a whole. As a result, society fragments, and more and more people come to feel (in Arnold Toynbee's phrase) that they are 'in' but not 'of' the society they live in.

The inflation of big government in Britain over the past century is best illustrated by A. J. P. Taylor's remark that 'until August 1914, a sensible, law-abiding Englishman could pass through life and hardly notice the existence of the state, beyond the post office and the policeman'.[23] A British citizen could travel as he pleased, without a passport and without the bother of currency restrictions. Taxes were bucolically minimal by present-day standards, because public spending remained fairly constant. Less than eight per cent of the national income went in taxation, and progressive rates, introduced in 1910, ascended to the dizzy height of 8¼ per cent. Social services were limited, but the state guaranteed education for children up to the age of thirteen, offered meagre pensions for people over seventy, and contributed to the cost of insuring some categories of workers against sickness and temporary unemployment. This, of course, was the Indian summer of *laissez-faire*.

War, depression, the Keynesian prescriptions for unemployment, a second war, and the Beveridge blueprint for the Welfare State changed everything. Between the beginning of the century and 1970, the non-industrial civil service increased its manpower from 116,000 to more than half a million, and the second figure does not take account of an additional 300,000 postal workers.[24] The greatest expansion of government intervention was in the realm of the social services. Today, more than a quarter of Britain's national income is poured into the social services. The apparatus of the Welfare State has extended far beyond its original goals, which were accepted by all parties: the creation of real equality of opportunity and the provision for the basic necessities of people who are unable (because of age, or infirmity, or the hazards of economic life) to fend for themselves. The Welfare State has instead become a means of shielding its beneficiaries from every risk that is likely to confront them between cradle and coffin. Worse still, its bureaucratic apparatus functions as 'a veritable egalitarian engine, an infernal machine for redistribution'.[25]

Such developments were criticised *in advance* by the nineteenth-century liberals, who raised questions about the limits of government that it would have been exceedingly difficult to transpose to the Continent where, as John Stuart Mill observed, 'those who admit any limit to what a government may do, except in the case of such governments as they think ought not to exist, stand out as brilliant exceptions among the political thinkers'.[26] The difference of approach is philosophic as well as social. The concept of limited government depends upon recognition of the need for the dispersal of power in a free society. It also depends on an awareness of the frailty of human reason and the existence of universal laws that transcend the legislators. The danger of our times is that the socialists have set out to concentrate all power in the hands of the state, to enshrine an egalitarian ideology above individual liberties and established conventions, and to legislate not in the name of universal laws, but in the interests of 'class-justice'. The modern workings of the Welfare State are one example of where this can lead.

Herbert Spencer, a radical exponent of libertarian thought in nineteenth-century Britain, maintained that 'the great political superstition of the present is the divine right of parliaments'.[27] Spencer regarded states as 'incorporated nations'. He argued that the citizen should assess government actions exactly as a shareholder would assess the actions of a board of directors, or as a member of a club would assess its committee: if they deviated from the original purpose of the association, even with the support of a majority of its members, there would be no obligation on an individual member to accept the decision. The members of an incorporated body are bound 'severally to submit to the will of the majority in all matters concerning the fulfilment of the objects for which they are incorporated; but in no others'.[28] If a majority of the members of a book club, for example, reached the conclusion that in present circumstances rifle practice was more important than reading, and decided therefore, to devote the society's funds to the purchase of arms, ammunition and targets, could it be seriously maintained that the other members should agree to be bound by this eccentric decision?

Of course, the analogy is no analogy at all. You cannot opt out of a state that has 'departed from its original purpose'—except by emigrating or overthrowing it. Herbert Spencer's libertarian logic can result only in a kind of anarchism. If he were living in Britain today, and was consistent in his beliefs, I presume that he would either refuse to pay whatever proportion of his taxes and rates he thought was going towards unjustified forms of public spending (in which he would have the sympathy of many injured taxpayers) or head off to the Scottish highlands to found a libertarian commune.

The problem for anyone who has doubts about the growth

of government intervention is that the acceptable limits of state
action are nowhere meticulously defined. Some countries have
written constitutions and bills of rights that state broad
guidelines, but these have rarely proved adequate in practice.
Britain relies on a body of custom and precedent and the
enduring medieval tradition of 'liberties under the law'; but the
dykes have broken down under the flood-tide of socialist
legislation. There is a surviving, unwritten consensus about
some of the things that government should *not* do. Few
Englishmen, for example, would readily accept the idea that a
parliamentary majority has the right to decide how people
should cut their hair (unless they are in uniform), what clothes
they should wear on Sundays, or the contents of the liturgy. By
the same token, few people (excluding anarchists and far-out
pacifists) would dissent from the idea that it is the duty of
government to provide for the physical defence of life and
property, both against foreign enemies and against criminal
elements within.

But there are vigorously contrasting views on just about
everything else. The immediate political debate revolves
around how far the state should intervene in the economy, on
the extent and definition of 'social services' and on the public
role in education and other crucial areas of social life. The
underlying issues of principle involve (i) the definition of basic
liberties, which include an assured private sphere for the
citizen; (ii) the clash between those who believe in equality of
opportunity and those who believe in 'pure' equality, which are
two violently contrasting aspirations; and (iii) the difference
between law and legislation—between universal justice and the
whims of transient political majorities.

Unlimited government—whether its mandate is parliamentary election, or the bayonet, or the divine right of kings, is like
a river without banks. It is uncontrollable, and is liable to flood
rather than irrigate the surrounding soil. The principal
condition for a free society is that a large number of things
should remain beyond political control. A government that
refuses to operate according to this principle is not only
charting a course towards totalitarian rule, but is in danger of
dividing a society against itself, precisely at the moment it is
trying to make it more homogenous. As Milton Friedman
argues, 'the fewer the issues on which agreement is necessary,

the greater is the likelihood of agreement while preserving a free society.'[29]

Hayek defines liberty as 'that condition of man in which coercion of some by others is reduced as much as is possible in society'.[30] Liberty is an opportunity, not a commodity, a condition in which 'each can use his knowledge for his purposes'.[31] It depends upon respect for a private sphere of thought and action, which must necessarily include the ownership and transfer of property. As Acton said, 'a people averse to the institution of private property is without the first elements of freedom'. Liberty is also a condition of progress in any society, because a state that imposes its own rigorous ideology and closes off the channels for self-expression and experiment will stifle innovation and become stagnant in most senses.

In this sense, perhaps, the pursuit of liberty is a negative ideal; the onus is on the individual to make his own choices in life and to accept the penalty for failure. It is not an ideal that will attract everyone, and it is worth remembering that truly liberal societies have been extremely rare in human history. Most people want to be led. Hitler's notorious statement that 'the masses are like a woman who will submit to a strong man rather than dominate the weak' reflected an accurate perception of the fear of freedom. Totalitarians offer more than psychological relief from the burden of individual choice. They offer relief from the risks of competing in a market economy, whose operations do not always reward the noblest or punish the worst.

Egalitarians are rarely impressed by the argument that man should be captain of his fate. The concept of liberty, they say, means nothing to the man who does not have enough to feed himself. It is a concept that appeals to the successful, to those who know where they are going. Equality is the cause that moves the masses, and, when they are honest, the egalitarians will add that they want to maximise, rather than minimise, state coercion in order to attain it. Enlargement of the 'general liberty', we are told, will mean 'curtailment of such particular liberties as may conflict with it'.[32] Inequalities of wealth are said to be intolerable, so there can be no freedom to earn more than a specified figure—£6,000, in the view of some British trade union leaders. Inequalities of environment—in schools, medicine and even housing—are also apparently 'unacceptable', so the freedom to choose a school or a doctor and perhaps eventually even a place of residence will also be taken away, in the name of a 'general liberty' that cannot, by definition, exist. You can have liberty for each man, or equality for men *en masse*; the two things are mutually exclusive. The word 'equality' itself has a multitude of meanings. There is an unbridgeable gap between the idea of equality of opportunity— *la carrière ouverte aux talents*—and the idea of equality of conditions, of unmitigated equality.

Since men are not equal, you can treat them equally only if you allow them to be treated differently. The trouble is that the assault on property and above-average earnings through new kinds of taxation that sometimes approximate to outright confiscation, is remarkably popular with most people who do not have to pay. Here de Tocqueville and the Marquess of Salisbury were right. The *revanchist* appeal of redistribution is fed with regular exposés in the press and television of what so-and-so is earning—exposés that hardly ever mention the proportion of income that goes in tax. The appetite is enlarged by the gross materialism that is the staple diet of public debate, and by the role of television in raising consumer expectations. And the appetite grows with the eating.

The effects of the mania for redistribution should be familiar to any student of the Welfare State in Britain. No one is encouraged to increase the size of the national cake; they fall to squabbling over who gets the crumbs that remain. But a diverse society that fosters initiative will, inevitably, be better equipped to deal with poverty than one that concentrates on liquidating its inherited assets. The paradigm was what Robert Owen discovered in his 'New Harmony' settlement in America in the early nineteenth century: the only socialist sentiment that survived the rigours of the New World was the passion for redistribution, which took the form (quite literally) of eating the seed-corn and other commodities in the community store. Finally, only two commodities were left; one was glue, the other was soap.

The religion of equality, which, dressed up in various guises, is the apology for unlimited government in the democratic societies today, has three main elements in its credo. First, it denies what is obvious: that there are inherent differences of ability in different men. Second, it perpetuates the mythical labour theory of value.* Third, it canonises the 'we want it now' mentality—the clamour for immediate consumption—and appeals to those dark springs of envy that flow within most men. As Ludwig von Mises observed, 'the incomparable success of Marxism is due to the prospect it offers of fulfilling those dream aspirations and dreams of vengeance which have been so deeply embedded in the human soul from time immemorial. It promises a paradise on earth . . . and, sweeter still to the losers in life's game, humiliation of all who are better or stronger than the multitude.'[33]

The 'strategy of equality' in modern democracies has involved the expansion of government on several fronts: as the agent of redistribution through taxation and the Welfare State; as the curtailer of economic freedom through legislation—and through tolerance for the coercive tactics of trade unions; and as state capitalist, through the takeover of vital sectors of the economy. The classic pretext for state intervention is that it is 'socially desirable' to run certain industries at a loss (financed, of course, by the taxpayer) in order to keep prices down, or to preserve jobs; the losses regularly mount to astronomical levels in the absence of a market discipline. But the argument is progressively shifting ground with the increasing volume of uncritical applause for all state takeovers, regardless of cost.

Many socialists (including those who are inaccurately described as 'liberals' in the United States) now talk as if there were something progressive and inherently desirable about any increase in public spending (apart from defence spending), any increase in economic controls, and any increase in trade union power relative to the power of capital. The fact that such 'advances' can usually be shown to have prevented or reduced the growth of real national income, to have sped up inflation, and to have had a dangerously divisive effect on society as a whole is either complacently accepted as proof of the socialist *machismo* of those responsible, or drives them to fling back logical non-sequiturs about the number of Rolls Royces and fur

---

*In Britain, this had already been left far behind. The argument is no longer merely that the labourer is entitled to the 'full produce' of his labour (and that capital is only a parasitical excrescence to be sloughed away) but that the state owes everyone a 'suitable' standard of living, regardless of labour. The taxpayer has to shoulder the bill, and when he fails, the new expectations are fed by inflation.

coats still on display in the West End of London—the kind of
reply favoured by the poet Yeats who, when put on the spot in
a discussion, would say mysteriously, 'Ah, but that was before
the peacock screamed.'

The moral corruption that goes with the bureaucratisation
of economic life and the extension of the Welfare State has
been widely observed. The entrepreneurial or inventive
mentality gives way to the 'employee' or 'pensioner' mentality;
indeed, the overwhelming majority of us are either employees
or pensioners. The danger implicit in this new occupational
pattern is the apathy that often accompanies job security.
Some of the big American corporations overcome this by
building pressures, stresses, and a competitive element into the
job that may well kill off executives at fifty. I am not
recommending *that*, but it is arguably preferable to the
clock-watching and lay-about syndromes that have become
depressingly apparent elsewhere. The danger of homogenisation of thought and social behaviour in the new socialist state is
as real as the loss of risk and adventure, despite the superficial
overlay of the 'permissive society'. The political perils of an
incipient state monopoly of education or medicine are equally
evident—quite apart from the decline of standards and
efficiency that are inevitable when an institution is not exposed
to the challenge of the market. (This is the overwhelming
argument for the voucher system in education and medicine.)

These are some of the costs of increasing government
intervention. One of the things that makes it possible is the loss
of the belief that governments and parliaments should operate
within a framework of agreed general rules. One of the
preconditions for limited government is this belief that law
precedes the legislators and is superior to them. The rationalist
Continental tradition has encoded such rules in writing as an
interpretation of 'natural law'. But what are set up as
commandments by one generation can be torn down by the
next, following Voltaire's advice that 'if you want good laws,
you should burn those you have and make new ones'. England,
in contrast, has preserved the medieval concept of law, as a
body of rules that are discovered, not invented, from precedent
and convention—a body of rules binding on all who exercise
power. It was the hope of early lawyers, such as Sir Edward
Coke, that the common law would serve as a constraint on the

folly of parliamentary assemblies. The underlying principle was that law was superior to power—whether embodied in a monarch or a parliament. There was a justice that transcended the interest of any social group. Unfortunately, it seems that parliament no longer legislates against the background of an all-encompassing customary law. As Lord Justice Scarman put it recently, 'social justice, as our society now understands the term, requires the law to be loaded in favour of the weak' while there is no effective curb on parliamentary legislation.[34]

To sum up so far: the mis-shapen hulk of the modern democratic state poses a serious threat to the ideals that it was originally intended to serve. The tentacles of bureaucracy and egalitarian socialism are strangling private enterprise in many senses besides the exclusively economic one. There no longer appear to be accepted or enforceable limits to government action, which is steadily cutting away the social and economic basis for a free society. The attempt should be made to reimpose those limits; suggestions for a bill of rights and a new constitutional settlement are taken up in the last part of the book. This attempt will involve the more aggressive and articulate advocacy of the values and traditions that are now at risk. Without them, mass democracy could lead us into Animal Farm.

3
The Nature of Subversion

> What is the bravery of soldiers worth if their masters are not aware that the art of self-defence consists of understanding your weak points?   *Curzio Malaparte*[1]

The former Italian Prime Minister Giolitti said wistfully after the March on Rome that Mussolini had taught him that in dealing with revolution, you should worry about the tactics, not the programme. His remarks echo those of democrats in other situations who have been hopelessly outmanoeuvred by totalitarians of left or right. We cannot understand the present dangers to democracy without coming to terms with Marxist ideologies and the way that—in certain quarters—they constitute a new intellectual orthodoxy. But our main task is to study the totalitarian *method*, which counts for more than ideology and infinitely more than those reassuring professions of democratic faith that are put out from time to time by Communist Parties in Western countries. 'Defend democratic rights—join the Communist Party', reads a frequent advertisement in the British Communist organ, *The Morning Star*. And Georges Marchais, the French communist leader, had the temerity to entitle a book that was published before the 1973 elections in France *Le défi démocratique*—'The Democratic Challenge'.

We must begin by defining the nature of subversion. Subversion is a technical term with a precise meaning: it may be defined as a systematic attempt, by an organised group, to overthrow an existing society. Many forms of subversion are, at first sight, indistinguishable from legitimate forms of protest and dissent. Groups opposed to the fluoridation of the water supply or vivisection may use some of the same techniques to get their views across in the media, for example. But there is an underlying difference which is fundamental. The subversive recognises no limits to his political action, which is designed, not to modify the existing form of society, but to destroy it and to substitute some new revolutionary model. Yet democratic politics are only viable, as we have seen, when it is generally accepted that there *are* limits to political action; that there are, for example, fundamental liberties which lie beyond the political sphere.

Because of his totalitarian view of politics, the subversive is prepared to use any and all weapons in pursuit of his aims. It may be tactically expedient to work within democratic institutions and to avoid breaking the law. But the subversive is opposed both to the law (which he may dismiss as 'bourgeois legality') and to the constitution ('bourgeois democracy') and will be ready to overthrow them when he judges that the time is ripe.

It is vital to grasp these basic distinctions, because subversion works under the cover of semantic confusion. Marxist-Leninists are thus often to be found championing greater 'democratisation'. Indeed, the frequent appeal to undefined forms of 'democracy' by extremist groups is a case of hypocrisy in its classical sense: the homage that vice pays to virtue. The uncompromising phraseology of Marxist literature is translated, for the benefit of the Western public, into appropriately liberal-sounding blandishments. The language of social concern is substituted for the language of armed revolution; that way, the communicators and the educators are more easily won. So, to understand the way that subversion works in those delicate but all-important areas—the media, the schools and the universities—we have to grasp a second concept, that of 'propaganda mediation'.

The Marxists today find resounding echo chambers among well-meaning people who are seduced by the rhetoric of social concern, among the familiar type of fellow-traveller, hypnotised by the iron certainties of a totalitarian order,[2] and among those who are possibly best described as *inverted patriots*, people who share in a guilt complex derived from the colonial past or the inevitable inequalities of the capitalist system. The 'down-with-my-country-right-or-wrong' syndrome is particularly characteristic of contemporary 'liberal' opinion in the United States.[3] From such sources are recruited the propaganda mediators—the light foragers who spread intellectual defeatism about the values and goals of a free society, and so clear. a trail for the advance guard of subversion that

approaches behind. The subversive process starts here, with
those who disparage the Western liberal democracies, reserve
the charge of 'imperialism' for the Americans and their Nato
allies, and labour mightily to perpetuate the dangerous 1930s
illusion that there are *pas d'ennemis à gauche.*

This leads to a further aspect of contemporary subversion. In
the 1930s, with the Axis powers overshadowing Europe, and
with fascist movements or fifth columns at work in many
Western countries, the argument that the most immediate
enemy of democracy was on the 'right' was irrefutable.* This
argument was not, even at that stage, an adequate reason for
Western intellectuals to gloss over the Stalinist purges and
prison camps—as an unfortunate number of them tended to do.
But the argument was reinforced by Russia's role in the Second
World War, which seems to have largely erased the memory of
the Nazi–Soviet pact in 1939 and Stalin's subsequent
snatch-and-grab operations in the Baltic countries. The
argument survived the post-war satellisation of Eastern Europe
and the era of the 'cold war', and the intellectual pacifism of
Western liberals towards the Marxist left was fortified by the
excesses of Senator McCarthy and the Un-American Activities
Committee.

We are left today with a situation in which it is notoriously
more popular—among many journalists, church groups and
'do-gooders' of all descriptions—to seek out and denounce the
nefarious activities of 'fascist' regimes in Spain, Brazil, Chile
and, until recently, in Portugal, Greece and South Vietnam
than to examine conditions behind the Iron curtain. The
number of candidates for the role of fascist *bête noire* in the
left-wing imagination seems to be falling fast, partly because
some of the regimes that could plausibly be described as
'fascist' (the Velasco regime in Peru, for example)† are immune
from criticism because they have denounced the Americans,

---

*I should not let it pass, however, without reminding the reader that fascism was a
variant of socialism; Mussolini's early career as a socialist leader was not some passing
aberration and the insertion of the word 'socialist' in the title of Hitler's party
reflected its early commitment to many collectivist ideas. The use of the term
'right-wing' for fascist movements is merely an inaccurate form of shorthand.

†The *Guardian* newspaper devoted an entire page late in 1974 to the confiscation of
newspapers by the Peruvian government as an interesting 'experiment' for the
British to study at a time when the control of the press was under debate.

learned to pronounce the progressive Newspeak, and admitted Soviet advisers.

It seems that the mental attitudes characteristic of the period of the Spanish civil war survive at a time when there is no external threat to the Western democracies from a fascist or right-wing authoritarian regime—unless you believe that Spanish paratroops are about to descend on Gibraltar, or that a Chilean flotilla is likely to shell Senator Teddy Kennedy's summer retreat in Massachusetts. On the other hand, there is a clear and growing threat to Western Europe from the Soviet Union, which treats its own subjects considerably worse than any of the right-wing regimes that are so often held up for execration. I am not saying that it is improper to expose and to attack the abuses of civil liberties that are evident in countries such as South Korea or Chile—or, for that matter, to investigate what the CIA and other Western security services get up to. But there are reasons for thinking that some of the recent effusions on such matters—in the absence of equal or greater attention to the situation in communist countries that pose a direct threat to Western security—are designed as diversionary exercises, part of the softening-up process that smooths the way for subversion.

A symptomatic example was the CIA 'scare' in London that preceded the visit of Alexander Shelepin, the former chief of the KGB who was then the boss of the Soviet trade union federation (AUCCTU) in April 1975. The news of Shelepin's impending arrival had inspired hostile columns and editorials in many newspapers and had focused public attention on the value (or otherwise) of east—west trade union contacts. Attention was momentarily diverted when an MP belonging to the left-wing Tribune group tabled a parliamentary question on CIA activities in Britain; the aim was apparently to convince the public that intelligence officials from an allied country— who were posted to Britain with the full knowledge and acceptance of the British government—posed an equal, or greater, threat to domestic security than intelligence officials from a hostile communist power. The parliamentary question was brought forward after the left-wing press had prepared the ground. Shortly before, photographers purporting to represent three different publications (*The Guardian,* the Trotskyist *Worker's Press* and *Time Out,* a remarkable magazine that manages to sell *agitprop* on the back of a guide to entertainment in London*) turned up simultaneously at nine o'clock in the morning on the doorsteps of three members of the American embassy. The result was the appearance of well-illustrated 'dossiers' on the CIA's activities in London in the *Worker's Press* and *Time Out*. *The Guardian's* editors appear to have retained a certain cautious scepticism—if the photographer in question really represented that paper in the first place. The whole incident looked suspiciously like a well-executed diversionary exercise.

The nub of my argument is that the Soviet Union is the only major power that stands to benefit from anything that weakens West European societies. We do not need to assume that there is *necessarily* Soviet (or East European) involvement in subversion and internal warfare; the most disturbing developments are essentially home-grown. But we need to be fully aware of who stands to gain—and of the fact that it suits the interests of the Soviet Union to camouflage its policy objectives and its channels of action and, so far as possible, to divert Western attention to other issues. The Russians are obviously concerned, on the one hand, to distil all possible advantages—in terms of imported technology, grain and cheap credits—from the process of *détente* diplomacy. They will be careful to avoid actions that might cast doubts on the 'democratic' credentials of the Communist Parties in France and Italy, or might provoke a strong reaction to communist infiltration of trade unions and political parties elsewhere. But, on the other hand, they are bound to be tempted by the waning military strength of the Nato alliance and by the signs of social and economic confusion in Western Europe—by what Boris Ponomarev, the head of the international department of the central committee of the Soviet Communist Party (CPSU), described early in 1974 as 'a qualitative shift in the crisis of capitalism' which had opened up 'new possibilities' for revolutionary change. The Russians are keeping several irons in the fire.

What the dwindling band of believers in *détente* (a word that has never found an English translation and, therefore, perhaps

---

*An ingenious formula, which explains the magazine's relatively large circulation, of some 60,000 and the fact that—alone amoung radical left publications—it is sold over the counter in W. H. Smith's huge chain of newsagents.

has meaning only in French) often ignore is that the debate in Moscow is over means, not ends. The ends remain constant; the situation will determine whether the most suitable means involve appeals to 'peaceful coexistence' or the promotion of subversion or armed insurrection. Indeed, the two tactics are by no means incompatible, especially if the Russians, or their proxies, can conceal their responsibility for certain developments.

We can glean some evidence on the Russians' approach to subversion from their own published statements. An interesting book entitled *The International Communist Movement* was published in Moscow in 1972, edited by a certain V. V. Zagladin on behalf of the CPSU. It represents Soviet orthodoxy in its most rigid form, and contains the revealing statement that support for the world revolutionary struggle 'through propaganda, moral support, or material support' is the mission of the Soviet Union 'in all countries without exception'. We have been too inclined to interpret Soviet intentions by a curious kind of transposition. Because the 'cold war' has ended on our side of the fence, we assume it has ended on theirs. Because ideology has gone out of fashion in the West—except for the revolutionary left—we assume that the communists cannot be serious about propagating their beliefs. Because the aims and methods of Western imperialism have been discarded, and the Western public is disinclined to spend heavily on defence, we assume that Russian imperialism died with the Tsar and that the SS-18 heavy ballistic missiles and the vastly expanded Soviet navy are playthings, or, if destined for use at all, must be aimed at the Chinese. A few quotations from the recent Soviet literature are enough to set the record straight: we can then go on to look at the instruments of subversion that the Russians have at their disposal.

Communists have always maintained that the capitalist system is 'incapable of stability and of eradicating its characteristic faults'.[4] But Marxist scenarios for the demise of the capitalist societies have had to be revised substantially since Marx and Engels wrote that falling profits would drive the entrepreneurial class to cut wages to the bone, provoking inevitable revolution. It may just have been possible to cling to the basic ideas of *Das Kapital* through the 1930s Depression, when many people became convinced that capitalism was finished. But the rise of fascism showed that the revolution can move in more directions than one, and the period of unprecedented affluence and technological innovation that followed 1945 confirmed what the existing evidence should have already told Marx even at the time he sent *Kapital* to the printers: that continued growth has brought the classes closer together rather than further apart, at least in material terms.

The new problems of world-wide inflation, the energy crisis and industrial chaos in the West clearly present fresh opportunities. But Soviet commentators, having been burned in the past, have displayed a certain understandable caution about pronouncing deathbed orations over the tomb of capitalism in the 1970s. Typical of this approach was an article on the 'Twilight of Capitalism' which appeared in the Red Army newspaper at the end of 1974. The author declared that the collapse of bourgeois society was unavoidable in the long run, but that it was likely that it would survive its present crisis.[5]

Historical memories still count for a good deal: there are frequent references to the risk of a resurgence of fascism or extreme right-wing tendencies in the context of economic recession. There are also openly-expressed doubts about the readiness of Western Communist Parties to exploit the crisis. Professor Sobolev, one of the leading students of Western societies, warned early in 1975 that although conditions for the 'transition to socialism' in some capitalist countries were improving day by day, the economic crisis would not lead automatically to communism. He appeared to have serious reservations about whether the non-ruling Communist Parties were prepared for their task. In his view, the 'political maturity and organisational level of the working class [a standard euphemism for the Communist Party] and the solidity of its alliance with the other strata of working people' were still inadequate. The bases did not yet exist for bringing about the 'new social system'. His own counsel appeared to be that communists in the West should continue to work for 'interim goals' rather than outright revolution. But he also warned that events could accelerate unexpectedly and that communists would need to prepare for possible violent clashes with the bourgeoisie.[6]

It is always possible to balance one Soviet quotation against another which appears to contradict it. This is not just the effect of selective quoting; the contradictions are genuine, particularly when it comes to the delicate subject of 'peaceful coexistence'. We need to remember that Soviet policy statements are tailored to suit the audience that is being addressed. We need not expect to find detailed manuals of subversive tactics among the public statements. But to the careful reader, some are extraordinarily revealing. One of the most useful recent clues to Soviet thinking on the possibilities for subversion in the West was supplied by an article published by Professor M. Banglay in the Moscow trade union paper *Trud* at the beginning of 1975.

Professor Banglay began by noting that 'the dark forces of reaction' were trying to sabotage the 'relaxation of international tensions' that was the aim of the peace-loving Soviet Union. 'Reactionary imperialist circles in the West have by no means disappeared but are attempting to wreck the process of positive changes which has begun.' He returned to a familiar theme in Soviet literature: that peaceful coexistence does not imply any relaxation in the ideological struggle, and it does not rule out communist support for armed insurrection by 'oppressed peoples'. On the contrary:

> Peaceful coexistence does not eliminate the class struggle, including that between socialism and capitalism in the international arena. This struggle objectively arises from the opposition of the fundamental principles of organising social life—*something which excludes the ideological coexistence and interpenetration of these social systems.* [my emphasis] For this reason, the attempts by certain circles in the West to incorporate in peaceful coexistence some sort of 'total reconciliation', an effacement of the differences between the two systems and the elimination of the class struggle are completely bankrupt, or at best Utopian.[7]

So much for the wistful idea of ultimate 'convergence' between the communist and capitalist systems. The reader is left in no doubt that in Moscow, *détente* is regarded as war by other means.

Banglay goes on to say that the Soviet leadership is opposed to the idea that revolutions can be exported. But at the same time 'the fate of the world revolutionary process is not a matter

of indifference to us and we frankly stress the favourable
influence of peaceful coexistence on its development. Lenin
said that the world socialist revolution must be helped, and we
are helping it.' The difference between trying to export the
revolution and trying to give it a friendly push is less than
obvious, but Professor Banglay is obligingly specific about the
resources that are available. This time, he needs to be quoted at
length:

> We are waging the ideological struggle jointly with the
> working class in the capitalist countries . . . Communist
> Parties always note the presence of certain aims in common
> with social democracy and advocate unity of action with it
> on both political and socio—economic questions. Co-
> operation is possible in this area without damage to one's
> ideological position, and the experience of France, Italy,
> Japan, Finland and a number of other countries confirms
> this . . .
>   At the same time it is obvious that ideological barriers are
> no obstacle to unity of action among trade unions of
> different orientations. It is no accident that, despite
> ideological differences, unity of action between Soviet trade
> unions and Western trade unions which are headed by social
> democrats and left-wing Christians, has been organised with
> particular success over the past few years . . . We do not
> exclude compromises, including political ones; without
> them, there can be no progress. But no one will force us, even
> for the sake of the most useful cooperation, to compromise
> on questions of convictions and world outlook.

There is no need to seek further than Professor Banglay's
article to identify the main thrust of Soviet subversion in
Western countries: (i) towards infiltrating and forming tactical
alliances with the social democratic parties and (ii) towards
manipulation of the trade union movement.
One of the most depressing developments of recent years has
been the unwitting, as well as the deliberate, blurring of the
fundamental difference between communist and social
democratic politics and between free trade unionism and the
repressive apparatus for the control of labour in the communist
states. Take the British case. The left within the Labour Party
has been engaged in a successful attempt to rehabilitate
communist front groups, and achieved an important forward

leap at the party's Annual Conference in 1973, when the decision was taken to lift the ban on proscribed organisations, including

The British-Soviet Friendship Society
The British-Czechoslovak Friendship League
The British-Romanian Friendship Association
The World Federation of Democratic Youth
The World Peace Council
The World Federation of Trade Unions

and many more. Roy Hattersley, a right-wing Labour figure, was sufficiently unperturbed by this move to be able to comment on a television programme that his party had previously tried 'to prevent its members from joining a number of altogether admirable associations and I think we are a great deal more civilised about that than we were in the late fifties'. It is difficult to see what is 'uncivilised' about a democratic party attempting to deny access to totalitarians and their fellow-travellers—and I use the word 'attempting' because it would be foolish to ignore the phenomenon of *covert* penetration.

The Labour Party decided in 1973 to retain the ban on political organisations which had their own programmes, principles and policy, or which fielded their own candidates in elections. So dual membership of the Labour Party and the Communist Party (or other revolutionary groups) was still ruled out. But for how long? Even in the absence of recognised 'dual membership' there were many *overt* means for the Communist Party to influence Labour policy: through the bloc vote of the trade unions, for example. A large number of Labour MPs—mostly from the left-wing Tribune Group—had no hesitation in the early 1970s about writing for the communist *Morning Star,* appearing as guests of honour on Communist Party platforms, sitting on the committees of well-known communist front-groups, or reaping handsome profits through commercial operations with Soviet bloc countries where they could make use of special *entrée.* The analysis of such personal contacts—and of that confusion about the aims of a social democratic party that enabled the British Labour Party to accept 'fraternal' East German observers at its Annual Conference in 1974—could be pursued a long way further.[8] The reader who is curious to know how Soviet bloc officials seek to penetrate the Labour Party could do worse than consult the work by the Czech defector, Josef Frolik. But I do not want to digress too far from my general argument.

We do not have to imagine foreign involvement—although there is a mounting body of evidence on Soviet activities—to find many examples of subversion in the sense that I have defined it. The implementation of Clause IV of the constitution of the British Labour Party (as amended at the Blackpool Conference in 1972) according to the letter would produce a form of society that would be 'communist' in the original sense of the term, incompatible with any conception of a liberal society and, I would argue, incompatible with political freedom as well. The aim, according to Clause IV, is:

> To secure for the workers by hand or by brain the full fruits of their industry and the most equitable distribution thereof that may be possible upon the basis of the common ownership of the means of production, distribution and exchange, and the best obtainable system of popular administration and control of each industry and service.

The language is not far removed from the *Communist Manifesto,* with the significant difference that Marx and Engels were much more honest about the true nature of 'common ownership'. There is, of course, no such thing: you can have private ownership, or cooperative ownership, or state ownership, and that is that. Marx and Engels did not talk about common ownership, but the need 'to centralise all instruments of production in the hands of the state, that is, of the proletariat organised as the ruling class.'[9] That is what Clause IV is really about, and it is only possible, in any meaningful way, to describe the British Labour Party as a social *democratic* party because a precarious majority of its members in Parliament are still opposed to implementing their own constitution as it stands. That blurring of fundamental distinctions that I mentioned must therefore be understood not merely as the work of revolutionary Marxists and their foreign patrons, but as something that stems from a basic confusion about the conditions of a free society—a kind of confusion, as Britain has found, which is extremely auspicious for totalitarians.

The same confusion is evident when we consider the case of

the trade unions. In a pamphlet published in 1949, the British Trades Union Congress described the contest between communists and anti-communists inside the trade unions as 'an issue of democracy or dictatorship, unity or disruption; that is fundamental'.[10] On 27 October 1948, the TUC's General Council urged its members 'to counteract every manifestation of communist influences within their unions; and to open the eyes of all work-people to the dangerous subversive activities which are being engineered in opposition to the declared policies of the trade union movement'. It was on the basis of this appreciation of communism that the British trade union leaders, who had been prime movers in the creation of the World Federation of Trade Unions (WFTU) in 1945, decided to pull out of it four years later, when it was already clear that the Russians had succeeded in converting the organisation into a political weapon. But a lot of water has flowed under the bridge since then, and the river is muddied.

The trade unions have long been viewed by the communist world as a possible Trojan horse within Western societies. The recent process of east—west trade union contacts has found many apologists. It has been argued that communist and non-communist unions have a common purpose in defending workers' interests against multinational corporations. It has even been argued (by Clive Jenkins, the leader of the British white collar workers' union, the ASTMS) that we should consider 'whether we might not have something to learn' from East European trade unions in 'inflation-free' societies. (In the article in *The Times* in April 1975 in which he made this point, he also argued that the KGB was more brutal than Western security services because the Russians had 'suffered' more.) Such comments reflect a—possibly disingenuous—ignorance about what the communists stand to gain from the process of trade union *détente*. Alexander Shelepin put it in dramatic language at the Eighth Congress of the communist-run WFTU in 1973, when he remarked that 'what the trade unions of capitalist countries are now struggling for has already been implemented long ago in the Soviet Union'. The short-term goals of the Russians and their accessories in the recent rounds of east—west union contacts may be summed up as follows:

1   To bring about a rift between west European unions and the American AFL—CIO, whose splendid old warrior

George Meany, has been an uncompromising critic of the whole process of east—west *détente*. In February 1975, the AFL—CIO's executive council put out a statement in which it declared that it viewed the 'fraternisation of democratic western European labour centres with Communist Party labour fronts with disgust'. One example of Soviet hopes on this score was a report by *Trud* after the east—west union conference on 'the humanisation of the work environment' held in Geneva early in 1975. The Soviet paper commented that the 'success' of the conference was due to the 'permanent and untiring efforts of Comrade Brezhnev, personally, and all peace-loving, progressive forces' and was a major rebuff for the 'cold-war' designs of the AFL—CIO.[11]

2 To secure admission for West European communist trade union federations to the European Trade Union Confederation (ETUC) which was founded in February 1973. They had made notable progress in this area by mid-1975: the Italian Communist Federation (CGIL) was admitted in 1974; there were signs that its French counterpart, the CGT, would soon gain entry also; and the Portuguese Intersindical and illegal Spanish *comisiones obreras*—which were represented at Geneva—were next in the queue.

3 To ensure the quiet demise of the leading non-communist world labour federation, the International Confederation of Free Trade Unions (ICFTU), whose headquarters staff in Brussels was sternly critical of accelerating east—west links.

4 To set up east—west 'trade secretariats' on individual industries which could provide vehicles for subversion.

5 To make extensive propaganda use of east—west contacts both to demonstrate to the East European audience that the merits of the communist system are applauded in the West and to erode the position of anti-communists in Western trade unions.

A longer-term goal for the Russians was to gain entry into the ETUC for the East European labour organisations and to establish a dominant position within it—thus finally accomplishing what they failed to achieve with the WFTU in the 1940s. The WFTU and the international department of the

Russian trade union federation are crucial instruments of communist subversion. The WFTU, which is based in Prague but is directly controlled from Moscow, and supervised by a notoriously tough team of Russians on the spot, contains a special department concerned with expanding and coordinating strike action throughout Western Europe. The spread of multinational companies has provided a splendid pretext for the multinational strike; the stoppages in Dunlop-Pirelli plants in both England and Italy in 1972 set the pattern for later action along the same lines.

The WFTU has a cosmopolitan leadership. At the time of writing, its president, Enrique Pastorino, was an Uruguayan; its general secretary, Pierre Gensous, was French; and its secretaries included Evgeny Cherednichenko from Russia, Albertino Masetti from Italy and Mahendra Sen from India. Although Czechs were prominent in the permanent secretariat, the key man in each department was always Russian. Western employees of the WFTU enjoy diplomatic privileges and receive part of their salaries in hard currency in foreign banks, usually in Switzerland.

The key functions of the WFTU are to promote Soviet propaganda; to identify and support sympathisers and agents in Western countries; and to organise an ambitious training programme for Western trade unionists, who are invited to institutions such as the International Trade Union College in Moscow, the Georgi Dimitrov Trade Union School in Bulgaria, or the Fritz Heckert College in East Germany.

The head of the international department of the AUCCTU, Boris Averyanov, was transferred to the WFTU headquarters in Prague in January 1975, but suffered injuries in a car accident shortly afterwards, so that the effect of his appointment could not immediately be gauged. But low-level employees of the WFTU were in agreement that his appointment represented a definite upgrading of the WFTU in Soviet strategy. Averyanov had an interesting background. Born in Kalinin in 1925, he first visited Britain to attend the TUC conference in 1949 and returned almost every year since; he also turned up at meetings of the Scottish TUC. From May 1959 until September 1961 he was second secretary at the Russian embassy in London, responsible for trade union affairs. He had also been active on a wider plane. His travels often took him to Africa, especially to

Lagos, where he was usually accompanied by Anatoli Botvinov, the chief of the African bureau of Averyanov's former department. Botvinov was thrown out of Gabon in 1961 on charges of 'subversive activities'. One of Averyanov's last trips in his former job was to Lisbon in November 1974.

Averyanov was identified as a career KGB officer by the celebrated double agent, Penkovsky. His case is just one example of how the WFTU, the AUCCTU and the KGB are bound together. Among the other well-known KGB men in the international department of the AUCCTU was Igor Konstantinovich Klimov, who was also the labour attaché in the Russian embassy in London before his expulsion in 1971. He made several trips to Britain as an 'interpreter' for trade union delegations.

The international department of the AUCCTU is not to be compared with counterparts in western union federations; its European department alone employs over a hundred people. It functions, in close coordination with the KGB, as the nerve centre of Soviet attempts to penetrate Western trade unions. Its modus operandi becomes apparent when we consider the experience of West Germany's trade unions.

The German trade union federation (the DGB) banned all contacts with Soviet labour bosses after the Russian invasion of Czechoslovakia in 1968. But contacts were resumed in 1969, when Shelepin entertained the leader of the DGB, Heinz Vetter, in Moscow. In 1970, some 50 East European and West German union leaders exchanged visits. The number doubled in 1971, doubled again in 1972, and rose in 1974 to more than four hundred visits. A curious sidelight on this is that for more than a year the man who vetted DGB travellers to the east was Guenther Guillaume, Chancellor Willy Brandt's former aide, who was subsequently arrested as a communist spy. One of the most vigorous advocates of east–west union contacts in West Germany, Hans Feltermeier of the Public Service and Transport Workers' Union, was arrested on suspicion of espionage in August 1974; he was eventually released but was not hired again by the DGB. The West German case brings us to the crux of the matter: the extent to which the Russians have been using their contacts with West European unions to promote subversion and recruit agents.

But such evidence of KGB involvement in the communist

union apparatus had little apparent effect on the policy of British union leaders. The Soviet invasion of Czechoslovakia interrupted but did not long delay the decay of Western resistance to Soviet policies that was already visible in the mid-1960s. The TUC congress in 1971 adopted a resolution calling for the encouragement of 'fraternal relations' between the WFTU and members of the ICFTU. At its congress in 1973, the TUC supported the idea of an international union liaison committee to pull communist and non-communist unions closer together.

In the course of the 1970s an expanding number of British trade unionists visited eastern Europe; Vic Feather (now Lord Feather), then the general secretary of the TUC, turned up in Moscow in December 1972, and went back on the eve of an important east—west gathering in Vienna in July 1973. The joint declaration issued by the TUC and the AUCCTU in Moscow in 1973 set the tone for what was to follow. It was agreed, for instance, that 'the trade unions of the Soviet Union and Great Britain had similar objectives and had adopted common attitudes over many issues'.

Such contacts resulted in the first major east—west union conference, held under the auspices of the trade union section of the International Labour Organisation in Geneva in January 1974. The Russians made it plain then that the agenda at such meetings would not include the condition of East European workers. As Shelepin put it in a statement that refutes the idea that trade union *détente* may help to relieve the plight of the economic serfs of Eastern Europe: 'cooperation must be based on the principle of non-interference in each country's internal affairs and recognition of present-day realities.'

A list of the major British trade union delegations in Eastern Europe in 1974 gives some idea of the way that a trickle of east—west contacts has broadened into a torrent:

Month	Union	No. of Persons	Country
May	Scottish TUC	?	Bulgaria
May	National Union of Mineworkers	4	Russia
May	National Union of Railwaymen	3	Hungary
May—June	National Union of Mineworkers	20	Poland

June	National Union of Railwaymen	3	Russia
July	TUC	1	Russia
July	Amalgamated Union of Engineering Workers 2		Russia
August	National Union of Mineworkers	3	Hungary
September	National Union of Hosiery and Knitwear Workers	3	Russia
September	National Union of Mineworkers	1	Romania
October	Amalgamated Union of Engineering Workers 2		Czechoslovakia
October	National Union of Mineworkers	4	Russia
November	Amalgamated Union of Engineering Workers	2	Yugoslavia
November	TUC	6	Hungary
November	TUC	6	Czechoslovakia
December	TUC	1	Yugoslavia

Such contacts may seem unexceptionable to some readers. But the point that surely needs to be stressed is that East European trade unions enjoy *none* of the rights that the WFTU congress in Varna defined in 1973 as fundamental for unions in capitalist countries. These included the right to strike, to elect union leaders, to influence the hiring and firing of employees, and to conduct collective wage negotiations. As Karel Hoffmann, the Czech union leader, put it at the Eighth Congress of his federation in 1972, 'for socialist trade unions, theories of independence or of neutrality in relations with the Communist Party are not acceptable. Lenin said that there could be no question of any sort of neutrality on the part of the trade unions.' The point is repeated in the resolutions adopted at the Fifteenth Congress of the Soviet union federation in March 1972: 'The Communist Party's concern is that trade unions successfully perform their role as a school of control, economic management and communism.' No similar 'schools of control' exist in the west. I am drawn to conclude that the appropriate bodies to deal with the East European labour managers, if such dealings are necessary at all, are governments, not trade unionists, and that contacts conducted on the present basis are not helping workers on either side of the iron curtain, but would seem to be helping someone else.

Baudelaire wrote that the Devil's greatest art was to persuade people that he did not exist. The world does not work according to simplistic conspiracy theories, but it would be very foolish to assume that there are not real conspiracies which demand more than our casual agreement that yes, indeed, they may exist. The crisis in the Western democracies is partly related to what the French describe, in an untranslatable phrase, as the *démobilisation des esprits*. This is not essentially the work of Trotskyists in the press, or communists in the House of Commons: it stems from our own confusion, our reluctance to look at things as they are, our good-natured refusal to name names. Thus when communist trade union leaders are interviewed on television, no one is ungracious enough to suggest that their interpretation of 'social injustice' may be related to their political affiliation: in short, that they are communists—members of a party once described by Léon Blum as a party that 'is neither a national party, nor an international party, but a *foreign* national party'.

Take an alternative example. BBC television in London produced a two-hour film at considerable expense which was shown during prime time in October 1974. It was entitled 'Leeds United' and purported to be an objective description of a strike by clothing workers. No one saw fit to mention that both the producer and the script-writer were members of the Workers' Revolutionary Party, a Trotskyist revolutionary group. I am not advocating the muzzling of Trotskyists, nor even denying their right to present their views on prime time television, although this would be intolerably tedious for the viewing public, and I labour under no illusions that if they had their way, people who disagreed with them would be excluded from *all* the media. What I would suggest is that, at the very least, it is the responsibility of a broadcasting authority to make it clear that a film like the one in question is, in fact, not the work of a normal professional team, but of people who have a revolutionary ideology to sell.

Subversion works at several distinct levels, which have been classified by the Soviet theorists themselves as: sedation, diversion, penetration and activation. We are not at a loss for examples of how sedation works. We are assured that we need not be concerned that the communists in Italy (in the regional elections of June 1975) pulled in a third of the votes, because the Italian Communist Party is 'different'. Different from what? Well, the answer comes back pat, Enrico Berlinguer has criticised the Soviet invasion of Czechoslovakia, and expressed his doubts about the way his comrades are operating in Portugal, and Bologna (whose local government is Communist) is a clean and pleasant town, and Berlinguer is photogenic. If the claims that the Italian Communist Party is 'independent' were true, that would not actually reduce the problem for those Italian voters who are worried that the country may find itself governed before long by an Allende-style coalition. But the claims are open to serious question anyway, since the Russians are said to provide about half the annual budget of the Italian Communist Party.

I have already skimmed over some British examples of the soporific effects of sedation: the creation of a climate in which Labour Members of Parliament can speak from communist platforms or publish their articles in the communist *Morning Star* without drawing a storm of adverse criticism; in which non-communist trade unionists swap visits with East European labour bosses; in which the annual elections for the committee of the National Union of Students turn out to be contests between more and less orthodox types of communists without anyone raising the perfectly proper question, why should the taxpayer continue to support such a body? But the most important case of sedation involves the reduced public consciousness of the strategic threat from the Soviet Union, and the widespread enthusiasm for forms of *détente* that are, at the best, more cosmetic than real. The British government—the government of a country with a gaping balance of payments deficit—was able to extend credits totalling £1,000 million to the Soviet Union early in 1975 at about half the world borrowing rate, and was allowed to get away with the argument that this was 'good for trade'. The agreement was in fact a commercial disaster (like the American grain sales); it could not remotely be justified in the dubious category of 'aid for developing countries', and was negotiated at a time when the Socialist left in Britain was successfully pressing for a boycott of credits and profitable arms sales to 'fascist' countries like South Africa, Spain or Chile—which, after the Allende regime was overthrown, promptly made compensation for some British enterprises that had been expropriated.

This is already leading us towards that second category: diversion. Here again, we find that the communists have achieved wonders in diverting public attention from the real dangers to Western society. Thus, when the evidence suggests that there has been a qualitative as well as a quantitative increase in Soviet-sponsored subversion in Western Europe, we find many countries besides the United States caught up in a debate about the past record and future purposes of the CIA. Several hundredweight of pamphlets, books and broadsheets have been produced on the human rights situation in Chile, but there is no corresponding interest in what is happening behind the iron curtain (or the new bamboo curtain that has descended in Indochina). The prime practitioners of diversionary tactics, of course, are not necessarily communists or even Marxists—the most successful are in fact unlikely to be either. They are likely to belong to those categories that the Soviet theorists describe, by an unflattering insect analogy, as 'termites' and 'maggots'— the types of people who seek to discredit those institutions, values and individuals that it suits communist interests to discredit, or who follow suit because they think the wind is blowing that way. They all belong to the same class that Lenin described, in an equally brutal phrase, as 'useful idiots': people who, without understanding revolutionary strategy and without belonging to the revolutionary party, are simply but resolutely against the existing order.

The terms 'penetration' and 'activation' are self-explanatory. The aim of a subversive campaign is to infiltrate and make use of all the key institutions of the state: government, the civil service, the armed forces, the educational system, the media, the trade unions. Some are harder to 'get at' than others: for example, while it may be relatively easy to organise a protest movement on the basis of the grievances of conscript soldiers, it is generally extremely difficult to penetrate a professional officer corps. 'Activation' is based on the well-known device of maintaining long-term agents, or 'sleepers', who will be exposed only at the climax of a campaign. Philby was an example in the spy world; his equivalent in internal subversion might, for example, be a cabinet minister professing views that are *systematically* contrary to the goals of his real political masters—a prominent man who is being 'saved up' for the moment of crisis.

But I do not wish, in this book, to adopt an overly *technical* view of a problem that, at its core, is moral and psychological. I have suggested in this chapter that, after prolonged burrowing by the 'termites' and 'maggots' (their words, not mine!) the foundations of liberal democracy may no longer be as sound as they used to be. The response I would advocate is a crusading, rather than a repressive one. As Hayek puts it, in the great battle of ideas that is now under way, we must first know what we believe. It is only on the basis of a restored awareness of the values and purposes—and innate *superiority*—of a free society that we can begin to contest the many-pronged assault that is now being made on it.

But there are some *structures* that will need to be changed. The survival of freedom of expression, for example, is at risk when a printing union can intervene in an attempt to censor newspaper articles—as one tried to censor an article by Lord George-Brown in June 1975—or even to censor an advertisement, as happened in the case of an announcement inserted by Mr Ross McWhirter in *The Guardian* that same month. His announcement warned of the dangers of the abuse of trade union power, and offered to help to arrange car transport for commuters who might be unable to get to their jobs in the event of a railway strike. It had previously been offered to another daily paper whose proprietor, obviously a cautious man, asked for 'danger money' in addition to the standard charge, but then called back to say that SOGAT (one of the printing unions) would 'black' the paper if the advertisement were carried. To its credit, *The Guardian*, which is not exactly a conservative paper, carried the advertisement. No other daily newspaper did. In a free society, the power to control editorial copy cannot be vested in the hands of a union.

The opportunities for subversion, in short, are presented by intellectual confusion about the fundamental difference between liberal democratic and totalitarian politics, about the presence of a growing external threat to the Western societies, and by the fact that doors have been left open that should now be firmly shut. I shall take up the argument that there is a case for *civilised intolerance* in a later chapter.

4

The Disease of Money

Shall I be sold up? Am I to become a beggar?
Shall I flee? Shall my flight come to an end?
Question addressed to an oracle
in the reign of Diocletian (284-305 A D)

Order is precarious. A stable society is one that constantly strives for, and attains, an equilibrium between the need to change and the need to conserve. If the balance breaks it cannot easily be restored. Yet the balance is always at risk in a rationalist age that has cast doubt on all the traditions, moral values and social conventions of the past, an age in which society is no longer seen as Burke saw it—as a compact between the dead, the living and the unborn. The loss of reverence for the past is something specifically modern, as is the idea that mankind is embarked on a forward march through history towards some secular paradise in which the lion will lie down with the lamb. This historical rootlessness, and that vision of a shimmering city on the other side of the desert have produced a contempt for the idea that there are unwritten boundaries for political (as well as personal) action. It is not understood that the cost of transgressing them will be a period of social disintegration followed by a new age of authority and belief, in which a lost religion will be supplanted by the idols set up by the state, and those boundaries that were so arrogantly ignored will be redefined on tablets of stone and policed with guard-dogs and electronic devices. This is the tragedy of Faustian man, of the man who thought he could transcend all laws, violate all limits. Yet

The stars move still, time runs, the clock will strike,
The devil will come, and Faustus must be damned.

The Editor of *The Times*, William Rees-Mogg, was right in a recent essay to identify inflation, the characteristic economic malady of many Western societies, as a 'disease of inordinacy'.

'The reigning error of the twentieth century', he writes, 'is the rejection of the idea of external discipline.'[1] And he associates the damage done by Dr Spock's assault on family discipline (for which the good doctor has since apologised—too late to help the millions of mothers who read him) and the Freudian erosion of sexual restraint, with the Keynesian attack on the idea of discipline in money. His view of inflationary man is profound, but perhaps it needs to be taken still further. The recent trends that are pulling us towards strato-inflation are related both to an inflation of expectations in the post-1945 consumer society, and to a loss of broader concepts of patriotism and citizenship. Politicians have contributed to the tragic impoverishment of social life by couching their proposals—and often their whole *weltanschauung*—in terms of what new economic benefits the state can offer its members, and rarely in terms of what *they* can offer society. The psychology of inflation is deeply implanted.

A society that does not attack the sources of inflation (and whose politicians and television pundits may even be instructing the public that 'a little inflation is good for you') is in the same plight as a society that fails to respond to systematic breaches of the law. Indeed, both those failures are characteristic of Britain today. Rules, written and unwritten, are being cast aside. The process is especially damaging in three interlocking pieces of economic life: the fuelling of inflation, the monopoly practices of the trade unions, and the vendetta against private enterprise and private property in general. This chapter deals with the social causes and effects of inflation—those other problems are taken up in subsequent chapters.

The behaviour of modern democracy does pose a huge problem for those who believe that political and economic order depend upon prescribed limits for what a central authority or a private pressure group can legitimately set out to do. The barter process that goes on between politicians and voters in elections has led many serious observers to ask whether the necessary corrective measures are 'politically possible'. Worse still, the belief that certain desirable measures (for controlling inflation or curbing trade union power) are 'politically impossible'—that is, the voters would not buy them—has led a great number of economists and assorted experts, as well as politicians, to apply a kind of self-denying ordinance to themselves. This self-censorship takes the form of not mentioning what needs to be done if it is felt to be politically unacceptable.

This is one variant of intellectual pacifism, of which I shall have more to say. The immediate point is that if X or Y needs to be done for the sake of preserving social order or keeping the economy off the rocks, but is 'politically impossible', the political system, in the long run, will have to be changed—not only *has* to be changed, but will *inevitably* be changed if the original analysis is correct. But no one can tell whether X or Y is politically possible or not until it has been fully debated and the proposals have been placed before the bench of public opinion.

To take two especially sensitive examples: if a rate of unemployment of six per cent (which Keynes would have considered to be not a long stretch from 'full employment') or ten per cent is the *only* alternative to Weimar-style inflation, then that must be said plainly, and the consequences of both action and inaction will need to be spelled out in full detail. If the *only* way to preserve a working market economy is to ban certain types of strikes and limit the process of collective bargaining in other ways, that also needs to be said, and the public will have to be led, once again, to take full account of the penalty for inaction. That is the only way you can determine whether a measure is 'politically impossible' because the electorate in a democratic society will not (as we are frequently told) swallow the strong medicine that may be necessary for its own survival, or, alternatively, because its political leaders were too timorous to offer it—in other words, because they failed to lead.

This whole problem is explored in a stimulating recent work by Professor W. H. Hutt[2], who concludes that 'the most urgent problem of our age for those who give most urgency to the preservation of democratic institutions is that of restraining the vote-buying process'. Hutt is profoundly depressed by the way that modern electioneering so often degenerates into a fatuous kind of auctioneering: the politicians bid each other up with similar promises of greater material rewards, better social services, full employment and stable prices. Radical proposals for reducing inflation, for redistributing income away from consumption and towards savings and investment, and for blunting the edge of the 'strike-threat weapon' get left outside in the cloak room—even as the urgency of the economic crisis mounts, and such measures begin to appear as essential to the survival of parliamentary institutions. Popular columnists and party *apparatchiks* are on hand to reassure those grooming themselves for re-election that such ideas are too hot to handle. Political 'realists' agree in their club-rooms that success will depend on the flattery and ever more costly bribery of Welfare Man, *homo gratificator,* that supreme achievement of natural selection in the Socialist holiday camp—the ultimate consumer who has been spoon-fed night and day with the pleasing idea that it is the responsibility of the state to provide for his every want, and some of his fantasies as well, without regard for merit or exertion.

La Rochefoucauld said of the court of Louis XVI, on the eve of the French revolution, that political decision-making had been debased to the point where 'promises were made to the extent that men hoped and kept to the extent that they feared'. So it would seem that some features of modern democratic behaviour are neither modern nor democratic: the doubt that remains is whether a democratic electorate is fatally drawn to reward those who offer the wrong sort of promises. Peter Jay touched on the problem in a provocative article[3] in which he suggested that four essential features of Britain's political economy may be found to be irreconcilable. He listed them as:

1 Government whose authority rests on renewable popular consent.
2 The commitment to full employment—not just as an ultimate objective, but as a necessary requirement year by year and quarter by quarter.
3 The dependence on stable prices, or at least on stable rates of inflation or some stable basis of economic exchange.
4 The durability of collective bargaining as the primary means of determining pay in the labour market.

A politician becomes a statesman by standing on basic principles and by aiming at long-term goals; but elections, and the management of precarious parliamentary majorities seem to depend upon short-term success—perhaps as 'short-term' as the monthly unemployment figures. So there is a dangerous tendency to offer bread and circuses while Rome burns.

In practice, recent British governments have usually found it expedient to fuel inflation rather than risk 'politically unacceptable' rates of unemployment; the fear of the dole queue is more acute, at any rate among politicians who remember the 1930s, than the fear of Weimar-style inflation. But it is at last beginning to be discovered that these are false alternatives in the end, and that the sub-Keynesian argument (Keynes was not a Keynesian, just as Marx was not a Marxist) that you can inflate your way out of recession has to be paid for at the price of a constantly accelerating depreciation of the currency and that the end reward is not an economic boom but 'slumpflation', *à la 1923*. The West Germans—who remember Weimar—appear to understand this better, which perhaps explains why they were curbing their rate of inflation in 1975 while Britain's was building up to a doom-laden twenty-five or thirty per cent.

Weimar remains the classic example of where economic inordinacy can lead.[4] The statistics, and the political consequences, were so spectacular that many people simply refuse to believe that the experience could be repeated. The injustice and cruelty of high inflation have had revolutionary consequences everywhere; it helped to bring about military coups in Brazil, Argentina, Uruguay and Chile, fascist takeovers in Portugal and Germany and communist revolution in Russia, Hungary and China. When the monthly wages of Chiang Kai-Shek's troops had fallen in 1949 to the point where they would no longer buy a few handfuls of rice, his fate was sealed.

A rate of inflation of 'only' twenty or twenty-five per cent, sustained for a few years, is quite enough to wreak havoc in most democratic societies. Democracy itself comes to appear impotent before the problem. Someone once said to Churchill, 'I admire the exaggerated way in which you tell the truth'. In just that sense, the Weimar experience offers a cautionary tale that we can hardly afford to ignore.

The value of the mark in Germany fell from about eight to the dollar in December 1918 to 4,200 milliards (4,200,000,000,000) to the dollar in November 1923. Over that same period, the face value of the currency in circulation rose from just over 33 milliard marks to 92 *trillion* marks (92,000,000,000,000,000,000,000). Yet ironically, the real value of the money in circulation had declined sharply; people were constantly complaining that there was 'not enough money'. Before the end of that period, most banknotes were literally worth less than the paper they were printed on. The Weimar experience exemplified the notorious two-stage progression of inflation: in stage one, money increases faster than prices; in stage two, prices outstrip the expansion of the monetary supply. By 20 November 1923, when the value of the currency was stabilised and Schacht successfully introduced a new currency, the Rentenmark, the German mark was worth exactly one *billionth* of its pre-war value.

The background to the Weimar lunacy—which had the blessing of the president of the Reichsbank, Rudolf Havenstein—was no doubt unique. Germany after the First World War was a country on the brink of revolution, and the new republican government was beleaguered by both communist and right-wing insurrectionists. It had suffered defeat in war, the humiliation of the Versailles settlement, the burden of reparations payments and the final insult of the Franco—Belgian occupation of the Ruhr in 1923. The calculation of Havenstein and those who thought like him was that deficit financing was the means of escaping revolution and satisfying patriotic sentiments; in the early stages, the depreciation of the floating mark in relation to the hard currencies produced a transient export boom and a low rate of unemployment. Later on, the printing presses covered the cost of 'passive resistance' in the Ruhr.

It did not work for very long. Herr Havenstein and his friends soon had to contend with a very simple psychological factor. Paper money has value only for so long as people are willing to suspend their disbelief that this can be money at all. If confidence wanes, there is a flight into 'real values' (*Sachwerte* is the German word) which will become more and more frenetic unless the authorities can find a way of restoring faith in the currency. If they cannot, the flight into gold, jewellery, foreign currency, commodities, property and *objets d'art* may become a universal rush to buy anything at all that will hold its value as the currency collapses—canned foods or cigarettes or a pair of shoes. The end, in Weimar, was the death of money as a means of exchange. Society went back to the barter system.

The public understanding of what high levels of inflation

actually mean is generally delayed. There is usually a long breathing space for the politicians and the speculators, during which ordinary respectable people go on making the same motions as before. As prices soar, thrifty families cut back on their weekly expenses, give up small luxuries, and try to set aside a little more each week towards that holiday or that new suit that they are hoping to buy. They go on putting money into deposit accounts or building societies even when the return, in the form of interest, is far too small to make up for the way that inflation—and the people responsible for it—are robbing them of their savings like thieves in the night. The people who are often utterly crushed by high inflation—pensioners, people on fixed incomes, middle-class families living on a small income from gilt-edged securities—are frequently the last to grasp what inflation actually means. When the understanding finally sinks in, it may be too late for them to save themselves. But when everyone begins to base his economic behaviour on the expectation of high inflation, the whole inflationary process accelerates out of control.

It is of course nonsense to argue, as do the authors of a recent popular book, that inflation 'does not involve much waste of real resources. It does not produce dole queues—its statistics do not have a human, photographable face.'[5] By forcing most people to turn to speculation instead of productive investment, inflation will, in the end, result in serious wastage of 'real resources'. Its statistics become highly photogenic if the currency breaks down altogether and people revert to a primitive barter-trade: witness the old Weimar photographs of men paying the barber a few eggs for a haircut. And yet the authors of that statement have latched on to an important half-truth that is very relevant to the way that politicians behave in Britain today.

In the early stages, inflation and unemployment may take their toll of different people. Perhaps the misery of a clerk or a professional man whose earnings are not keeping up with inflation, whose firm cannot afford to pay him more, who is not defended by a powerful and aggressive trade union and who has just seen the value of his savings and the insurance policy he took out to pay for his children's education wiped out, is 'less photographable' than that of a line of workless men outside a social security office. But it is certainly no less real. In the long run, in any case, you are more likely to end up with both kinds of misery at once. What many socialists appear to believe is that they can live in the short term, using inflation as a form of taxation without representation* in order to redistribute income away from the middle-class towards their own favoured constituency. For the conscious revolutionaries among them, this may in fact be a rational and politically-motivated policy; Chile provides a recent example of a Marxist attempt to skew the effects of inflation to destroy the middle class. What is certainly clear from Weimar, as from the more recent examples, is the truth of Lenin's remark that the surest way to destroy a society is to destroy its currency.

When money died in Weimar, so did lifelong habits of honesty, thrift, self-discipline, productive labour, concern for others. Those who clung to them longest were brutally pushed to the wall by a new breed of speculators who grasped precisely what was going on and saw how to profit from it. Hugo Stinnes, who made himself the richest man in Europe by buying up anything he could lay his hands on with money borrowed from anyone who would lend, and who systematically bankrupted his creditors by repaying them in valueless marks a few weeks later, became the living symbol of the Great Inflation. Men like Stinnes, who played off depreciating loans against appreciating assets (like property speculators in inflationary Britain in the early 1970s) became the focus for hatred and murderous envy. The type is not unique to periods of high inflation, but it thrives upon them. The French inflation of the 1790s produced a similar representative figure: Tallien. The successful career of the charming confidence trickster, Stavisky—whose fiddle with municipal bonds brought down a police chief and a prime minister in 1934—was related to the corruption of middle-class values as a result of successive devaluations of the franc. As an adventurous recent historian of the Third Republic concluded, to understand Stavisky and his like, 'you have to take account of how the stable resources of old middle-class families, which had been nourished in a tradition of honour and honesty, had been methodically destroyed through the game of successive devaluations. Thus the way into the very heart of the

---

*Which it is literally, if the tax grid is not readjusted upwards with inflation, so that men whose salary increases may not have been sufficient to keep them abreast of rising prices find themselves taxed more than before.

establishment was opened, little by little, to all sorts of people who were poorly prepared, by their backgrounds and attitudes, to appreciate a Stavisky at his real value.'[6]

The demoralisation of the middle-class—of precisely those social groups that are most committed to saving and among which the work ethic is most pronounced—is a national tragedy. Their justified resentment at the effects of the lottery of inflation, in which most of them are bound to draw losing tickets, will naturally seek a focus in those who are winning, who tend to be either profiteers reaping fortunes with borrowed money or the members of powerful trade unions; both types of winners, of course, have a vested interest in keeping the rigged roulette wheel spinning as long as they think they can get away with it.

The world of the pimp and the profiteer, of the 'pusher' (*Schieber*) and the 'snatcher' (*Raffke*) was a world fit for Hitler, whose storm-troopers, under their banners and crosses, succeeded in a macabre imposture of an older, sterner order that was not tainted with the corruption and social decomposition of the Republic of the early 1920s. The gaslit debauchery of 'Cabaret' led on to the gas chambers. The irony of Hitler's imposture of Teutonic virtue was compounded by the fact that his financial backers included some of the most notorious inflationary profiteers, who were able to divert public resentment at their own performance towards the myth of the world-wide conspiracy of 'Jewish bolshevik-capitalists'.

People who have a vested interest in inflation, like trade union leaders in Britain, are sometimes heard to opine solemnly that it was unemployment, not inflation, that brought Hitler to power. Len Murray, the leader of Britain's Trades Union Congress, said just that in an interview at a time, early in 1975, when many major trade unions were pressing wage claims in excess of thirty or thirty-five per cent. The argument clearly appeals to anyone whose earnings outstrip inflation, or who believes that the government should resort to the printing-press to preserve jobs or fulfil more grandiose egalitarian demands. And superficially, Mr Murray is right. Hitler came to power more than nine years after Germany's hyper-inflation had been brought under control. He came to power when the market economies were still reeling from the effects of the stock market crash in the United States and when unemployment had soared. He came to power as the leader of a party pledged to full employment.

But the German government's mishandling of the slump can in turn be traced back to the fear of inflation that was generated by the experience of the 1920s. Far more important, it was during that earlier period—and largely as a result of hyper-inflation—that the democratic parties in the Weimar Republic suffered a heavy blow from which they were never able to recover. This was after all the period of the Kapp putsch, of Hitler's 'beer-hall' putsch, and of communist insurrection in Bavaria. In the 1919 elections, the parties that were unequivocally committed to the Weimar constitution— the Democrats, the Centre Party and the Social Democrats— were able to win a majority of the seats in the Reichstag. In the elections the following year, when the mark had declined to one-tenth of its pre-war value in relation to the dollar, they lost their parliamentary majority. They were never able to recover it, despite the eventual stabilisation of the currency. In the next elections in March 1924, when the hyper-inflation was over but its sting was still fresh, the Nazis made their first appearance in the Reichstag with thirty-two seats; the right-wing Nationalists, led by Alfred Hugenberg (one of the foremost inflationary profiteers) were the real victors of that ballot, although they were to lose out in the long run. The Great Inflation ensured that the defence of the Weimar constitution remained a minority cause in pre-Hitler Germany.

The origins of Weimar inflation must be sought in deficit financing—and here, there is a direct parallel with our own situation. The growth of public spending is almost always inflationary, even if a government makes out that it can cover its new expenditure by increased taxation. Modern experience shows that there is a kind of Parkinson's law involved in public spending, which is summed up very well by Milton Friedman: 'legislators will spend whatever the tax system will raise plus a good deal more'.[7]

The explosion of public spending in Germany came during the First World War, when deficit financing came to be regarded as a public duty. The stage was set when the convertibility of marks into gold was suspended on the eve of the war, in August 1914. By the end of the war, the government had accumulated an unfunded debt of over 50 milliard gold marks. It is worth noting that in wartime Germany, as in other countries, the inflationary effects of monetary inflation were not fully felt, since saving was presented as a contribution to the war effort and the consumer market was very restricted. Reluctant to raise taxes, post-war governments reverted to the wartime practice of printing money to cover public spending. With the brief hiatus of Erzberger's draconian tax increases in 1920 colossal quantities of banknotes were issued and prices moved even faster. By late 1923, only three per cent of public expenditure was covered by taxes and other government revenues.

The lunacy had its temporary reward. Unemployment remained relatively low until mid-1923, with the exception of the few months in 1920 when the government was trying to restore some measure of monetary stability; between March and July 1920, the rate of unemployment rose from 1.9 per cent to 6 per cent. But Weimar Germany at last presented a surrealistic model of 'slumpflation'. As all remaining confidence in the currency collapsed and the internal value of the mark plummeted downwards even faster than its exchange rate in the dollar markets, the number of jobless men shot upwards—from about 1 per cent at the start of 1922 to 2.8 per cent at the end of the year, 6 per cent in August 1923 and 23 per cent that November. The Great Inflation was bringing in its train an autonomously-generated Great Depression which was only averted by the stabilisation of the currency.

What cannot be stressed enough is that hyper-inflation in Weimar was the product of two interlocking factors: calculated deficit financing, which was based on the bad habits acquired in the First World War and the myopic belief that this was the way to minimise the effects of the reparations burden and promote an export boom, and the panic that set in when society at large finally woke up to what was happening. The panic was what the advocates of inflation—and there were many of them—were not prepared for.

But it is the social effects of the Weimar inflation that should concern us most. The destruction of money, the index of economic value, brought about the collapse of all social values. As Stefan Zweig noted grimly, 'amid the general collapse of values, a kind of insanity seized even those middle-class circles that had hitherto been unshakeable in their order'. Social decomposition was apparent in all sorts of ways: in the increase in crime (the number of thefts trebled between 1913 and 1923), in the behaviour of the parasitic *nouveaux riches* with their whores and their gaudy display, in the despair of retired professional men who saw their savings turned to dust overnight and were reduced to living on charity in newly-established hostels.

Society was very clearly divided into the losers and the winners; there were not very many of the latter in the end, and their wealth looked too much like the product of illegal gambling to be readily accepted by the rest. As one author commented, inflation under Weimar was possibly 'the vastest expropriation that has ever been effected in peacetime'—but an expropriation that proceeded according to no known laws or morality. Its logic was apparent to most people only in hindsight. Afterwards, it was clearly appreciated that rapid inflation turns normal economic life upside down. The creditor loses, the debtor gains. The cautious saver is ruined, the profligate can resell his consumer goods for a profit. Any form of investment with a fixed money value—an insurance policy, a treasury bond, a bank deposit, a mortgage loan made to someone else—is about as profitable as burning money in a public place. Even the owners of property lost out in many cases, since capital gains tax was applied on the old basis if the property were sold—as if money had held its value—while tenants' rents were held down by regulatory legislation. Shopkeepers and manufacturers had fun for a time, but rapidly discovered that they could not replace the goods they had sold or the raw materials they processed without paying out vastly more paper money. Businessmen learned that, in order to survive, they had to buy and sell goods rather than manufacture them. The logic was described by Mark Twain in his tale of a sack of flour in a Wild West mining town where money was plentiful but goods were scarce: it changed hands again and again but was never consumed. The same logic explained the scandal of Centre Point, the large commercial office block in London that was kept vacant for years by its owner, the millionaire speculator, Harry Hyams, in the expectation of capital gains.

As inflation accelerates, people who owe money—to an employee, a creditor, or the tax authorities—discover the beauty of masterly inertia. By delaying a payment even for a few hours in 1923, a debtor in Germany could reduce its burden to zero. The bureaucrats and the bankers never caught up with the merry-go-round. As late as August 1923, the standard rate of interest on a bank loan was only thirty per cent. No one seemed to have heard of indexation.

There is a story of a child in Germany in 1923 who received a gift of a one-dollar bill from a foreign relative; her family decided to set up a trust fund to administer it for her. We are unlikely to sink quite as low as that. But the Weimar experience should have taught us something about how the debauching of the currency has a profoundly corrupting effect on society as a whole and rewards speculation at the expense of productive investment. And of course you do not need to go back to Weimar to observe that. Recent economic policy in Britain—which has fuelled inflation and clamped down punitive rates of taxation on productive businesses—has driven private capital into increasingly speculative forms of investment and punished and demoralised precisely those social groups that are traditionally most inclined to saving.

Unlike an earthquake or a hurricane, inflation is a man-made disaster. There is not much that a community of Pacific islanders can do about a volcanic eruption, apart from getting off the island as fast as their canoes will carry them. But inflation is an artificially-induced disease of money which can be cured by known anti-toxins. There are perhaps three ways of tackling it: you can either (i) let the fever rip in the hope that the patient will somehow survive; (ii) offer sedatives in order to keep the patient calm; or (iii) apply a vaccine that may have extremely painful side-effects. We can hardly agree on the right treatment for the disease if we cannot agree on what causes it. But when we turn to the consultants for advice, we find that they are attacking each other with scalpels outside the surgery.

I confess that I have nothing original to contribute on this subject, and I do not propose to review the recent course of inflation and stop-go policy in Britain, which has been done admirably elsewhere.[8] But it seems to me that there are three fairly obvious points to be made. The first is that there is no inflation without an expansion of the monetary supply, whose effects may be delayed for a year or two.* Oil sheikhs, trade

*The only partial exception to this statement that so far appears to have been

unions and speculators are equally powerless to cause inflation—which is a *general* upward movement of prices, as opposed to specific price rises—if the government refuses to increase the quantity of money in circulation. Thus the whole concept of 'cost-push' inflation confuses causes and effects. Inflation is always, quite literally, a question of too much money chasing too few things. If there were a further hundred per cent increase in the cost of oil, or a doubling of miners' wages, and the quantity of money in circulation were kept constant, other sectors of the economy would suffer severely from the diversion of resources to pay for those price increases—but in the long run, the *overall* rate of inflation would remain unchanged. It would be *relative* prices, not prices in general, that would change. But of course, things do not work like that in real life, and few people—including governments—are ready to tailor their economic behaviour to the need to maintain some optimal statistical average. Fear of strike action, fear of unemployment, fear of losing the next election, the spread of inflationary *expectations* (whose effects in Weimar we have already observed) usually get the better of them.

This brings me to the second point. When it comes to explaining the *mechanism* of inflation, every economist worth his salt is in some sense a 'monetarist'—a term that, for some inexplicable reason, is used as a boo-word by many people who have never heard of Ricardo or David Hume, and have certainly never read Keynes thoroughly. That is to say: it would be extraordinarily difficult to sustain the argument that you can have inflation if the supply of money remains constant—that is, if its increase is limited to the growth in the national product.

But control over the monetary supply depends on political decisions, which in turn are influenced by all sorts of extraneous factors, some of which—the need to pacify trade unions, for example—I have already mentioned in passing. So the oft-heard argument, 'trade unions cause inflation' (or, in a historical context, 'war causes inflation') which cannot possibly be accurate as it stands, is irrefutable if it is rephrased:

---

unearthed is the case of the inflationary explosion triggered off by the Korean war in the 1950s. In this case, according to Professor Friedman, it was the increased *velocity* of the money in circulation rather than an increase in quantity that fuelled American inflation.

'trade unions can cause governments to cause inflation by expanding the monetary supply'—in order to cover excessive wage claims, maintain uneconomic levels of employment and, in short, to save a labour monopoly from having to accept the logical economic consequences of its sustained abuse of power.

Or, as Professor Hayek puts it, 'there is, strictly speaking, no such thing as a cost-push inflation: all inflation is caused by an excessive demand. . . But unions can force a government committed to a Keynesian full employment policy to inflate in order to prevent the unemployment which their actions would otherwise cause; indeed, if it is believed that the government will prevent a rise of wages from leading to unemployment, there is no limit to the magnitude of wage demands—and indeed even little reason for the employers to resist them.'[9]

To push Hayek's argument a little further, the causes of inflation are political and psychological rather than purely economic. In Britain, expansionist monetary policy is indissolubly linked to the fear of the trade unions and a widespread intellectual commitment to the sub-Keynesian argument that you can maintain full employment simply by manipulating aggregate demand. Political discourse in Britain is still peppered with theatrical appeals to the wraiths of the 1930s dole queues. Thus a highly capable Labour MP was recently asking (in an article supporting wage control) whether a Conservative government 'or any government' would 'be able to stand the political tension that would be generated by a further, massive and deliberate increase in the numbers out of work. Would they be able to face the halt that would have to be called on school, road, house and hospital building?'[10] We are back to the 'politically impossible' argument, and the language of false alternatives. A hyper-inflation, developing at ever greater speed over several stop-go cycles (each one, in Britain, shorter than the last) will bring a major depression with it. It is a question of whether you halt it before it has gone completely out of control, when the cost—in unemployment and reduced social spending—is still manageable, or whether you wait until all hell has broken loose, and the cost of restoring social order may mean unemployment in the high millions, the suspension of collective bargaining, or even authoritarian government.

This brings me to the third point. It is that it is necessary to look for the secular trend that runs through those stop-go

cycles of the modern economy. Hyper-inflations, as Professor
David Laidler puts it, 'build up very slowly over time through
stop-go cycles . . . until eventually one cycle gets too big to
handle. I do not know how many cycles we are away from
ultimate ruin at the moment in this country. I suspect two or
three. But we are close enough now that I think we ought to be
feeling uncomfortable'[11]. Modern British experience has shown
that simultaneously—in the context of a stagnant economy and
constantly escalating inflationary expectations—is greater in
each successive cycle, in terms of inflation. A return to
economic ordinacy would mean sharply reducing public
spending and a commitment to bring about a yearly reduction
of the rate of expansion of the monetary supply so that it
would eventually be brought down to the same level as the rate
of growth of the country's real wealth, as measured by the gross
domestic product.

There is a widely canvassed alternative approach which is
actually no alternative at all: a wages and prices freeze. The
only favourable thing to be said about 'incomes policy',
whether voluntary or compulsory, is that it may serve to curb
inflationary expectations and to restore confidence in the
government's determination to deal with the problem. That in
itself can count for a good deal, but only, of course, if the
government is willing to police its own controls with an iron
hand. This was done in Argentina under a military government
and had a salutary, but only very transient effect; the
government continued to pump money into the system and
there was a pent-up wages explosion when controls were lifted.
This went to show that official controls only suppress the
symptoms of inflation. This was also, in all essentials, the story
of the Conservative experiment in Britain in 1972–4, which
coincided with a dangerous expansion of the monetary supply;
Mr Heath's government was gambling on an 'export-led boom'
to compensate for the monumental inflation its policy was
helping to bring about.

Against the temporary advantage of a freeze in lowering
inflationary expectations, you have to weigh the inevitable
distortions and inflexibility that it imposes on the economy as
a whole. This remark may not apply to some kinds of
'voluntary' restriction, but there is no evidence that these are
likely to work in conditions of high inflation. Even if it does

work, a 'voluntary' incomes policy based on keeping wage increases level with prices will only serve to build inflationary expectations into the system; it will lead to endless haggling over 'special cases' and whether a wage-earner should be given extra money if his wage increase puts him into a higher tax bracket. And it may well be, of course, that in some sectors men are overpaid and that the condition for restoring economic viability would be a drop in real wages. Since 1945, in Britain and most other Western countries, wages have been resistant to downward movements.

My basic point is political. It is that the necessity is for governments to transcend the vested interests and habits of mind that support ultimately fatal inflationary policies. Wages controls, if resolutely applied, may allow a breathing space and may even serve as an effective instrument in the psychological warfare that may need to be waged with trade union leaders. But, at best, they are merely a lid clamped down on a steaming pressure-cooker. Unless you can turn off the gas, the pot will boil over when the lid is removed—or blown off.

Indexation is a more interesting device. Where it has been successfully used—as in Brazil—it has been designed to prevent the distortions of the economy that are normally associated with inflation. Perhaps it is worth running through the list. High inflation eats up the earnings of people on fixed salaries. It profits people who borrow money at the expense of those who lend—unless they have been thoughtful enough to charge outrageous rates of interest, and there are often laws that prevent them from so doing. It imposes a hidden tax on anyone who lends to the government; advertisements in British papers in 1975 for government bonds or local authority loans at thirteen and a half per cent or even sixteen per cent did not tell the reader that even if he got his interest tax-free it would not preserve the value of his money. It erodes a country's payments position by pulling in more imports and inflating the cost of exports, and even a government with the political nerve to ram through realistic devaluations will have to contend with currency speculators and will usually be caught lagging behind events anyway. High inflation will hurt a lot of honest businessmen by generating illusory company profits that will then be taxed, while depreciation will continue to be calculated on the basis of outdated prices. Inflation will, in short, go a long way towards breaking down a country's credit system, eroding its export drive and ruining the lives of wage-earners and self-employed people who have not banded themselves into labour monopolies capable of holding the national economy to ransom.

But none of this has happened in Brazil since the overthrow of the Goulart regime in 1964, despite rates of inflation that are still running at eighteen or twenty per cent. Indexation—or monetary correction—has become the whole art of living with inflation in Brazil. The Brazilian system is based on the assumption that no one will lose (or win?) through inflation if most things with a paper value—capital, earnings, pensions, rents, savings, loans, government bonds, private securities, fixed assets—are revalued on a regular basis. The adjustments are made annually on the basis of a wholesale price index prepared by an official foundation. The accuracy of the index has been challenged, and there is no doubt that many people in the semi-subsistence sectors of the Brazilian economy have continued to suffer from some of the classical effects of inflation.

What cannot be gainsaid is that monetary correction has brought about an impressive increase in private savings in Brazil since 1967, contrary to the normal deterrent effect of inflation, and that it has worked equally well to protect the capital of private companies. But it must also be conceded that the fears of those critics of indexation who think that it serves to institutionalise inflationary expectations—and thus to perpetuate inflation—also seem to be borne out by the Brazilian example. I have looked at the Brazilian case in more detail elsewhere.[12] The point to be made here is that indexation may be, as Milton Friedman has described it, 'a first-best device for a second-best world'. If you cannot persuade a government to do the 'politically impossible' things that may be necessary to end inflation, you can at least try to induce it to take action to limit some of the more destructive economic and social side-effects.

The kind of price rises we are familiar with today are strikingly different from those that were possible under the rule of the gold standard. Over the two and a half centuries between 1661 and 1913, according to an index published in *The Economist* (13 July 1974) prices in Britain actually *declined* by ten per cent. Now they are increasing by twenty-five per cent a year. This has led to a revival of the argument that a return to the gold standard is the surest way of restoring monetary stability. This particular suggestion raises tremendous technical difficulties; it is the psychology, rather than the suggested method, that is right. Locke defined money as 'some lasting thing that men might keep without spoiling'. This is plainly not how the paper currencies of the West are seen today. And if men can no longer keep their money without it spoiling, that is essentially because public spending— expenditure that is not sufficiently covered by revenues and genuine borrowing out of savings—has been the tool for managing the economy in the name of full employment since 1945. Mr Rees-Mogg's argument for gold is that 'gold belongs to the family of finite economic resources whose exchange it is supposed to regulate'; internal and external convertibility of the currency into gold would lower interest rates and wage demands, stabilise prices and, most important, close off most of the opportunities for governments—and society as a whole—to spend more than it earns. It would restore the rule of the gods of the copybook headings who are so casually flouted today.

This may be nostalgia for a lost world. But the case for gold is similar in kind to the arguments that are sometimes heard for a currency linked to commodities or for a binding constitutional amendment (if that were ever possible!) forbidding the expansion of the monetary supply by more than three or five per cent per annum. There is an underlying scepticism, fully justified by their recent inflationist behaviour, in the capacity or willingness of elected governments not to print money to fulfil demagogic promises or buy support. Hence the need for an external discipline. In the meantime, the politicians will go on playing dice with the economy. They will be encouraged to do so, in the British context, by the trade unions—a group that is always strengthened by inflation, which not only makes constant wage readjustments and disputes over relativities and cost-of-living allowances inevitable, but eventually drives almost everyone to behave like a trade union militant in order to defend his income. This behavioural pattern is encouraged by the loss of that patriotic resolve and civic responsibility that carried Britain through earlier times of peril; the challenge of the Wehrmacht united society, but the challenge of inflation pits each man against the rest.

5

In Fear of Strikes

> The Party must more than ever and in a new way, not only
> in the old, educate and guide the trade unions, at the same
> time bearing in mind that they are and will long remain an
> indispensable 'school of communism' and a preparatory
> school that trains proletarians to exercise their dictator-
> ship, an indispensable organisation of the workers for the
> gradual transfer of the management of the whole
> economic life of the country to the working class. *Lenin*[1]

This chapter is largely about Britain, because the growth of
trade union power in Britain—and the challenge that it presents
to the country's economic and political system—is without
parallel in the other advanced democratic societies. Why this
should have happened in Britain is debatable. It is probably
easiest to begin by pointing to some of the reasons why it has
not happened in other democratic societies. In France, there is
a relatively large agricultural population and a variety of
powerful and highly effective middle-class pressure groups to
counter-balance the trade union movement, which is further
weakened by its division into three ideological federations. No
such countervailing forces survive in Britain, although there
have been recent attempts to create them.

In West Germany and the United States, there has been a
highly visible process of *embourgeoisement* of industrial
workers, a process of absorption into the broader community
of the affluent society, that has removed many of the classical
symptoms of class struggle. This process has been complemen-
ted, in the German case, by what Ralf Dahrendorf identifies as
the traditional 'German ideology' of the classless society[2] and,
to a lesser extent, by experiments in workers' participation
(*Mitbestimmung*). In contrast, despite the narrowing income
gaps and the growth of the service sector, this process of
embourgeoisement seems not to have taken place in Britain,
and the present generation of trade union militants seem
wholly dedicated to keeping the dangerous doctrines of class

war alive.

This horizontal identification with class or union rather than with community, enterprise—or nation—is less characteristic of Japan than of any other industrial democracy. As a recent Japanese author puts it, people there tend to stick together because they are 'complementary' rather than because they are 'similar'.[3] Members of the same enterprise may even refer to it as the 'household'. Vertically integrated societies like Japan may lose their stability in a time of crisis but will then tend to turn towards the principles of authority and national unity in exaggerated forms. They are likely to prove far less strike-prone and far less inclined towards Marxist conceptions of class struggle than horizontally integrated societies—of which Britain is becoming an increasingly problematic example. The company union with its specific loyalties is also unlikely to present the same kind of challenge to government as a national union led by men who—so far from identifying with the enterprises for which their members work—may be avowedly committed to the revolutionary transformation of society.

It is possible to seek vertical integration of the trade unions on a different basis, through the institutions of the corporate state. This is what the pre-war fascist movements purported to be doing, and what the structures of the Spanish *sindicatos* are intended to achieve—although they have steadily lost ground to the clandestine *comisiones obreras*.

But it might be argued that the corporative ideal has also been served by at least one post-war social democratic state, Sweden, where the centralised settlement of wage claims in periodic conferences involving the trade union federation, LO, the employers' federation and the government takes place behind a façade of ritual haggling. This should not be allowed to mask the fact that LO functions virtually as an arm of government and that 'industrial democracy', as one critical observer puts it, is interpreted by the trade unions as 'a means of extending the power of their *organisations* into the management of industry, which means the invasion of one corporate power by another'.[4] What Sweden seems to have achieved is a degree of vertical integration behind the smoke-screen of socialist rhetoric—a kind of integration, it must be conceded, that favours the interests of the trade unions and the Welfare State bureaucracy rather than those of the private sector. It is hardly surprising, therefore, that some British trade union bureaucrats with a taste for the good things of life, such as Clive Jenkins of the white-collar workers' union (ASTMS) look yearningly towards Olof Palme's Sweden.

What all the societies so far mentioned have in common is a standard of living above that of Britain (but only recently attained in the case of France), rising growth rates (if we discount the recent downturn in the United States and Japan, which will be seen to be transient) and high levels of productivity. They belong to a league in which Britain looks increasingly out of place. Britain's gross domestic product declined from 156 per cent of Japan's, 112 per cent of France's and 93 per cent of West Germany's in 1960, to 72 per cent, 85 per cent and 76 per cent respectively in 1972. If the same rate of decline continues over the period up to 1980, it has been calculated that the value of Britain's national income will have shrunk to about sixty per cent of France's and Germany's and a mere third of Japan's by the end of the decade.[5] This alarming shrinkage of the economy as a whole has been accompanied by a decline in living standards relative to the rest of the developed world, and a laggardly growth in real wages which has only partially been camouflaged by rapid inflation.

The sharper edge to labour disputes in Britain and the new uses that are being made of trade union power are not unrelated to the evident economic stagnation; they are both cause and consequence. The fear of strikes (and the Keynesian commitment to full employment) goes some way towards explaining why successive British governments have abandoned market principles and so eroded the incentives for new investment and the country's trading position. The economy's failure to grow has not, as a result, served to limit expectations.

The squabble over who gets what slice of the national cake becomes progressively more envenomed; after all, if the size of the cake remains constant, you can only get a bigger slice by taking away from someone else. Some romantics retire into the ecological crusade, the case for zero growth, or a nostalgia for lost imperial glories that has given rise to one of Britain's livelier industries—the production of historical sagas for television— but few people who survey the changing pattern of industrial relations, and of class attitudes in general, would now be inclined to endorse the view that 'kindliness, or lack of aggression' still 'characterises British social relations' in the old way.[6]

Monopolies subvert the market principle, which is the basis for efficient production, technological innovation and economic democracy in its genuine sense: consumer choice. Yet those who manage to establish a monopoly of any kind will tend to hold on to it until someone stronger dislodges them. Such a person can only be the government, if the monopoly in question is the perquisite of a powerful commercial trust or trade union. It is the duty of governments to curb private coercion of this kind. Yet successive governments have failed (and often enough failed even to try) to curb the abuse of power by labour monopolies in Britain. As a result, the British trade unions enjoy a position of legal privilege that is without parallel in any other country, and the industrial power that they are able to wield—at least by repute—has grown to such proportions that it is hardly an exaggeration to say that the key economic decisions that are taken, or not taken, by governments in Britain are taken in fear of strikes.

The existence of trade unions is one of the conditions for a free society. But equally, it may prove to be a condition for an unfree or ungovernable society if trade union power is not exercised within the common framework of law and is not kept within the bounds that apply to other economic interest groups. The guiding-reins in Britain have snapped completely. As a result, a danger to democracy and an opening for revolution has developed that John Strachey foresaw in a quite prophetic book which he wrote during his communist phase in the early 1930s. In this book, entitled *The Coming Struggle for Power*, Strachey singled out the reasons why Britain was a particularly favourable ground for communism'. He dwelled on the high proportion of industrial workers in the British labour force, and the absence of a large class of farmers of the type who are 'necessarily conservative'. He was delighted by the intellectual and political confusion he found among the British ruling class, which was losing the capacity for 'swift and ruthless action' that would be needed to ensure its own survival.

But one of the most prescient observations that he had to contribute was that

Capitalism is doomed unless it can curb and restrain the enormous and now almost universal interferences with freedom of exchange, the manifold distortions and dislocations of the market, which today characterise the policy of every important state . . . The free market cannot function properly, the glittering mechanism of the economists' perfect market can never work, unless *all* its interconnected parts are movable. If one of them sticks, then naturally the whole machine will jam and ruin itself.[7]

The part that he thought was already starting to jam was the mobility of labour. That cog in the glittering market mechanism (which has never been seen outside a textbook) has now stuck completely and does not seem to budge under any normal pressure. Almost half a century ago, Strachey was encouraged by the fact that 'powerful trade unions have to some extent succeeded in creating monopolies . . . of labour and so in obtaining monopoly prices for them'. They have come some distance in Britain since then.

British trade unions enjoy a position of unique legal privilege. The general rule of law, quite simply, does not apply to them. This is not a novel situation. The removal of legal constraints from the trade unions is, as Professor Abrahams noted, a quite remarkable case of 'law-making in advance of public opinion'.[8] Most legal restraints were removed by the Acts of 1871 and 1875; but the veritable charter of immunities was the Trade Disputes Act of 1906, passed by a Liberal government, which inspired Sir Edward Carson to comment that the House of Commons had enunciated a new constitutional doctrine; that trade unions could do no wrong. The new Act established that no trade union could be sued in tort in any court whatsoever. 'Any action against a trade union . . . or against any members or officials thereof on behalf of themselves and all other members of the trade union in respect of any tortious act alleged to have been committed by and on behalf of the trade union shall not be entertained in any court'.

With the Act of 1906, many of the remaining legal weapons for controlling trade union power were thrown on the scrap-heap; prosecution for conspiracy, breach of contract, restraint of trade, interference with other people's freedom of contract (for example, through sympathy strikes) and various practices that might formerly have been attacked as 'intimidation' was no longer allowed. The irony of the 1906 law is that it was introduced at a time when British trade unions were still extremely weak. Trade union membership was under two million; high unemployment reduced the unions' bargaining power; and members had actually been drifting away since the Taff Vale affair—when a company successfully sued a trade union for damages inflicted during a strike. The country had no experience of the latter-day forms of 'industrial action' that were to be practised under the protection of this law. 'The power of the strike weapon for personal vendetta, or for victimisation of blacklegs; the usually disingenuous Luddism, which takes the form of discouraging full performance, 'go slow', 'work to rule'; the Luddite doctrine of the 'spreading of the load'; the vice of overmanning that was to wreck so many newspapers; these were to reach full expression only after freedom was attained.[9]

So the Liberals who blithely passed a Bill drawn up by the first generation of Labour MPs in keeping of an electoral promise quite literally had no idea what they were doing. Asquith, it is true, had forebodings, but the Prime Minister (Campbell-Bannerman) and most of the cabinet were confident that British trade unionists were moderate, responsible men who could be trusted not to abuse their freedoms. In any case, as Asquith himself was to argue, 'when trade unions abuse their powers, Parliament can interfere'. A reassuring doctrine, but it did not fit subsequent events. The recent conflicts over trade union law go to show that it is better to keep legal powers in reserve than hope to acquire them when the need arises. The Conservatives did not try to exploit the obvious opportunity to revoke the 1906 Act that arose after the defeat of the General Strike in 1927. Indeed, the moderation displayed by many trade union leaders in 1926 and the subsequent plight of the unions during the Depression (when membership fell by a third) encouraged the belief that no legal action was necessary.

The first significant case of government interference with trade union liberties was Statutory Regulation and Order 1305, issued in 1940, when the country was at war with Hitler. This law, acceptable to trade union opinion because of the imminent danger of Britain's survival, made all strikes illegal unless the Minister of Labour failed to acknowledge an 'apprehended dispute' within twenty-one days. But it is interesting to observe that there was some resistance to this law even in wartime; it was defied, for example, during the Betteshanger colliery dispute in 1941. The Order remained in law until 1951.[10]

The only post-war attempt to bring the trade unions back within a legal framework was the Conservative Industrial Relations Act (1971), bitterly resisted by the unions at the time and subsequently rescinded by the Wilson government in 1974. The Labour government had drawn up an Industrial Relations Bill of its own in 1969, but trade union and backbench opposition ensured that it never got outside the parliamentary draughtsman's office. Previous Conservative governments had been reluctant to act because of the 'good chap syndrome' that is accurately described by Stephen Fay[11] and was best exemplified by Harold Macmillan's benign view of the men who helped to wage war with Hitler. Untrammelled trade unions were still regarded, like the Commonwealth or the parity of sterling, as 'institutions reflecting the greatness of Britain's past, and they must be clung to if Britain were to remain great in the future'. It was evident well before the Heath government took office in 1970 that this was no longer the case. The great swing to the left that began in the British trade unions in the mid-1960s produced a new generation of radical or openly revolutionary leaders fully prepared to exploit the rising material expectations generated by full employment policies and post-war affluence, the hugely increased vulnerability of centralised industries to low-level disruption and the legal immunities preserved since 1906. The new generation of trade union militants viewed the world rather differently from those sober men who—according to the solicitor-general in a speech to the Commons in 1906—could be 'prudently trusted with exceptional powers'.

The upshot was the Industrial Relations Act. Borrowing from Canadian and American practice, it was a radical departure from the pattern of collective bargaining in post-war Britain. It is enough to remind the reader of a few of its most important clauses. First, the Act banned 'unfair industrial practices' (a new concept in British law); such practices included all unofficial strikes and strikes by unregistered unions, sympathy strikes, stoppages designed to make employers infringe workers' rights (for example, to secure the sacking of a non-union man) and the breaking of legally binding agreements. All contracts between employers and employees were now assumed to be legally binding, unless it was explicitly stated that they were not. Second, the Act created the National Industrial Relations Court as an adjunct of the High Court to deal with the major cases arising under the Act. The initiative to take a union to court rested solely with employers. Third, the right to strike was restricted to unions that registered under the new Act. Registration was not automatic; one of the conditions for recognition was that the union rules had to specify who was entitled to call an official strike, and under what circumstances. Fourth, the Act outlawed the closed shop, except in some special cases (actors and seamen) and substituted the novel concept of an 'agency shop'; if an agency shop was agreed between workers and employers, then the workers had either to join the union or pay the equivalent of the union subscription—unless they qualified as 'conscientious objectors'. Finally, the employment minister was given emergency powers—subject to a ruling from the National Industrial Relations Court—to order a 'cooling-off' period before a strike began and to order a strike ballot. These powers, it subsequently transpired, were used only once: against the National Union of Railwaymen. Their ballot produced an impressive show of support for the strike leaders, although there had been reason to believe that the strike had not been a popular move inside the union; this convinced many observers that loyalty to the union was likely to prove decisive in the event of direct government intervention of this kind.[12]

This is not the place to continue the debate over whether the British Industrial Relations Act was poorly framed, and whether it might have been more readily accepted if, for example, the registration clause had been omitted. The way that the trade union leadership made martyrs out of five dockers (the 'Pentonville Five') who were imprisoned under the Act led some people to argue that you must not seek a legal solution to trade union power; the answer must be found outside the courts. There are perhaps three general points that need to be made. The first is that there is little sign that the militant leadership of the major British trade unions is losing ground to that moderate majority whose views are rarely made felt, although there is a great deal more that can be done to help rank-and-file members to assert their views. In the meantime, the *carte blanche* that is offered to purely destructive strike activities by the legal situation is dangerous and incompatible with any general concept of the rule of law.

Second, it is clear that public opinion in general is in favour of imposing legal curbs on the trade unions. The opinion polls showed majority support for the Industrial Relations Act throughout its brief life, and it is interesting to note that in a series of opinion polls on the subject since 1958, a majority of those interviewed expressed support for draconian measures banning *all* strikes. The man in the street in Britain still believes, on balance, that trade unions are a 'good thing' but there is widespread alarm at their abuse of their monopoly position.

Finally, in the aftermath of the Industrial Relations Act, Britain is left in the situation described by the American Henry C. Simons, where 'government, long hostile to other monopolies, suddenly sponsored and promoted widespread labour monopolies, which democracy cannot endure, cannot control without destroying, and perhaps cannot destroy without destroying itself.'[13] Let us stand aside from the current political rhetoric about how governments should not 'confront' trade unions and how industrial relations are not a matter for gentlemen in lawyers' wigs. This has served only to confer a spurious legitimacy, based on the appeal to class or trade loyalties, on forms of private coercion that are at odds with the interests and purposes of the community as a whole. The rights of groups and individuals in a free society cannot be extended to the point where they detract from the rights of others and place in jeopardy the liberties from which they are derived. Trade union militants and their apologists in Britain have propounded—within a legal void for which the legislators are responsible—the extraordinary doctrine that the right to strike is limitless. The doctrine is monstrous, and if it is henceforth to remain unchallenged by governments the situation will at last arise where other sectors of the community—taxpayers and ratepayers, for example—will, with equal if not greater legitimacy, demand equally limitless rights to apply economic sanctions to defend their interests. Only the xenophobia or selfish ambition of trade union leaders in Britain has prevented them from conceding that their position is

unique in the democratic world, and that legal proposals that
they reject as intolerable are standard practice in many other
countries.

We had better also take account of the logical economic
consequence of union wage-fixing. If wages are not determined
by the market, we will at last be confronted with a brutal
choice of action in the effort to restore a viable economic
system; authoritarian wage-fixing by the government, or the
denial of the right to strike. It really will not do to adopt an
ostrich-posture in the face of developments that should
concern democratic trade unionists as well as everyone else.

It seems to me that trade union power is compatible with a
free society only if it is subject to the following limitations,
some of which were embodied in the Industrial Relations Act:

1   If the trade unions exercise the same rights and
    responsibilities as other groups and individuals under the
    common laws of the land—which would mean, *inter alia*,
    that collective agreements, like other contracts, should
    be legally binding.
2   If the rights of employees to belong or *not* belong to a
    union are fully guaranteed—which would mean safe-
    guards against the closed shop of the kind that exist in
    most West European countries apart from Britain.
3   If strike action is subject to an agreed procedure and legal
    protection against intimidatory tactics. The right to
    strike should not be regarded as universal; there is a case
    for suspending it in the case of stoppages in vital services
    that pose a menace to life and health and in the case of
    political strikes unrelated to trade disputes.
4   If there are guarantees for internal democracy within
    trade unions, which is most likely to be encouraged in
    Britain by the use of the postal ballot—subject to
    impartial supervision—in the election of officials and as
    the condition for calling a strike.

None of these conditions applied in Britain in 1975, and
there appeared to be no immediate hope of bringing them into
force. The trade unions were left to function in the condition
that Durkheim described as *anomie*, or normlessness, in which
the norms of society as a whole do not apply and the code by
which one lives is separate and self-regarding.

Two other singular features of British trade unions are their intimate relations with a political party that was initially founded to advance their interests, and the power of the 300,000 shop stewards across the country who take the initiative in organising unofficial strikes—often enough on the basis of an unbelievably petty local dispute or the pursuit of an extremist ideology. Lenin was clearly not informed of developments in Britain when he wrote in 1906 that 'there can be no question in free countries of identity between the organisation of trade unions and the organisation of the Social Democratic Party'.[14] Half the total members of unions belonging to the Trades Union Congress are affiliated—through their unions—to the Labour Party. Their union leaders manipulate a crushing bloc vote at the party's annual conference. Of the 6,200,000 bloc votes cast at the 1973 conference, for example, delegates from the trade unions cast nearly 5,500,000. The unions' influence over party policy is greatly enhanced by the fact that it is almost wholly dependent on them for finance. Two-thirds of the Labour Party's annual income is derived from trade union contributions.

Needless to say, the special relationship between the unions and the Labour Party has made them a still more attractive target for Marxist groups bent on entering British politics through the back door. Behind the surface fireworks of the recent internecine feud in the Labour Party is a fundamental power struggle between the Marxist elements in the party's industrial wing and the precariously-placed social democrat group in parliament; the industrial big battalions have been steadily gaining ground.

The power of shop-floor organisers is another characteristic feature of labour conflicts in Britain, and it has again provided the subversives (in the sense defined in an earlier chapter) with a major opening. The Donovan Report found in 1968 that some ninety-five per cent of British strikes are unofficial—that is, organised without the official blessing of the national trade unions. Such disputes are often non-economic in origin, concerned with demarcation disputes between rival trade unions or with the enforcing of closed shops. In fact, union disintegration—the decentralised and anarchic trend in labour conflicts—has gone hand in hand with the greater integration and centralisation of industry. Huge enterprises can be paralysed by a dispute involving a few dozen workers in a subsidiary plant, especially when workers are organised to cut off alternative sources of supply. The influence of the Communist Party and of Trotskyist and Maoist groups is particularly marked at the level of shop stewards. Some of the most celebrated organisers of the new-style strikes in which a large firm is paralysed by a handful of strategically-placed men are Communist Party members—such as the key men at Chrysler's Ryton plant or at British Leyland's Longbridge plant—while the communist-dominated Liaison Committee for the Defence of the Trade Unions has been effective in organising coordinated stoppages through the shop stewards.

The new militancy in British trade unions cannot be explained without reference to the systematic infiltration of union bureaucracies by communists and Marxists and the succession of two left-wingers, Jack Jones and Hugh Scanlon, to the top posts in the two biggest unions, the Transport and General Workers' Union (TGWU) and the Engineers' Union (AUEW) in the 1960s. The swing to the left—which brought control of some ten per cent of the key union posts into the hands of the communists by the early 1970s—is related to some of the factors already mentioned: the legal vacuum, the rise of inflationary expectations, the undemocratic election procedures of many trade unions.

There has also been a failure of communications; failure by governments to translate macro-economic figures into the popular psychology, so that the payments deficit (to which trade union disruption was contributing) was never sufficiently understood as part of a national crisis that demanded restraint from everyone. At the same time, trade union militants appeared to demonstrate that their tactics paid off, so that less ideological men felt obliged to borrow the same techniques— with varying success. Finally, trade union militants were able to argue, amid the general intellectual confusion about 'what's wrong with Britain', that their *raison d'être* was to protect jobs by obliging governments to dole out subsidies and keep bankrupt firms open—in other words, they actually contrived to blind many people to the obvious fact that the trade unions themselves are responsible for the unemployment that is bound to result from the pushing of wages above natural market levels—unless governments resort to the printing press. They were assisted in this by the emotional commitment of post-war governments to full employment policies and by the effusions of shrewd self-appointed tribunes of the people like Anthony Wedgwood-Benn who was ever on hand, to remind those whose policies implied higher unemployment that people in comfortable jobs shouldn't joke about the dole queue—an argument that emerged oddly from the mouth of a scion of the aristocracy who was engaged in the full-time defence of a labour oligopoly that was showing less and less concern for the welfare of those who did not belong to one of the dozen strongest unions.

Two final elements in the leftward swing in the British unions in the late 1960s and the early 1970s: the extent to which the public was subsidising stikes, and the organisational and conspiratorial flair of the Marxist left by comparison with the 'moderates' (an unsatisfactory description of men who are often prepared to fight doggedly for their beliefs but which has entered the shorthand of political discourse). The importance of the first factor—supplementary benefits and tax rebates for strikers—is frequently exaggerated. Supplementary benefits are paid to the family, rather than the striker, and the British experience is that it is still only a minority of those eligible who claim. But tax rebates did appear to play some considerable part in the behaviour of lower-income groups which came out on strike in 1972, and the literature of the various claimants' groups points the way to a qualitative expansion of strikers' claims on the social services.[15]

Ballot-rigging and similar practices are by no means unknown in sections of the British trade union movement, and it would seem that one of the preconditions for the containment of the Marxist left is a thorough reform of union election and decision-making procedures. Unfortunately, the Trades Union Congress is unlikely to give the moral lead against the communist left that it provided in the late 1940s and 1950s; we have already seen how the British TUC is promoting east—west union contacts of the kind that offer opportunities for Soviet subversion and seem designed to blur the fundamental distinction between democratic trade unions and the agencies of the communist police state. The coup that was engineered in the British engineers' union (AUEW) in May 1975 brought home the difficulty of dislodging the Marxist left from its entrenched positions and inspired a moderate Labour Minister, Roy Jenkins, to speak of 'ballot-rigging'—for which the union president, Hugh Scanlon, promptly threatened to sue him.

The AUEW, like most unions, was characterised by a very low level of member participation until 1971, when the national committee—by a one-man majority—agreed to introduce the postal ballot. This decision was bitterly unpopular with the Marxists within the union, who had profited from the low turnout in branch elections; Hugh Scanlon, a former communist who is still openly bent on destroying the capitalist system, was elected president with only six per cent of his members' votes. The full effects of the postal ballot—which increased the voting percentage to over thirty per cent—were fully felt in 1975, in elections for a new general secretary. John Boyd, an anti-communist and a dedicated member of the Salvation Army, romped home, triumphing over his left-wing rival, Bob Wright.

The union's rules revision committee (its national committee under a different name) met afterwards in Blackpool to discuss whether the system of postal balloting should be retained. Everything seemed cut-and-dried when the Blackpool meeting decided (by twenty-seven votes to twenty-five) to keep the system. Then an extraordinary series of incidents served to reverse the decision. First, a member of the union's South Wales division sent a letter challenging the credentials of one of its delegates on a technicality. The delegate was disqualified, and a substitute was sent who was then discovered to have been an 'adult member' of the union for only five years, instead of the requisite seven. He was also disqualified. This reduced the majority in favour of the postal ballot from 2 to 1.

Hugh Scanlon now came up with a new trick. He proposed (through the union's standing orders committee) that the vote of the remaining delegate from the South Wales division should be expunged from the record on the grounds that he had been 'improperly elected'. The charge was that the minutes of the meeting that elected him had not been properly kept, since they did not show the votes cast. (It was subsequently proved by a leading labour correspondent that the practice was the same in at least one other division; the difference was that its delegates were left-wingers.)

The next step was for the union's executive to rule—in the absence of Boyd, and on the casting vote of Scanlon—that the vote of the second South Wales delegate should be disallowed. This left the conference divided 25—25. The time had come for Scanlon to deliver the *coup de grâce*. Acting as chairman, he again used his casting vote—in favour of abolishing the postal ballot.[16]

The whole affair seemed an attempt at a Marxist coup in miniature, against the chance of real democracy inside Britain's second largest union, whose left-wing leaders survive through dubious branch elections involving five per cent of the members or less—and who were determined not to lose out to more representative leaders. The only consolation was that the way the vote was stacked resulted in a major law-suit in which Mr Scanlon's vote was declared invalid—although not of the kind that broke the communist hold over the electricians' union in 1961 and cleared the way for a determined right-wing union leader, Frank Chapple, who proceeded to introduce the postal ballot and ban communists from holding office.

One of the most disturbing features of the new unionism in Britain is its undercurrent of violence. Few union leaders have openly advocated the use of violence; but the militarist metaphors used by Reg Birch, a Maoist member of the national executive of the Engineers' Union, the AUEW, are a sign of the times. In an interesting pamphlet entitled *Guerrilla Struggle and the Working Class,*[17] he discussed the need to apply 'the strategy of guerrilla war to the economic arena'. He rebuked the hospital workers who went on strike in 1972 (for the first time) and were subsequently defeated for their failure to comprehend the 'guerrilla line of struggle'; it appears that 'they were still too gentle, not ruthless enough, ever conscious of the social, humane nature of their work'. This would seem to imply that they should have been more prepared to put patients' lives at risk.

Mr Birch's voice is hardly representative, even among trade union militants. But as the union leadership has shifted to the left, work stoppages have been combined with what can fairly be described as industrial guerrilla tactics. Two notable examples are the use of flying pickets and the occupation of factories. The model for intimidatory picketing was set by the miners' and building workers' strikes in 1972, and for factory occupations by the sit-in at Upper Clyde Shipbuilders when the firm was threatened with closure in 1971. These cases, and the tactical thinking derived from them, bear some examination.

Illegal picketing was crucial to the success of the miners' strike in 1972, although it was arguably a less critical factor than the widespread public sympathy for face-workers (who had not participated in a nationwide strike since 1926). The government seemed well-equipped to sit out the strike; coal stocks had reached the record level of fourteen million tons. What the government had not counted on was the systematic picketing of power stations, coal depots and ports and the new militancy of the miners' leaders. At one stage the 'moderate' Mr Joe Gormley, president of the National Union of Mineworkers, told a mass meeting that 'there are going to be casualties as in any other battle and people are bound to be hurt'.[18] Mass picketing was clearly illegal, and 263 pickets were arrested. But the police were either unable, or were not encouraged, to deal with large numbers of pickets, even when the miners were stationed far from any coal mine. At the huge Saltley coal depot outside Birmingham six thousand pickets forced the police to lock the gates.

Despite the occasional violence of this strike, public sympathy was largely with the miners; but the apparent success of illegal picketing set a disturbing precedent which was taken up by the Marxist extremists who sent strong-arm squads onto the building sites during the construction workers' strike in the summer of 1972. Given the decentralised nature of the building trade, and the high proportion of non-union men involved in it, this strike would probably not have got off the ground but for the widespread use of intimidation—applied by squads organised at an almost military level of efficiency, and financed, according to the chairman of the Commission on Industrial Relations, from 'dubious sources'. Some of the worst cases of violent intimidation occurred on 6 September (remembered by building employers as 'Black Wednesday') when flying pickets descended on a number of building sites in the west Midlands in a coordinated attack.

The lack of a forceful official response to large-scale picketing in both these strikes in 1972 ensured that the weapon would become part of the arsenal of future strikers. It was subsequently used by dockers in a Luddite campaign against container firms. Mass picketing obviously appeals to militants both as a means of maximising the economic damage done by a strike, and thus increasing its chance of success, and as a means of creating confrontation situations in which the authorities are forced to choose between law enforcement (which may produce 'martyrs') and a humiliating retreat.

The other tactic that is relatively novel to Britain—the occupation of factories—has numerous parallels abroad. You do not need to go as far back as the factory occupations in the revolutionary Turin of 1920; the prolonged occupation of the Lip watch factory in France is a celebrated recent example of a method that has sometimes produced notable rewards—especially if the workers are appealing to a weak or sympathetic government to intervene in a declining firm in order to save jobs. Workers' sit-ins were used systematically by the left in Chile after 1970 to produce the kind of economic chaos that supplied a Marxist government with the excuse to install a 'temporary' state manager in order to preserve jobs or maintain production quotas. The Socialist left in Britain was clearly thinking along the same lines when it managed to insert the following proposal in the 1973 Labour Party programme: a future Labour government would take power 'to put in an official trustee to assume temporary control of any company which fails to meet its responsibilities to its workers, to its customers, or to the community as a whole'. How news travels! No steps had been taken to carry out that proposal, at least at the time of writing. But we should bear such further possibilities in mind—together with the way that Socialist ministers have made it plain that they will finance workers' 'self-control' in failing industries—in looking at the tactic of factory occupations in Britain.

The Trotskyist left, which is small in numbers but fertile in ideas (and of rising influence in health workers', teachers' and journalists' unions) has produced some interesting recent guides to the sit-in strike in Britain. One such 'how to do it' kit[19] recommends that the strikers, having put up the barricades and formed a committee, should take precautions against summary eviction by immobilising machinery and smuggling out key parts. They should sustain interest by holding daily mass meetings, political indoctrination sessions, film shows and other light entertainments. They should spread news of their cause by leaflets and roving propaganda teams and try to organise sympathy strikes and the 'blacking' of alternative sources of supply. They should try to raise strike funds through a public appeal for a sympathy levy and through a lottery. Full use will be made of all company amenities—telephones, telex, stationery and so on—and (most interesting of all) the company files will be rifled to dig out 'dirt' on the directors and shareholders.

The myth of the revolutionary general strike (of which there has never been a successful historical example*) is popular with sections of the Marxist left in Britain. It is interesting to note British communist thinking on this score. Jack Woddis, head of the Party's International Department, suggested in a recent publication that 'a national strike in British conditions today, and accompanied by factory occupations, mass demonstrations, and other actions by the working class, could have a most powerful effect . . .' He goes on:

> In a highly developed capitalist country like Britain, based on a complex interplay of industry and technique, everything—industrial production, sources of fuel and energy, communications, transport, public services, press, radio and television, as well as Government administration—is increasingly dependent on the operations of large armies of workers, including scientific and technical personnel. These latter are becoming organised and integrated with the whole working class movement.
>
> The full, determined and united action by all these sections of the working people could deliver a hammer blow to the ruling class, helping to restrict and paralyse some of its powers.
>
> Deprived of the press, radio and TV, unable to use the telephone, without heating, lighting or any sources of energy or transport, the ruling class would face unprecedented difficulties . . .
>
> During the nine days of the 1926 General Strike many towns were virtually in the hands of the workers, and it was they who decided what material, if any, would be moved in or out of the town.
>
> We have come a long way since then. The working class is

---

*The closest approach to it was possibly the Russian experience of 1905. An interesting, and less distant, attempt was the Perónist industrial uprising in Argentina in 1964. Some 500,000 workers occupied factories, but the strike petered out in the end.

much more highly organised; the left is stronger; the Communist Party larger, and more organised. In these respects the working people are today much better equipped to face up to the capitalist class.[20]

There is no historical evidence that an offensive general strike has ever brought down the state, as Sorel and others preached that it would.[21] But it could, in different circumstances, provide the conditions for a revolutionary political transformation—if combined with a well-organised *political* scenario for the seizure of power, possibly by parliamentary and (at least superficially) legal means. Nor can the risk of a government defeat in a general strike be overstated; the problem of dealing with any large-scale strike action by other than passive means (that is, by sitting it out) are obvious when one remembers that more troops were used to control the docks in the 1949 dockers' strike than were stationed in Northern Ireland in mid-1975. No government will willingly bring about a nationwide confrontation with trade union power. The British problem is that such a confrontation may be unavoidable if trade union leaders cannot be brought to understand the problems of the national economy as a whole, and if the country is not to be governed permanently *in fear of strikes*.

What is possibly not sufficiently understood, even in the aftermath of the British miners' strikes of 1972 and 1974, is that the strike is a form of internal warfare. This is not to suggest that strikes are never justified; but what should be observed is that in war, victory goes to the strongest, not the most righteous. There has only been one general strike in British history, the strike of 1926, which was a defensive strike, fought by men resisting a drop in their wages, and which was eventually defeated. Yet the recent successes of strikers in Britain, and the new tactics that they have deployed, have made the 'strike-threat weapon' a powerful deterrent to any government bent on reducing inflation or restoring the universal rule of law. Trade union power is *the* political issue in Britain, and the way that it has been allowed to develop almost uninhibited by law or by countervailing social forces is a tribute to the short-sightedness of successive generations of politicians who failed to grasp that one of the primary duties of governments is to curb private coercion. The problem seems unlikely to be solved without a power confrontation whose outcome is uncertain.

A socialist friend of mine has sketched out a scenario for that confrontation which is rather different from the fantasy presented in Chapter 1. He imagines a peaceful outcome, in which a government bent on wages restraint will find the trade unions ready to support its policy—on condition, that they are given a hand in running the country. The mechanism that presents itself is elevation to the peerage; trade union leaders outside the House of Commons could then be made ministers. He foresees the leaders of the transport workers, miners and engineers taking over the Home Office and other key ministries. This, like my first chapter, is political science fiction. But this alternative scenario reflects one fundamental truth about current British politics: the wide subscription to the forlorn belief that, by giving the trade unions still greater power (or, as some would put it, by formally recognising the political power that they have already acquired) you can turn the poachers into gamekeepers. At all events, the argument runs, you must avoid a showdown on such fundamental issues as the legal immunities of trade unions (restored after the repeal of the Industrial Relations Act in 1974).

However faint-hearted, this corporatist approach (because that is what it actually boils down to) is at least arguably more realistic than the arguments sometimes heard from those who have got their monetary policies right but appear to believe that they could be carried through as if the trade unions did not exist or would not be prepared to use the strike-threat weapon to influence overall economic policy on such matters as subsidies to state-run firms or unemployment.

Ludwig von Mises predicted that when trade unions established a monopoly of labour in the vital sectors of the economy, there would be only two classes left in the country: 'members of the trade unions for the branches of production essential to life, and the remainder of the people, who are slaves without rights'.[22] Von Mises' scepticism about the effects of trade unionism *as such* is not widely shared. But it may be justified in a situation where trade unions have been allowed to evade legal sanctions and exercise monopoly power. In that situation, we need to ask ourselves: what are trade unions actually achieving? And: to what extent does their interference with the economic market interfere with democratic politics?

The argument that the trade unions played a crucial role in defending workers' interests and improving living standards in the aftermath of the Industrial Revolution is readily conceded. But we are living in a very different age, and the confrontation now is no longer between some Dickensian Gradgrind, whip in hand, and his cowering employee, but as often as not, between a giant labour organisation and an employer poorly matched for the contest. We are told that trade unions are defending and advancing the causes of 'equality' and 'social justice'. But this seems, at best, to be only a half truth.

The evidence in post-war Britain suggests that strong trade unions have been successful in maintaining, or improving, the relative earnings of their members—but without notable regard for the condition of anyone else. What they have been able to do with notable success in post-war Britain has been to apply a 'profits squeeze' to private companies that is slowly asphyxiating a fair number of them. This is justified by doctrines of class war like the one enunciated in a TGWU education pamphlet in 1970: 'Care must be taken not to let members be persuaded that their interests are the same as the owners.'[23] This is not the attitude of trade unionists in general, but it is helping to perpetuate and to deepen those 'horizontal' tensions that are damaging British society. I shall have more to say about what can be done to resist the doctrines of class war—through the mobilisation of the democratic majority and through 'participation' in a constructive sense—in Chapter 14.

What needs to be said, in concluding this chapter, is that Britain need not be governed in fear of strikes. With adequate preparations—accumulation of stocks of coal and oil, organisation of private road transport, contingency planning for the use of military reserves and civilian volunteers—and with an intelligent political education campaign, a determined government can survive even a general strike. The confrontation would be more jarring in (say) 1976 than in 1926, and it is profoundly to be hoped that it can be avoided. But it is a curious kind of defeatism to maintain that, in the event of such a confrontation, the majority of workers would place the interests of an unrepresentative union bureaucracy before those of the country as a whole.

6

The Necessity of Property

> All free subjects are born inheritable, as to their land, so also to the free exercise of their industry, in those trades whereto they apply themselves and whereby they are to live. Merchandise being the chief and richest of all other, and of greater extent and importance than all the rest, it is against the natural right and liberty of the subjects of England to restrain it into the hands of some few.
>
> *Committee of the House of Commons 1604*[1]

Without economic pluralism, political pluralism cannot survive for long. We have seen already that the survival of a free society depends on the dispersal of power, on Burke's 'little battalions'. This is as clear in economic life as in politics. If the State is the sole employer, then anyone who objects to its policies risks going hungry. Yet the steady encroachment of state intervention in the economy has gone almost unchallenged, and private property rights have been treated as dispensable privileges. Here, once again, we need to go back to first principles. The argument of this chapter is not merely that the market system is demonstrably more efficient and more likely to improve the conditions of society as a whole than any other economic system, but that it is the precondition for liberal democracy and free trade unions.

Capitalism, an unsatisfactory name for what is probably better described as economic liberalism, has figured as an extremist and unpopular doctrine even in the countries where it came home to roost. It is looked upon that way in much contemporary discussion outside the United States and West Germany, where capitalist ideas figure in the 'simple traditional folklore'[2] and in one or two authoritarian third world countries such as Brazil, where the argument that private investment is the key to growth has taken root and appears to be at least partially justified by the results. But there is a general reluctance outside small groups of economists to offer an intellectual case for capitalism, which may have something to do with the fact that the word itself tends to conjure up Marxist stereotypes of a heartless *laissez-faire* system that buys and sells men like groceries, and historical memories of misery and sweated labour in the Manchester of the Poor Law. As Peter Utley observes, even in Britain—the birthplace of the philosophy of economic liberalism—'in so far as capitalism has come to be accepted, it has been accepted as an institution, not a system of ideas'.[3]

Looked at from a broad historical aspect, it would seem that the hard-fought victory of capitalism over medievalism in the period between 1500 and 1700 (and the subsequent migration of economic liberalism to the New World) was always precarious, and that the course of the present century may show that medievalism won in the end. If this is the case, it has far-reaching implications for those forms of representative democracy that at least partly owe their derivation to the triumph of the capitalist idea.

I do not mean to use the word 'medievalism' as a term of disparagement. The medieval ethical order, in which economic life is subordinate to higher values, the medieval form of society in which each man has his place in a natural hierarchy, the medieval economic system in which (at any rate in theory) goods are sold at their 'just price' and speculation and usury are treated as evils, all exercise a compelling appeal for almost anyone who adopts a strongly moral view of social life and is repelled by the moral limbo of the marketplace. The judgment of the medieval author of the *Elucidarium*, who saw in the free play of market forces nothing loftier than the struggling of wolves over carrion, is shared by the traditionalist right as well as the revolutionary left; it is entrenched in the philosophies of communism, corporatism and the Catholic counter-revolutionaries, and in the aesthetics of T. S. Eliot, Ezra Pound, Maxim Gorky and Berdyaev.

> With usura
> Seeth no man Gonzago his heirs and his concubines
> No picture is made to endure nor to live with
> but it is made to sell and sell quickly . . .
> Usura rusteth the chisel
> It rusteth the craft and the craftsman
> It gnaweth the thread in the loom[4]

The rejection of the market system is a common link between Marx and Mussolini, Hilaire Belloc and John Strachey, Pope Paul VI and Herbert Marcuse. R. H. Tawney remarked that, 'the last of the Schoolmen was Karl Marx'.[5] The Schoolmen would not have been flattered to think of that bearded atheist as one of their godly company, but in his subjection of economic freedom to the ethical hierarchies of a secular religion, perhaps he qualifies for associate membership. Tawney's mistake was that Marx was certainly not the last of the Schoolmen.

The source of this widespread aversion to the market economy is accurately described by Dr Van den Haag, who writes that 'the felt discrepancy between distribution according to the market value of services and distribution according to the moral value of services—justice—is the source of widespread dissatisfaction with income distribution, and of the consequent political attempts to adjust the economic to the moral. This felt discrepancy and the attempts to bridge it by political means are the major source of all threats to the market economy.'[6] All economic systems result in inequality, even when they are pledged to the service of pure equality: the rise of the bureaucratic 'new class' in the communist countries and the structure of nepotism and privilege associated with it is a well-known example. But the inequalities that result through the operations of the market—even the closely-circumscribed markets of recent years which bear only a faint resemblance to the Marxist caricature of capitalism—are widely perceived to be arbitrary or 'unjust'. This perception is strengthened when defenders of the market system explicitly deny the possibility of a *moral* justification for inequality[7] or adopt the gospel of mere utility—Bentham's view that 'pleasure and freedom from pain are the only things desirable as ends.'[8]

The rejection of a system for economic life that is not founded on moral sanctions is readily understandable, and the poverty of a political philosophy founded on nothing more than market principles explains the historical decline of the (truly) liberal parties. The mass movements of the twentieth century have been anything but liberal, and the defence of the market economy forms no part of their ideologies. Mussolini's contemptuous rejection of economic liberalism echoes down the corridors of history, and reminds us that the socialist left is not the only enemy of the market economy.

> Now liberalism is about to close the doors of its deserted
> temples because the peoples feel that its agnosticism in
> economics, its indifferentism in politics and morals, would
> lead, as they have led, the State to certain ruin. In this way
> one can understand why all the political experiences of the
> contemporary world are anti-liberal. . . . Faced with the
> continual, necessary and inevitable interventions of the state
> in economic affairs what would the Englishman Bentham
> now say, according to whom industry should have asked of
> the state only to be left in peace? . . . When one says
> liberalism, one says the individual; when one says fascism,
> one says the state.[9]

The danger is that although the forms of morality—the
medieval value-systems—proposed by the opponents of the
market economy are not always spurious, their application
may well restore the least admirable aspects of medieval life,
starting with serfdom, or compulsory labour. We are presented
with a remarkable contradiction: the market system seems to
be a precondition for democratic pluralism, and yet the market
system has only a limited political appeal in many Western
democracies.

Medievalism in economics is characterised by the refusal to
separate the two worlds—secular and religious. Translated into
today's irreligious language, it is the refusal to allow the market
to function independently from one's own value-judgements.
But who, in a secular society, is competent to judge the 'just
price' of a packet of soap powder or the 'equitable reward' of a
football player? The answer is supplied by the secular religions,
which substitute their own certainties for the belief in a
universal morality dictated by God. There is also the aesthetic
or even mystical attack on the profit motive and the pursuit of
economic growth which assumes a political form in the writings
of the New Left, but is shared, in most essentials, by many
other critics of the consumer society. We are all left, upon
occasion, with the taste of ashes in our mouths at the spectacle
of a society that has mastered its material environment but not
itself. We are irritated to read how much Liberace is paid for
thumping a piano, however gracefully, in Las Vegas
night-clubs. And it is obvious that many of the greatest
individual achievements—and the greatest human sacrifices—

have had nothing to do with the profit motive, even if it is true that Dostoevsky had to churn out his masterpieces like any anonymous hack in order to cover his gambling debts, and might never have finished some of the novels otherwise.

Capitalism, and the revolution in natural science that accompanied it, helped to disintegrate local communities and to produce a general scepticism towards established conventions and institutions—without providing a broad-based philosophy that could satisfy man's need for faith. Max Born, the German physicist, expressed one side of this moral crisis when he wrote in 1968 that 'the break in human civilisation caused by the developments in the disciplines of the natural sciences may not be capable of repair. The natural sciences are so opposed to the tradition of historical developments that they may not be capable of absorption into our culture.' The rise of modern capitalism was of course closely linked with the Reformation, and with Jean Calvin's sanctification of commerce, with the challenge to medieval assumptions that was flung down by his famous question, 'Whence do the merchant's profits come, except through his own diligence and industry?'

But the argument shifted ground long ago; the Calvinist devotion to godly industry gave way to the moral vacuum and grinding poverty of the early industrial revolution, from which Marx and Engels drew their indictments of the capitalist system. The cost of the capitalist revolution in all western countries was heavy, although it is probably still exaggerated. The catastrophic effects of the potato famine in Ireland in 1845 are a reminder of what was happening elsewhere, where the new techniques of production and forms of organisation had not been applied. But the condition of the economically weak under nineteenth-century capitalism produced an unanswerable case for government intervention to ensure the means of survival and supplied both socialists and traditionalists with ammunition for their assault on the 'irreligion of Manchester'. It also produced compelling prophecies of the eventual demise of capitalist democracy that were the basis for the mass ideologies of the twentieth century. The connection between economic inequality—the inevitable result of the market system—and political liberty was seen to be transient. In the long run, either capitalism would be destroyed, or democracy, or both.

Marx, who taught that the state is based on class conflict and the need for class domination, and that political systems and ideologies are a super-structure that depends on the prevailing forms of economic production, believed that the 'historical tendency of capitalist accumulation' would lead to its own destruction—and with it, the collapse of bourgeois democracy. The essence of Marx's argument is well known. He believed, first, that the tendency towards concentration of economic activity would eliminate small business and bring together large numbers of property-less workers. Second (borrowing from Ricardo), he believed that profits would fall as the scale of enterprises—and the capital investment in them—increased, so that employers would reduce wages to a bare subsistence level in order to protect their margins. This would in turn lead to a contraction of the domestic market and a crisis of overproduction in the capitalist industries. The result would be socialist revolution, as sketched out in a celebrated passage in *Das Kapital:*

> One capitalist lays a number of his fellow capitalists low. Hand in hand with this centralisation, concomitantly with the expropriation of many capitalists by a few, the cooperative form of the labour process develops to an ever-increasing degree . . . all the peoples of the world are enmeshed in the net of the world market, and therefore the capitalist regime tends to assume an international character more and more. While there is thus a progressive diminution in the number of capitalist magnates (who usurp and monopolise all the advantages of this transformative process) there occurs a corresponding increase in the mass of poverty, oppression, enslavement, degeneration and exploitation; but at the same time there is a steady intensification of the wrath of the working class—a class which grows ever more numerous, and is disciplined, unified, and organised by the very mechanism of the capitalist method of production. Capitalist monopoly becomes a fetter upon the method of production which has flourished with it and under it. The centralisation of the means of production and the socialisation of labour reach a point where they prove incompatible with their capitalist husk. This bursts asunder. The knell of capitalist private property sounds. The expropriators are expropriated.

Other prophets believed, as opposed to Marx, that the capitalists would overcome the crisis they provoked by introducing an age of iron repression. Hilaire Belloc, who attacked British capitalism from the Catholic right, produced a tract early in this century entitled *The Servile State*. Belloc's thesis was that capitalism, by its very nature, is an unstable state of affairs because it dismantled older forms of social integration based on religion and deference and because 'its social realities were in conflict with all existing or possible systems of law, and its effects in denying sufficiency and scarcity were intolerable to men'.[10] He defined the capitalist state as a form of society that was characterised, first, by political freedom and mobility of labour; and second, by basic social division between capitalists and proletarians, or property-less workers, that he thought would become more and more accentuated. He saw the permanent source of instability in the tension between liberal theory and harsh social facts. On the one hand (writing before television and the application of modern advertising techniques) Belloc foresaw growing frustration with the failure of the modern industrial state to satisfy the expectations it created; on the other hand, he believed (like Marx) that capitalism condemned the worker to poverty and insecurity. 'To solve capitalism', he concluded, 'you must get rid of restricted ownership, or of freedom, or of both.'[11]

Belloc identified two alternative strategies. The first was an essentially conservative solution: a 'distributionist' strategy designed to spread the privileges and risks of ownership to a much greater proportion of the population, thus giving them a stake in the system. He was sceptical about whether this would work. Alternatively, there was the collectivist solution: the attempt to establish 'public ownership' (that is, control by the politicians) of the means of production. The intellectual and political currents of the time, in his view, were flowing strongly in favour of the collectivist alternative. Capitalism bred collectivist politics; collectivism offered a safe harbour from the sudden storms of the market and satisfied the moral scruples of the many people who believed that men should be rewarded according to merit—or need—and not according to the 'going price'.

Yet Belloc had his doubts about collectivism and it is here

(although he got his predictions largely wrong) that he speaks to us most directly today. Belloc despised the bureaucratic socialist mentality, and concluded that 'all that human and organic complexity which is the colour of any vital society' offends the collectivist 'by its infinite differentiation. He is disturbed by multitudinous things.'[12] The pursuit of collectivism was likely to result, not in a land flowing with milk and honey, but in the servile state: a society in which men would bind themselves over in the manner of latter-day serfs, willingly bartering their freedom to give and withdraw labour in return for absolute job security and a guaranteed income. The beneficiary of this revamped medievalism, Belloc suggested, would be big business rather than communism; he believed that a devious and powerful capitalist elite would succeed in disguising itself in 'sham socialism' in order to consolidate and perpetuate its dominance. Things have moved in a different direction. But Belloc's perception that the rationalist and seemingly 'lawless' behaviour of capitalist society spawns collectivist doctrines which, in turn, lead on towards new forms of serfdom, goes to the heart of the problem of securing, through economic pluralism, the indispensable base for a free society.

The prophecies of Marx and Belloc, at least in the short term, proved to be equally false. The 'corrected market economy'—to use Samuel Brittan's phrase—proved capable, not only of safeguarding the economically weak, but of introducing a period of unprecedented growth and improved living standards after 1945. No modern economy fits Marx's definition of the capitalist system. The huge expansion of social services and of state intervention (or supervision) throughout the economy put an end to the reign of *laissez-faire*, and few people will mourn its passing. The danger is that we will succeed in recreating the servile state, not in the interests of a group of capitalist entrepreneurs (as Belloc believed) but in the name of social justice—that we will *evolve* into a communist society that is equally at odds with liberty and economic efficiency. It is the challenge to political liberty that concerns me here.

The market is the only genuine form of 'economic democracy'—a phrase that rolls easily off the tongues of modern medievalists who would like to deal with capitalists as Dante dealt, in his imagination, with the Cahorsine moneylenders, who were assigned to a very warm place in Hell. The market system is a means of coordinating economic activity in which people 'cooperate because it is in their private interest to provide others with what they require'.[13] The main alternative model is the command system, applied in communist and third world socialist countries, which is a means of coordinating economic activity by issuing government instructions. In practice, all economic systems have elements of both. There is no known example of a literally *free* market system, which is why many economists now follow the West German lead and describe the Western economies as 'social market' (*die soziale Markwirtschaft*) systems. The commissars in Eastern Europe discovered long ago that it is impossible to determine every minute detail of economic life by central decision—and that the effort is disastrous anyway.

The market is economic democracy in action. The exercise of consumer choice is in fact a form of balloting. A teenager who buys the records of a pop group called Led Zepellin or Mud is helping to determine that more of them will be produced, however horrifying his parents might consider the prospect. His father, similarly, by choosing a certain brand of cigarettes or make of car, may be starting—in a tiny way—a chain process that will produce fortunes or bankruptcies, the 'election' of a captain of industry or his replacement. Certainly, suffrage is not equal in this kind of democracy, but it is universal. As von Mises put it, 'when we call a capitalist society a consumers' democracy, we mean that the power to dispose of the means of production, which belongs to the capitalists and entrepreneurs, can only be acquired by means of the consumers' ballot, held daily in the market-place.'[14] Those who object that consumer tastes are the creation of a cynical advertising machine and of backroom mergers (as Professor Galbraith has suggested, in a vastly more sophisticated way, in his critiques of the affluent society) would do well to remember that in a market economy, you cannot sell anything you like, whatever resources are committed to promoting the product. The position is different in command systems, where the consumer, deprived of his vote, must accept whatever goods are foisted upon him or go without.

If the market is replaced by some central planning agency, there is about as much choice for the consumer as there would be for a voter in a one-party state. It will immediately be argued that there is little choice for the poor man in a capitalist society who cannot afford to send his children to public schools or to buy colour television. But our liberties are at risk because this sort of argument has been made the pretext for the usurpation of choice by governments. If you want to help lower-income groups, you should do it by a negative income tax—by subsidising individuals or families—rather than by subsidising *things*. Instead, the 'corrected market economies', with Britain well to the fore, have set about nationalising service industries on the pretext of maintaining low prices, and expanding the role of the state in schooling, housing and social services—all in the name of protecting the economically weak. The results are notorious.

Not only has state intervention proved to be far more costly than private enterprise, but it has resulted in a sad narrowing of choice. This is perhaps nowhere clearer than in the zoning of comprehensive schools in Britain, which means that parents who cannot afford private education are often left with no choice but to send their children to the local school, even if its standards are notoriously bad. The cost of abandoning the cardinal principle of an operative social market economy— which is that governments should subsidise people, not things—applies here as in other areas. A voucher system in education of the kind that has been experimented with in the United States would guarantee adequate schooling for the children of the under-privileged, without granting a monopoly (and thus relief from competitive standards) to the state.[15] In other words, a government bent on maintaining ambitious welfare programmes and raising the living standards of the poor can and should operate according to market principles. The capitalist approach is not a prescription for static privilege, but a fundamental condition for liberty.

True economic democracy involves freedom of access—to employment, to housing, to means of publicity—for the critics of the system. Milton Friedman makes a powerful case for economic liberalism in his book, *Capitalism and Freedom*, when he recalls that the victims of the McCarthyite witch hunt in the United States were still able to find jobs and publishers. Can the same be said for political dissidents in state-run economies? A political democracy that creates a government monopoly—or tolerates a private monopoly—over any of the information media (the press, broadcasting, or publishing) has put the knife to its own throat.

The trouble is that the *political* necessity (as well as the economic benefits) of the market system has become obscured by pseudo-moralistic appeals to equality or regulation in the public interest. The first kind of appeal is based, as often as not, on dubious statistics about the relative spread of wealth and income—which, in the case of Britain, never seem to take account of concealed sources of income for lower-paid workers who benefit from welfare supplements, subsidised housing, and other gifts of the Welfare State. A recent study[16] demonstrated that the fashionable proposition that ten per cent of the British population owned seventry per cent of the wealth could only be substantiated if it were true (which it clearly is not) that twenty-four million adults own nothing at all, that anyone whose wealth exceeds £5,600 is in the top ten per cent, and that the value of the contents and motor-car of the average British household is only £200. Egalitarian arguments of this kind bypass many real cases of 'unacceptable' inequality, such as the fact that compositors on some Fleet Street newspapers are paid £8,000 to £10,000 a year (more than most journalists) not because of skill—since on Russian newspapers their jobs are often done by girls with six months' training—but because they enjoy the protection of strong trade unions. Such arguments rarely take account of the effects of progressive taxation. The post-tax earnings of a British Air Chief Marshal, for example, are about four times the net wages of a corporal in his early twenties—a minute differential compared with those that prevail in the Soviet armed forces.

The second kind of appeal—to the 'public interest'—is as pervasive as the appeal to envy and complaints about Rolls-Royce cars in the streets of London, and can be equally dangerous. There are some kinds of intervention which can fairly be said to be in the 'public interest', such as the curbing of private monopolies. But there are other sorts of intervention— the determination of how much a man should earn, for example—which are not in the public interest at all, unless that interest is defined as pertaining to a politically-motivated bureaucracy. Who is qualified to determine what a man's maximum income should be, or to decide in detail where society should invest its resources? The essence of the market system is that *it lets the public choose*. The choices are real, so that (as Samuel Brittan argues) capitalism, the *bête noire* of the trendy left, is actually also 'the biggest single force acting on the side of what it is fashionable to call "permissiveness", but what was once known as personal liberty.'[17], Collectivists who assume that state planners know best are saying, in effect, that the population as a whole is composed of mental defectives whose every step has to be guided by bureaucracy.

From what I have said so far, it will be apparent that the economic growth and efficiency that are demonstrably associated with the market system are not the nub of my argument—although it should be mentioned in passing that the 'public sector' is bound to be inefficient, since there is no compulsion on the government to produce a return on capital. Nor is the 'public sector' exposed to the same kind of scrutiny by the consumer as a private company, which has to pass through a kind of continuous electoral test. I have placed the phrase 'public sector' in inverted commas because it is not really public at all. Public ownership would mean that members of the public could behave as shareholders and influence the use that was made of their property. They cannot. Nor can they alienate their property. We are not talking about the position in a joint-stock company in which, as Montesquieu said, *le pouvoir arrête le pouvoir*. We are talking merely about a system by which civil servants manipulate taxpayers' money for 'public ends' designed by themselves.

If decisions are taken bureaucratically, spontaneity and innovation are likely to be minimal. To quote Peter Utley again, 'whereas ordinary services may be successfully commanded under threat, exceptional services (which it is in the power of only a few to perform) can be elicited only by reward.'[18] Centrally-planned blueprints for society reflect a dangerous arrogance about man's inevitable ignorance, and indifference to the need to allow scope for new ideas to burst forth in unexpected quarters. This is one of the conditions for a mobile and genuinely 'progressive' society and its absence in communist countries explains the tremendous technological lag of the Russians—except in areas where they have been able to play on the cupidity of western companies in order to import the needed technologies. State control and egalitarian redistribution also implicitly deny the need for the *pacemaker*. Societies do not move at the pace of the fastest individual, but the effort to keep up is healthy. Deny the scope for rapid advancement for those in the lead, and everyone else will slow down sooner or later. Contrary to the old saw, societies in which the rich get richer *through the market* tend to be societies where the poor get richer too. In contrast, 'a redistribution that slows down the rate of advance of those in the lead must bring about a situation in which even more of the next improvement will have to come from redistribution, since less will be provided by economic growth.'[19]

The cost of turning socialist rhetoric into practice and abandoning market principles can hardly be clearer—outside the communist world—than in the case of Argentina. In a book published in 1940,[20] the distinguished Oxford economist, Colin Clark, placed Argentina in the First Division of wealthy countries—not quite as rich as America or Canada, but in the same category as Britain, Australia or New Zealand, and some way ahead of Germany or France. Argentina has come down some way in the world since then, and is now to be classed in the fourth division where (as Professor H. S. Ferns observes)[21] the average per capita income is less than £350. The sources of Argentina's sad decline, which has brought political chaos and apparently uncontainable violence in its train, are to be found in the brand of state socialism applied by General Perón in his first political incarnation (1946-55). The present-day advocates of the siege economy and of socialism through income redistribution, nationalisation and ever-burgeoning welfare schemes would do well to consider the effects of their policies in what once appeared as the Canada of South America.

Juan Domingo Perón was carried to power by the riots of 1945. His power was confirmed in the 1946 elections, when he received fifty-six per cent of the votes. He proceeded to rule according to mythology. The problems of the following years were attributed to foreign conspiracies hatched by Jews, Communists, Uruguayans, Brazilians, Americans, Catholic priests and even the Swiss. Collectivist measures were justified by complaints againt the oligarchic dominance of 'the two hundred families'—whose identity was to remain a puzzle. Clemenceau had declared, in the course of a visit to Argentina early in the century, that the country was so immensely rich that no governor, however incompetent, would be able to ruin it. Perón was to prove him wrong.[22]

Perón was a great nationaliser and, for the lofty purpose of purging the country of capitalism, he worked wonders in converting profitable and innovative private firms into loss-making bureaucratic sinecures. Within three years of the state takeover, Argentina railways were employing more men per kilometre than any other railway system in the world. By the time the armed forces ousted Perón in 1955, the government controlled 60 per cent of Argentine banking, 80 per cent of electricity production, 65 per cent of air and marine transport, 80 per cent of the iron and steel industry, and had established monopolies in coal, gas and the railways. What's wrong with that? Readers may well ask. After all, most other governments have done the same. Those that have not insisted that state-run enterprises should be made to operate according to normal commercial principles will also have discovered what Argentina found out: that subsidised state-run industries sometimes prove to be infinitely 'leaky', with the government inflating the currency in order to keep them afloat, and almost infinitely prone to providing 'jobs for the boys' regardless of the need. (The state airline, Aerolíneas Argentinas, for example, employs three times as many people per plane as private local airlines like Austral or ALA.)

Like most doctrinaire nationalisers, Perón was also a great inflationist. Argentina's monetary supply increased fourteen times over the period between 1941 and 1955; the supply of goods and services increased by only fifty per cent over the same period. The two main reasons for keeping the printing presses in action were (i) Perón's political commitments to the industrial trade unions, the continuing power base for the Peronist movement, and (ii) the use of deficit financing to 'pay' for over-ambitious public spending programmes and nationalisation schemes. The inflationary legacy was heavy. Since 1950, Argentine inflation has fallen below ten per cent on only two occasions, and has often climbed to over fifty per cent. In the conditions he had created, Perón was led to impose rigorous exchange controls; the government seized all foreign currency earned by exporters and distributed it quite arbitrarily to favoured importers. Successful exporters were discouraged, traditional export markets were lost (through official price-fixing) and ruinous import businesses were subsidised and encouraged. The state export agency, IAPI, set itself up as the sole buyer of crops for export, paying farmers a fraction of the world price for beef or wheat. The surplus was not—contrary to Peronist propaganda—used to encourage rational industrial-isation, but to pay for the consumer goods from abroad that local industry was not producing. The Alice-in-Wonderland system of price controls set up to regulate foreign trade was extended over the Argentine economy as a whole, with the inevitable results. As an Argentine critic of Peronism observes, 'when the free market is broken down, the official takes upon himself the monstrous right of deciding what, how, and how much must be produced, overstepping the citizens' free will.'[23] But you cannot actually determine what or how much people will produce unless you introduce slavedrivers, or their modern equivalent. Perón's interventionist economic policy could not, for example, prevent a tremendous flight from the land of farmers who had been ruined by price controls—and a consequent decline in the production of staple crops that has never been effectively reversed.

The American economist Paul Samuelson, looking back on the opportunity that was lost, hazarded the opinion that the answer has to be found in populist democracy. If in the time of England's industrial revolution men had had the political power to try to rectify within a generation the unconscionable inequalities of life, in which a few privileged lived well off the sweat of the multitude, it is doubtful that the industrial revolution could ever have continued. The outcome would have been legislated increases in money wages of as much as forty per cent a year.[24]

Samuelson was echoing an old, old fear—the fear of the Marquess of Salisbury, who feared that if the cat was put in charge of the cream-jug, nothing would be spared for the future. Joseph Schumpeter expressed his fear, in a famous work first published more than three decades ago[25] that there would prove to be an irreconcilable conflict between capitalism and democracy. It is a fear that seems justified in Britain today. More generally, it is likely to prove accurate whenever the public is persuaded that there are no limits to what governments are entitled to do in the name of the 'people'. But it is to be hoped that they can be persuaded otherwise—at least in a society where private property is as widely dispersed as in Britain, where a majority (albeit a slim majority) of families own their own homes.

Yet to the average householder, the management of a large private shipbuilding firm no doubt seems as remote as a government department in Whitehall—unless he happens to hold shares in it, in which case it will become of compelling concern to compare the loss-making record of state-run enterprises with the record under private control. The 'managerial revolution' and the rise of the multinational corporations have, as their prophets argued, resulted in a certain convergence between the private and the public sectors, leading in some cases to the ascendancy of 'bureaucratic' incentives (for example, status within some huge, impersonal enterprise) over the profit motive in its traditional sense, to the creation of semi-monopolies and to a decline of price competition. I have no wish to skirt around the problem for political decision-making that arises from the emergence of corporations that overshadow the governments of some of the countries in which they operate. Since, as already stated, one of the basic reasons why governments exist is to curb private coercion, they have a duty to prevent the emergence of private monopolies that would, in themselves, overthrow the market—although this may be extremely difficult in a case where a company has a clear technological lead over its competitors.

The question we are left with may be stated as follows. The market is more efficient than command systems, and the dispersal of economic power is a precondition for pluralist politics. Yet the inefficiencies of the state sector in countries like Britain are made a pretext for more, not less, state intervention in the economy (and for deficit financing) which in turn threatens to reduce the private sector to a pale shadow of its former self. The tensions created by this continued state intrusion into most sectors of economic life may become unbearable, and the dilemmas of a mixed, but unstable economy may finally be resolved only by either turning back or surging forward—which in a country like Britain, might well mean the resurrection of the Peronist siege economy, or even the state of affairs under the late Roman Empire, which enforced a rigid closed shop and instituted police surveillance and ferocious official harassment to ensure that price regulations were observed and that crippling taxes were met. A contemporary chronicler observed that 'spies went around all the cities listening to what people were saying. All temperate and just liberty of speech was destroyed and everyone trembled at his own shadow.'[26]

The restoration of choice will depend on the acceptance of some general propositions that seem to me self-evident, and of a programme for rolling back the frontiers of state intervention. The general propositions are these:

1 That the market economy was the basis for the most remarkable period of material affluence and technical innovation in human history.

2 That it is indissolubly linked with the rise and survival of representative government. 'Democracy and a free economy are as logically linked,' as Erhard put it, 'as are dictatorship and state controls.'[27]

3 That the desire to own and accumulate property is an ineradicable, and creative human instinct.

4 That individual choice can be combined with the pursuit of equality of opportunity through the application of market principles in health, education and welfare, but that the pursuit of unlimited equality is a totalitarian cause.

5 That no centralised agency is capable of coping efficiently with the focal problems of the modern economy in all their complexity—determining consumer preferences, allocating resources, deciding on production techniques, creating incentives and coordinating economic activity as a whole. If the market is no longer used to determine wages and prices, for example, who is to decide on the value of difference goods and services?

There are not many examples of a society that has entered into a phase of far-reaching economic collectivism successfully 'rolling back the frontiers'. Argentina, which has been mentioned, has carried on down the path that Perón marked out. The great and single exception to the pattern of steadily increasing state intervention in Europe is West Germany—but it took the holocaust of Hitler's war and the Allied occupation to make that possible. It did not happen spontaneously, and without the war the brilliant and far-sighted architect of Germany's new 'social market economy', Dr Ludwig Erhard, would never have found a hearing. Even as things were, he had to fight against the conventional unwisdoms of some of Germany's post-war occupiers in order to dismantle price and wage controls and restore internal competition. Other countries that have tried to restore the market mechanisms after a deep descent into state socialism have done so under the umbrella of an authoritarian regime—like Brazil or Chile—which is not exactly encouraging for those who seek to restore economic pluralism through democratic means. However, there is room for hope that if the case for the market economy is argued cogently enough, as the social and economic effects of runaway government spending and the manifold inefficiencies of state-run enterprises become inescapable, it will be widely accepted. If it is not, and the restoration of consumer choice is at last dismissed as not being 'practical politics', there is added reason for scepticism about the future prospects for political pluralism.

There is a final point to be made about the current and potential assault on certain forms of private property—through wealth tax, taxes on 'unearned income', and an almost vertically 'progressive' income tax—and on the inheritance and transfer of property. Again, the inverted commas are there because we find ourselves once more in a semantic jungle. The whole concept of 'unearned income' is founded on some dubious assumptions. Is the interest on a sum that a man saved during his working life 'unearned'? I do not want to burrow into the murky warren of existing tax legislation, but it does seem that the efforts to reduce economic inequality through taxation are jeopardising both the incentives for highly dynamic individuals to work and invest, while aiming to supplant the basic human instinct for the support and preservation of the family—which is surely the basic and most permanent unit of social life, and in itself the prime motivation for much economic activity.

The need to have and to hold, for the sake of self-preservation, for the sake of the family and the survival of the species, is one of the primal instincts in man—an instinct that no collectivist blueprint for Utopia has ever been able to eradicate. The first questions that I was asked, on a visit to

Poland, were: 'Do you live in a house or flat? How many rooms does it have? How many square metres does it contain? What kind of television set do you have?' When Fidel Castro, in the romantic early years of the Cuban revolution, tried to inspire workers and students to clear the fields by labelling different kinds of week 'Uncle Sam' or 'United Fruit', he found that this was no adequate substitute for material incentives. But the need for material incentives is only part of the argument for private property.

It is not by accident or merely because of advanced mechanisation that in Russia one peasant feeds one city-dweller, while in America one farmworker feeds a dozen townsmen. Nor is it simply because a market economy offers higher rewards—and greater choice in how they are deployed. It would seem to have a great deal to do with the fact that agricultural land in the United States is still divided between a large number of private farmers. The stimulant effect of a private 'territory' has been studied in the animal world, and the evidence suggests that the attachment to property is not, as behavioural psychologists and 'social engineers' would have us believe, merely the result of environmental conditioning in a wicked capitalist society. The robin sings only within the frontiers of the territory he has marked out for himself; beavers achieve prodigies of work—but only when a beaver colony has established a permanent site, secure from expropriation by others. Territory for animals, like property for human beings, satisfies three univeral psychological needs: the need for security, for stimulation, and for *identity* with something bigger than the animal itself. If those needs are frustrated, the result is bound to be alienation, a loss of creative energy, and a disastrous tendency towards social warfare.[28]

The time has come to offer, in place of Socialism, a kind of popular capitalism founded on the recognition of those basic needs. Profit-sharing and worker participation are positive concepts if they also entail the risk of *loss*—sharing and overall responsibility for the success or failure of an enterprise within the framework of a market system. Modern socialists and trade union bureaucrats tend to shy away such responsibility. But 'public ownership', carried to extremes, can result only in the substitution of the *apparatchik* for the entrepreneur.

7

Pseudo-Legality and Revolution

The irony of world history turns everything upside down.
We, the 'revolutionists', the 'overthrowers'—we are
thriving far better on legal methods than on illegal
methods and overthrow. The parties of order, as they call
themselves, are perishing under the legal conditions
created by themselves. They say despairingly with Odilon
Barrot: *la légalité nous tue,* legality is the death of us.

Friedrich Engels[1]

No government, however brutal and unpopular, rests solely
upon bayonets, and the success of an insurrection or *coup
d'état* depends on more than the violence that is employed. Of
course Mao was right, but only in a restricted sense: power
grows out of the barrel of a gun, but there are kinds of power
that are more important, and the first among them is the
authority that is derived from *legitimacy*. The claim to
legitimacy can be based on a revolutionary ideology, a religious
orthodoxy or some royal pedigree but it can only succeed if it is
couched in terms that most people can be brought to accept.
Totalitarians at work in democratic societies have long
understood the need to borrow some of the trappings and
much of the vocabulary of the systems they set out to destroy.
The rapid seizure of power by a revolutionary minority
depends on neutralising the majority, anaesthetising a large
part of the population with the notion that what has happened
is 'proper'. Thus in a politically sophisticated country where a
large proportion of the population is involved in public life—as
an electorate, through community groups and trade unions,
through membership of political parties—the overthrow of the
state will be difficult to engineer unless it takes place under a
cloak of pseudo-legality. The position is rather different in a
society that has entered a stage of total breakdown, or in a
primitive and politically demobilised society where most
people are entirely *hors de combat*. The classic example of the

first situation was the Bolshevik coup in Russia.

Curzio Malaparte, who cast a cold and cynical eye on the mechanics of the *coup d'état,* drew the conclusion that method is everything.[2] The Bolshevik revolution was made by Trotsky, the tactician, and by Antonov-Ovseyenko, the former officer of the Imperial Guard who studied insurrection as a chess-player studies his board. It was *not* made by Lenin, the strategist, or by the intellectuals of the Bolshevik central committee, who were planning proletarian revolution while the real conspirators were assigning their teams to the key pressure-points in the capital; to the railways, the electricity plants, the telephone exchange, the radio station, the petrol, coal and grain depots, and the fortress of St Peter and St Paul.

The lesson that the Comintern[3] and outside observers like Malaparte were to draw from the events of October 1917 was that, if you could make revolution in Holy Russia with a thousand men, you could set out to overthrow any regime with a group of technicians, of professional revolutionaries. This idea lingers on—in a grotesquely caricatured form—in the writings of Régis Debray and his quixotic mentor, Che Guevara. The success of the Bolsheviks was the success of a strong man striking a paralytic, as Trotsky was later to observe. The administration was invertebrate; the streets were given over to the mob, with 200,000 deserters scavenging for food, scoffing at all proclamations. The collapse of the Russian state, and Kerensky's incomprehension of the nature of revolution, provided the opportunity for a small band of disciplined men who knew precisely what they were doing; the chaos of the streets provided a mask for tiny assault-teams whose members had been well-tutored in the anatomy of the modern city, and who had been trained to see beyond the symbols of power—the ministries and parliaments—to the sinews and arteries.

Edward Luttwak supplies one of the most useful definitions of the *coup d'état:* 'A coup consists of the infiltration of a small but critical segment of the state apparatus, which is then used to displace the government from its control of the remainder.'[4] The coup is not an attack from outside the regime, but an attack from within. Its success depends upon the machine-like functioning of military and civil service chains of command; on the fact that men below the *effective* level of command (which will vary according to the situation—it may be colonels, captains or sergeants) will carry out instructions. The classical *military* coup also depends on speed and smooth execution to secure its goals and paralyse resistance; its immediate goals are likely to include vital services, communications, and above all the elimination of the potential leaders of the resistance, among whom a powerful shop steward may rank higher than an uncharismatic minister. The coup depends, by definition, on the *failure of reaction*. This is why it is most likely to succeed in backward countries, where there is limited political participation in the system and general scepticism or ignorance about the novel structures of government. Mass resistance in such countries is unlikely, whatever the aims of the makers of the coup.

The seizure of power is a more complex affair in an advanced democratic society, not just because more people are involved, but because power is diffused. 'Power in a sophisticated democracy is like a freely floating atmosphere—and who can seize that?'[5] But advanced democratic societies can become vulnerable. Disaffection becomes widespread in the context of economic crisis, defeat in war (or a drawn-out and unsuccessful war), sustained political violence inside the country, the merry-go-round of government under changeable multi-party coalitions (as in France under the Third and Fourth Republics) and the abolition of conservative institutions.

The last case is more important than it may seem at first sight. British democracy, for example, has grown up and flourished in combination with symbols and institutions derived from an older, hierarchic order; the monarchy and the House of Lords are the most obvious instances. Such institutions, which are frequently attacked as anachronisms, have in fact been crucial to the stability of the British political system under conditions that would have produced violent eruptions in many republics. Remember the famous conversation between Sir Arthur Paget, the commander of the British troops in Ireland, and the dissident cavalry officers at the time of the Curragh mutiny. 'He said that we must clearly understand that this was the direct order of "the Sovereign", and asked us "if we thought he would obey the orders of those dirty swine of politicians".'[6] Here an effective appeal was made to a loyalty transcending the government of the day. Only one of the European constitutional monarchies went fascist before

1939, and the House of Savoy in Italy was rather a parvenu among the continent's crowned families.* The point is simply, as S. M. Lipset notes in the kind of language that scars sociology,[8] that a system with a low 'effectiveness' rating but a high legitimacy rating may command greater loyalty than a system with a higher effectiveness rating but a lower legitimacy rating. The constitutional monarchies (which are more than merely decorative since they relate older conceptions of status and transcendent belief in the legitimacy of the system than do the republics) have provided a guarantee of stability, at any rate within the framework of western Europe.

In a politically sophisticated society, would-be revolutionaries (or counter-revolutionaries) must be able *either* to invoke a 'higher' source of legitimacy than the constitution, a legitimacy which is recognised by a significant section of the population or the armed forces, *or* to work through the constitution so that resistance will be paralysed by respect for a legality that is, in reality, being destroyed from within. The notion that political legitimacy rests on the will of the people is a relatively modern concept. The alternative ideas about legitimacy—that it rests on the blood-right of the king's first-born son, on universal law, on divine selection, or on the rule of the 'best'—are not only older, but have continued to provide a philosophic basis for challenges to democratic constitutions.

But as Sir Henry Maine observed, the concept that political legitimacy stems from popular sovereignty—which swept through Europe after Jean-Jacques Rousseau sat down and wept by the shore of Lake Geneva—in itself has far-reaching revolutionary implications. 'From this came the subordination of governments, not merely to electorates, but to a vaguely defined multitude outside them, and to the still vaguer mastership of floating opinion. Thence began the limitation of

---

*Monarchs, of course, were not unknown to seek their own authoritarian solutions to the problems of the 1920s and 1930s. One of the most interesting cases was the creation of a royal dictatorship in Yugoslavia in 1928, following the assassination of the leader of the Croat Peasant Party by a Serbian deputy in parliament, and a confused decade of coalition politics in which there were no fewer than twenty-three governments. In this case, royal intervention was primarily designed to overcome ethnic and regional differences. One of the king's first actions was to change the name of the country from the Serb-Croat-Slovene state (an admission of insuperable disunity) to Yugoslavia, or 'South Slavia'.[7]

legitimacy in government to governments which approach democracy . . . There has been no such insecurity of government since the century during which the Roman emperors were at the mercy of the Praetorian soldiers.'[9] The idea of a transcendent 'general will' provided the same kind of claim to legitimacy for left-wing totalitarians that the idea of a transcendent state or of the primacy of race provided for right-wing totalitarians.

In conditions of social collapse, it is often sufficient for those who are capable of seizing power in the name of 'order' to appeal to the general sense of crisis and to the need for efficiency and strong government. This was the pattern of many of the military or royalist coups in Europe in the 1920s—and of military intervention throughout the third world in more recent times. Such intervention is sometimes justified in terms of the Roman concept of the need for 'temporary' dictatorship—although of course, when constitutional restraints are lifted, it is difficult to guarantee that the dictatorship will be merely temporary. Such intervention is made easier by the presence of a 'man on a white horse', a well-known war leader like Marshal Pilsudski (who set up a limited military dictatorship in Poland in 1926 and who was already famous as the man who had raised and commanded the Polish legions in the Austrian army, and later inflicted defeat on the Russian army in 1920).

The declaration issued by General Primo de Rivera to justify his coup in Spain on 13 September 1923, is a representative example of the appeal to chaos and the corruption of politicians as a *sufficient* justification for military intervention:

We do not feel obliged to justify our action, which sensible public opinion demands and imposes. Murders of priests, ex-governors, public officials, employers, foremen and workers; audacious and unpunished hold-ups; depreciation of the value of money; the hogging of millions of concealed expenditures; a customs policy suspect for its tendencies but even more because whoever manages it boasts of impudent immorality; base political intrigues seizing on Morocco as their pretext; social indiscipline which renders labour inefficient and of no account; agricultural and industrial production precarious and in a ruinous state; communist propaganda unpunished; impiety and barbarousness; justice influenced by politics . . .[10]

It would seem that a fair number of Spaniards thought this *cahier de doléances* to be an accurate statement of the way things were. If Primo de Rivera's intention had been merely to 'sort things out' and then retire from the scene, he might well have confined his claim to legitimacy to a statement of the facts. But since he meant to stay on, he took the precaution to establish his 'democratic' credentials by holding a referendum. We must still distinguish between 'holding operations' of this kind and a *revolutionary* assault on the state by either right or left. Serious revolutionaries are well aware that the attack on 'bad government' or the appeal to the 'general will' may not be sufficient to paralyse resistance to the seizure of power in an advanced society. This particularly applies to the left, which is less likely to be able to win the support of the armed forces and the permanent apparatus of the state and will therefore need to play upon traditions of legality and constitutionalism, where they exist. Lenin supplied some important clues as to how this is to be done.

After the failure of the communist insurrections in Germany in 1918-19, Lenin published a pamphlet entitled *'Left-Wing' Communism, an Infantile Disorder,* which remains the definitive statement on the use of tactical compromise by Marxist revolutionaries. He attacked, to his right, social democrat 'opportunists' who, having gained access to parliament and the trade unions, became props of the system of bourgeois democracy that they had initially set out to destroy. But he turned with equal ferocity on those to his left who maintained that all compromises were to be rejected on principle and that revolutionaries should boycott parliament and the 'reactionary' trade unions and rely on the method of armed insurrection. Lenin resolved the old debate between would-be insurrectionists—should we rely on legal or illegal methods?—by saying quite simply that of course you need both. 'Revolutionaries who are incapable of combining illegal forms of struggle with every *legal* form of struggle are poor revolutionaries indeed.' But 'it is far more difficult—and far more precious—to be a revolutionary when the conditions for direct, open, really mass and really revolutionary struggle *do not yet exist,* to be able to champion the interests of the revolution (by propaganda, agitation and organisation) in non-revolutionary bodies, and quite often in downright reactionary bodies, in a non-revolutionary situation.'[11]

The important thing was to grasp the nature of tactical compromise, the basic difference between 'a compromise enforced by objective conditions . . . which in no way minimises the revolutionary devotion and readiness to carry on the struggle' and a sell-out, a 'treacherous compromise' with the other side in the class war. Communists, of course, do not wish to prolong the life of parliaments or free trade unions for a day longer than necessary, but by gaining a foothold within them they can bring that day closer. Lenin warned his readers that they should have no illusions about the political 'maturity' of the working class. The masses were not about to rally *en masse* to the revolution; and if the mountain would not come to Mahomet, Mahomet must go to the mountain. 'You should not fear difficulties, or pinpricks, chicanery, insults and persecution . . . but must absolutely work *wherever the masses are to be found*. You must be capable of any sacrifice, of overcoming the greatest obstacles, in order to carry on agitation and propaganda systematically, persistently and patiently in those institutions, societies and associations—even the most reactionary—in which proletarian or semi-proletarian masses are to be found.'[12] The most important of those institutions was the trade union movement.

Lenin's comments about the use of parliament are perhaps the most revealing. He did not suggest that communists were likely to come to power by parliamentary means, but that a revolutionary bloc in parliament could help to discredit the democratic system that it was exploiting and paralyse government response to mass upheavals in society as a whole. Communist participation—overt or covert—would help 'to prove to the backward masses why such parliaments deserve to be done away with; it facilitates their successful dissolution, and helps to make bourgeois parliamentarism politically obsolete.' Parliament would provide a convenient forum for revolutionary propaganda. But above all, a strong left-wing bloc could help to deny the government a mandate for responding effectively to 'extra-parliamentary revolutionary mass action', as in Russia in 1905.

Finally, Lenin was well aware that the Bolshevik insurrection was not about to be repeated in anything like its original form in the advanced industrial democracies. Armed communist uprisings were likely to be broken as the Spartakists in Berlin had been broken. But the opportunity for the communists was presented by the fact that the democracies' defences, like the guns at Singapore in 1940, were pointing the wrong way.

> The bourgeoisie sees practically only one aspect of Bolshevism—insurrection, violence, and terror; it therefore strives to prepare itself for resistance and opposition primarily in *this* field. It is possible that, in certain instances, in certain countries, and for certain brief periods, it will succeed in this. We must reckon with such an eventuality, and we have absolutely nothing to fear if it does succeed. *Communism is emerging in positively every sphere of public life;* its beginnings are to be seen literally on all sides [my emphasis].[13]

Lenin might have carried his reasoning a long way further if he had had greater personal knowledge of the Western societies that the Comintern had selected as targets. He saw clearly how democratic *institutions* might be exploited by the totalitarian left, which would set out simultaneously to educate the working class in the folly of those same institutions. He did not appear to see that the *psychology* of many advanced societies—and particularly those elements that Lenin and his comrades would have considered most 'reactionary', such as orderliness, a liking for 'doing things by the book' and simple patriotism—presented equal opportunities for anti-democratic movements if they knew how to dress themselves in the mantle of pseudo-legitimacy.

The appeal to these instincts is a natural prerogative of the right rather than the left, but there is no reason why a Marxist movement that pays sufficient attention to its costume should be unable to beat on the same drum. This is something that came home to George Orwell in England during the Second World War, when he noted that 'the patriotism of the middle classes is a thing to be made use of. The people who stand to attention during "God Save the King" would readily transfer their loyalty to a socialist regime, if they were handled with a minimum of tact.'[14] True, no left-wing organisation had ever been able to gain a foothold in the British armed forces, but the left could count on an all-important English trait, the deeply-ingrained respect for constitutionalism and legality, to deter any threat from that quarter. For Orwell, the twin appeals to nationalism and legality, if they could be mastered by the left (by which he did not, of course, mean the communist left) would make possible fundamental changes in social and economic structures that the victims of the process would not be likely, in other situations, to accept. Orwell was an enemy of the totalitarians; he spoke for a kind of idealistic and evolutionist socialism, that Lenin, the mechanic of absolute power, would have recognised only with contempt. Yet he pointed to some of the social attributes of a long-established democratic society that totalitarians would be able to exploit.

I intend to devote the rest of this chapter to the use of pseudo-legality by the revolutionary right and to pass on in the next two chapters to the two outstanding recent examples of the use of the same technique by the communist left: Czechoslovakia and Chile. It is worth mentioning, in passing, the case of Napoleon Bonaparte, who must surely figure as one of the great practitioners of pseudo-legality.

Napoleon's *coup d'état* of 18-19 Brumaire (9-10 November) 1799 was the latest in the whirligig succession of usurpations of power that began with the storming of the Bastille. But it differed fundamentally from the revolutionary *journées* and from the Thermidorean coup of 1799 not just because this was the first time, in the course of a revolution whose protagonists appealed to 'popular sovereignty', that the consultation of the people was used to supply a genuine mandate for the regime. The story of the events of 18-19 Brumaire, which brought about the overthrow of the Directory and Napoleon's elevation to the rank of First Consul, is well-known in the colourful version bequeathed by Count Albert Vandal.[15] It does not speak highly of Napoleon's resolution. When the assembly of Five Hundred moved to declare him an outlaw of 19 Brumaire, he fell into a 'half-fainting condition' from which he was retrieved by his forceful brother Lucien, who had the presence of mind to summon the grenadiers and persuade them to disperse the deputies at the point of the bayonet.

Napoleon was better-prepared for subsequent developments. He legitimised the new constitution, granting full powers to the First Consul, with a plebiscite in January 1800. He again received overwhelming support in the plebiscite on 2 August 1802, which made him Life Consul. And in 1804, after he was proclaimed Emperor by the senate and had placed the diadem on his own head, the new constitution was again approved by plebiscite. Napoleon himself observed that 'the appeal to the people has the double advantage of legalising the prolongation of my power and of purifying its origins. In any other way, it must always have appeared as equivocal.'[16]

The first of the major fascist *coups* in Europe legitimised itself after the event. The fascist seizure of power in Italy, unlike the Nazis' constitutional coup in Germany, was an attack from *outside* the system. But it succeeded only because (i) significant forces within the system—notably within the army—were sympathetic to Mussolini's aims; (ii) because the coup received legitimation from King Victor Emmanuel; and (iii) because the fascists had already succeeded in proving, to most people's satisfaction, that strike action and other forms of mass resistance would succumb to their violence.

Italy's democratic system pre-dated the First World War, unlike Germany's. In fact, the contrast between the two traditions was striking. Italy had been united under the most constitutionally-minded and 'progressive' state in the peninsula, Piedmont, while German unification came about under the country's most military-minded and authoritarian state, Prussia. And yet Italian democracy even after 1912 (when universal suffrage was granted) like British democracy throughout most of the nineteenth century, was the preserve of a narrow ruling class. Its stability—or so it appeared to historians in retrospect[17]—depended on the apathy or formal exclusion of the majority, and also on the system of constituency voting. Both factors changed after the First World War, with the irruption of modern mass movements onto the political scene and the introduction of proportional representation (in 1919) which, as in Weimar Germany, proved to be a condition for weak coalition government.

To return to the basic three reasons for Mussolini's success: the widespread support for fascism in official circles in the early 1920s is sometimes attributed by Italian writers to the phenomenon of 'cultural despair' that is also mentioned in connection with Weimar Germany. Certainly, Italy's laggardly industrial development and military enfeeblement in the post-Risorgimento period generated a kind of resentment towards the outside world, a feeling that Italy had not found its proper place. This was aggravated by the myth of the 'mutilated victory', Italy's own peculiar version of the 'stab-in-the-back' legend that circulated after 1918. The Italians, of course, were on the side of the victors, but complaints that 'just' territorial claims had been left unsatisfied indicated that 'Italy acquired the psychology of a defeated nation'.[18] This neurosis found an outlet in d'Annunzio's romantic expedition in Fiume in 1919.

But there was a more practical reason why a powerful section of the Italian establishment rallied to the fascists: they appeared to provide front-line defences against the threat of revolution from the left. The widespread occupation of factories in September 1920, at the tail-end of a great revolutionary wave throughout Europe, proved to be a strategic defeat for the communists; but it also prompted the mobilisation of threatened interests. The great leap forward for Mussolini's movement came in the winter of 1920-21 when, with support from the general staff and the tolerance of local police prefects, the *fasci di combattamento* waged war on the left throughout the northern countryside. The relations between the Italian fascists and the business and landed interests that felt themselves threatened by communism was less equivocal than the relations between the Nazis and similar groups in Germany. There was a strongly anti-capitalist current in Italian fascism, which was reflected in a key statement by Mussolini that was quoted in an earlier chapter. But the fascist credo was open to unlimited contradiction, and the general tendency over the period between 1919 and 1922 was towards the defence of property—although this met with considerable resistance from inside the movement.

The March on Rome on 27-28 October 1922 was not, contrary to legend, what brought down Italian democracy. Rome was held by twelve thousand troops under a loyal general, and it is probable that the capital would in no sense have 'fallen' had orders been given to resist. Things were rather different in many provincial capitals, where no clear directions had been given to the authorities, and the fascists were able to seize control of communications and command centres. Mussolini's 200,000 Blackshirts were more than theatrical: they had amply demonstrated their capacity for ruthless violence. But it was King Victor Emmanuel who gave Mussolini power. The open collusion of some generals with the fascists may have swayed him to revoke the state of siege that had been proclaimed and to accept Mussolini as head of a government that contained a Nationalist, a Liberal, three Democrats, two Popolari (the Church party) and two soldiers as well as three other fascists and the proto-fascist philosopher Gentile—a spectrum of party allegiances that shows that Italian fascism, although striking from outside the system, was very widely accepted within it. The road to absolutism now proceeded through pseudo-legality, albeit a very threadbare version. Mussolini supported his demand for 'full powers' from parliament with the interesting claim that 'I could have made this grey and gloomy hall into a bivouac for my legions.'[19]

Curzio Malaparte characteristically exaggerated the 'technical' element in the fascist seizure of power, but he made one critical observation that deserves to be recalled: 'It was not in October, but in the month of August that fascism gained the decisive battle in its conquest of the state.'[20] He was referring to the one serious attempt that had been made to organise effective mass resistance to the growing fascist power. It was then that the socialists, together with the trade union federation and other left-wing groups, attempted a 'legalitarian general strike' against Mussolini's movement. The aim was probably not specific enough to bring success anyway. But the whole wretched affair proved to be a devastating rout for the left and probably persuaded many people whose feelings towards the fascists were ambiguous that there was no hope of standing against them. The strikers' rallies were broken up by Mussolini's *squadristi* and the socialist *giunta* was forcibly evicted from the Milan town hall. The strike had provided the fascists with another chance to figure as champions of law and order. But its lasting effect was to suggest that a fascist coup would not have to contend with any serious trade union resistance.

Insurrection, to quote Trotsky, is a machine that makes no noise. The story of Hitler's rise to power is in part the story of how the extreme right in Germany came to understand, and successfully practise, the technique of pseudo-legality: that the democratic state must be attacked from within instead of without, and that the attack must be shrouded with the semblance of constitutionality. After the failure of the Kapp putsch of 1920 and Hitler's beer-hall putsch in November 1923, it came to be understood that in the seizure of power in the modern democratic state, force *completes* the process; it does not initiate it—although secondary political violence may help to establish the climate of collapse. Rauschning, one of Hitler's disenchanted former sympathisers, who wrote what probably still stands as the most perceptive explanation of the Nazi's constitutional revolution, described the mechanics of the takeover as a process of 'inoculating legality with the revolutionary impulse'.[21] He echoed Trotsky when he observed that the events of 1933 were to show that a coup 'can be carried out piecemeal, at intervals, and almost without a sound'.[22]

I do not propose to attempt any overall explanation of why Genghis Khan was resurrected in central Europe in the second quarter of the twentieth century; whole libraries have been devoted to the theme, and more remain to be filled. My concern here is with two contributory factors: (i) the nature of political legitimacy under the Weimar Republic; and (ii) the way that the Nazis were able to use democratic institutions, and the failure of both the authentic defenders of the Republic and the conservative authoritarians (who might conceivably have provided an alternative to Hitler) to prevent the Nazi seizure of power.

The first point to observe is that the Weimar Republic was the product of defeat in war, a humiliating peace settlement, and the abdication of the emperor. It was born half-strangled by its own umbilical cord, illegitimate in the eyes of the nationalist right and unfamiliar to everyone else. It was to suffer the whole pathology of internal warfare: revolution from below, coups from above, the manipulation of the institutions of democracy by its sworn enemies. It had to cope with the burden of reparations, the Franco-Belgian occupation of its industrial heartland in the Ruhr, the Great Inflation and the world depression. The range of problems that Weimar governments had to solve would have placed almost unendurable stress on a long-established democracy; but this was a foundling democracy whose own army, judiciary and civil service doubted its claims to legitimacy. To find a parliamentary majority that actually accepted the Weimar constitution—under a system of proportional representation—became another insuperable problem after the elections of 1920. The solution to political or economic crises became rule by emergency decree, on the authority of the president under Article 48 of the new constitution, or under enabling laws of the kind passed by the Marx cabinet in the early 1920s—and which set a precedent for Hitler.

Authoritarian critics of Weimar democracy could appeal, not only to the 'stab in the back' legend, but to the traditional Germanic conception of the state as an entity transcending governments and constitutions. Industrialisation in Germany had taken place within the framework of traditional feudal structures; the liberal cause had been defeated in the mid-nineteenth century, and the subsequent political evolution disproved the Marxist assumption that there is a *necessary* connection between industrialisation and liberal democracy. The German middle class looked for status in the traditional sense, through military or caste hierarchies, and thus the social basis was lacking for the creed of individual liberty and the political expressions that it found in England or the United States. The authoritarian welfare state, as it emerged in Bismarck's Germany, was a state that sheltered *subjects* but did not recognise citizens.[23] Bismarck himself, when challenged with proposals for constitutional reform, was to enunciate the classical Germanic doctrine of the state transcending political systems: 'Let us first create a solid structure, secure to the outside, firmly built inside and joined together by the national tie, and then you ask me for my opinion about how the house should be furnished with more or less liberal constitutional institutions, and you may find that I answer with, I have no preconceived opinions on this. . .'[24] The concept of *Staatsrason* as the permanent and supreme law transcending transient political division, whose full historical ramifications were explored by the historian Meinecke[25] supplied the authoritarian and revolutionary right under Weimar with the appeal to 'a law above the constitution'. The personification of the state in this way is probably inimical to democracy; as Carl J. Friedrich has observed, 'strictly, under a democracy, the state does not exist.' My point here is that the Germanic cultural tradition of statolatry laid the foundations of legitimacy for a modern totalitarian movement that did not recognise any of the restraints on power that were imposed by an adherence to religion, convention and the strongly-held idea of the state based on law (the Rechtstaat) under imperial autocracy.

Defeat in 1918 destroyed the pre-existing consensus on the exact nature and location of legitimate authority in Germany. As Professor Wheeler-Bennett[26] and later scholars have shown in detail, the army remained the real arbiter of power over the whole period up to Hitler's triumph. Despite its reduced manpower, the army could arguably have seized power at any point of crisis throughout the course of the Weimar Republic; but traditions of legality and 'civilianism' ran deep. Hindenburg leaned hard on President Ebert to make him crush the Spartakists in 1918-19. There was a ham-fisted attempt at a coup in 1920 (after the Allies had presented a list of 'war criminals') by General von Lüttwitz; significantly, the front man was Kapp, a civilian. The lack of a mass base and of any semblance of constitutionality for this irresponsible attempt explained its failure—and the lesson was not lost on later military schemers, and notably General von Schleicher, whose very name meant 'intriguer', and whose plots to set up an authoritarian dictatorship helped to bring down the final curtain on the Weimar Republic. But throughout most of the Weimar period, the aims of the general staff were essentially negative or limited: to restore the army as a powerful autonomous force within a unified state; to resist Allied demands for disarmament and reparations; to combat communism. The generals were certainly not enamoured of democracy, and they detested the social democrats. But, under Generals von Seeckt and Gröner, they were prepared to cooperate with the Republic. The disposition to intervene reached its height when it was actually too late. Karl Newman concludes that 'in the twentieth century, an authoritarian state which is based only on the armed forces, the police and the bureaucracy can no longer check the progress of a popular mass movement.'[27] The statement is only half-true. The 'presidential dictatorship' that Hindenburg and Schleicher were trying to establish in the last months of the Republic could not withstand the Nazis because (i) they operated within the framework of pseudo-legality and (ii) they appealed, however fraudulently, to the same nationalist values and the same professional desire for military supremacy as the armed forces.*

Hitler wrote a letter to Chancellor Brüning at the end of 1931 that defines the dilemma for a democratic society that is harbouring totalitarian forces *within its own institutions* as clearly as any paragraph in the literature of politics:

> You refuse, as a 'statesman', to admit that if we come to power legally we could then break through legality. Herr Chancellor, the fundamental thesis of democracy runs, 'All Power issues from the People'. The constitution lays down the ways by which a conception, an idea, and therefore an organisation, must gain from the people the legitimation for the realisation of its aims. But in the last resort, it is the People itself which determines its Constitution. Herr Chancellor, if the German nation once empowers the National Socialist Movement to introduce a Constitution other than that which we have today, then you cannot stop it.[28]

We have now to look at how a movement so explicitly and uncompromisingly opposed to the 'legality' of the Weimar Republic could come to power legally.

We should observe at the outset that the citizens of Weimar were as often as not living in a literal state of siege. The Weimar constitution remained in effective operation for some fifteen years; over nearly half that period, constitutional emergency powers were in force. There is always a danger in the use of emergency powers. Perhaps the man who drew up the Weimar constitution had forgotten that a 'state of emergency' was used to overthrow the Roman Republic. This is not a device favoured in many contemporary democracies; the famous Article 16 that de Gaulle insisted on writing into the constitution of the Fifth Republic is a notable exception. And yet it is a little too hasty to conclude that the 'dictatorship paragraph' of the Weimar constitution—Article 48—was one of

---

*Hitler delivered a speech in March 1929 in which he promised the army that 'if our movement wins, we are glad to assure you that we shall exert ourselves by day and night to create those military formations, now forbidden to us by the Treaty of Versailles.' He had it printed in a special 'Reichswehr edition' of the party paper.

the keys to its overthrow. In the early 1920s, and under Brüning's chancellorship (30 March 1930 to 30 May 1932) it was one of the keys to the Republic's survival. After all, the Republic was in an almost unbroken state of internal war and, as we shall see, there was no *parliamentary* basis for strong government over most of the period after 1920. The Republic might well have collapsed much sooner than it did but for the exercise of emergency powers. The scope for irresponsible executive action was alarmingly great, as Hindenburg's adventures were to show, and one can only agree with Karl Dietrich Bracher's observation that 'all components of a democratic state and a democratic society must be fully involved in an emergency regime'.[29] But emergency legislation would not have been essential under Weimar if successive ministries had not been *governing without consensus*—that is, if powerful social and political forces had not *refused* to be 'fully involved'.

The new government formed by the social democrat, Friedrich Ebert (a saddle-maker in a previous incarnation) faced enemies on all sides. Independent revolutionary governments had raised the red flag all over the country: in Kiel, Wilhelmshaven, Bremen, Hanover, Cologne and Munich, when the ancient Wittelsbach dynasty was overthrown in November 1918. Hordes of armed and disorganised veterans formed ready recruits for the revolution. The left-wing Spartakists controlled parts of Berlin itself, and the safe delivery of the Republic was only assured when the army was sent in full strength against them; Karl Liebknecht and Rosa Luxemberg were shot 'resisting arrest'.

It was against this background of mob violence and competitive attempts to bring the Bolshevik revolution to Germany that the new constituent assembly met in the sleepy town of Weimar in the early months of 1919. It is hardly surprising that the good burghers assembled there were more concerned to arm the new Republic with far-reaching powers of self-defence than, for example, the citizens who met in Philadelphia in 1787. One of the delegates rose during the debate to air his view that 'peace and order can be maintained only if the legitimate government has the right to repress violent disturbances of the peace by measures of equally drastic violence'.[30]

The social democrats, supported by the parties of the centre and the right, proceeded to write into the new constitution the most extreme emergency provisions adopted by a major democratic state in peacetime. Under Article 48, if 'public safety and order' were disturbed, the president was empowered to suspend temporarily the basic rights guaranteed elsewhere in the same document, including personal liberty, freedom of opinion, assembly and association, and the inviolability of dwelling places. Military tribunals could be set up to take the place of normal courts. The most extraordinary feature of this article was that it enabled the president—on the basis of whatever pretext fell to hand—to issue emergency legislation as well as to order administrative and military action. The role of the Reichstag was confined to being 'informed' of what was happening, with the right of appeal for the revocation of the emergency powers. Since the president had the power to dissolve parliament at will, this was hardly an effective check on his authority.

Many Weimar democrats were dubious about Article 48, but their doubts were silenced by the series of insurrections and economic crises that ensued. The purpose of emergency powers, after all, is to give soldiers the same freedom in dealing with their rebellious countrymen that they would normally exercise against foreign enemies, and to give the government power to act swiftly to handle a national crisis. Germany in 1920 was in a state of internal war, and the constitution was under attack from both flanks. The first taste of right-wing violence came with the Kapp putsch in Berlin in March 1920, which sent the government scurrying off to Stuttgart. (Kapp was not defeated by government action under Article 48, however; Ebert was not prepared to test the loyalty of the army. Kapp's archaically-organised conspiracy fell apart in the face of a general strike.)

This was the signal for the most dangerous attempt at communist insurrection that the Weimar republic had to face; some 70,000 armed workers were called out to man the barricades along the so-called 'Red Front' stretching from Essen to the Lippe. It was suppressed by making full use of Article 48. Military commanders were empowered to order the summary arrest of suspects for up to three months. All revolutionary publications and gatherings were banned wherever the ban could be enforced. Courts-martial handed out summary death sentences, and fear of their judgements was a major factor in the withering away of the communists' will to fight. The German officer corps, it should be noted, felt little or no compunction in using these methods against communists; the situation was rather different when it came to dealing with the extreme right.

But there is a more general point to be made about the suppression of the 1920 communist insurrection. As one legal historian notes, it was 'a striking illustration of the benefits to be derived from constitutional emergency powers as an aid to the prosecution of military operations. . . Within a period only slightly longer than the traditional six months of dictatorship in ancient Rome, the use of emergency powers was followed by the restoration of normal political methods.'[31]

The problem that the federal government was left struggling to master was how to assert its authority over state governments that were openly hostile to it. Towards the end of 1923, the right-wing government in Bavaria had become openly insubordinate, while communists had entered the state cabinets in Saxony and Thuringia and were calling for the formation of a Red army. Hitler's farcical 'beer-hall putsch' in Munich on 8 November 1923, was a crucial turning point in two senses. First, it finally brought the German army into direct confrontation with the extreme right, showing that—after a period of ambiguity—the Reichswehr would defend the legitimate government against *some* people on the right as well as the left. Second, it drove the Nazis to follow the communists' example by aiming at the seizure of power by methods other than violent insurrection. The beer-hall putsch and a brief spell in the Landsberg Castle taught Hitler the virtues of pseudo-legitimacy. Hitler himself supplied the definition of his new approach. 'The constitution gives us the ground on which to wage our battle, but not its aim. . . Of course, when we possess all constitutional rights we shall then mould the state into that form which we consider to be the right one.'[32] The Brownshirt strong-arm squads were retained; but they were no longer to be wasted in futile tests of strength with the security forces. They were to be used exclusively to intimidate political opponents and for defence against rival gangs of bully-boys.

The Nazis' gradual progress to the election 'miracle' of 1930—when their share of the vote increased by 5½million (to 6·4million) and their seats in the Reichstag from 12 to 107—is well known. There is no doubt that the landslide was closely related to the suffering inflicted by the Depression. Papen later commented on the dramatic swing of electoral support to the extremist parties in 1930-2 that 'the workers were so bemused by unemployment and by communism, socialism and Nazi propaganda, that they had lost confidence in the power of government to relieve their lot.'[33] The official unemployment figures showed a rise from 2million at the end of 1929 to 3·5million in November 1930, 4·36million by 1 January 1931, 4·76million in mid-January 1931, and 5·7million by the start of 1932.[34] Yet, as suggested in an earlier chapter, the Depression was only the proximate cause. The demoralisation of the German middle classes in the inflation in the 1920s was a vital contributory factor. And then we need to make full allowance for the immense propaganda skills of Hitler and Goebbels and for its impact on a voting system in which the list (and thus the party leader and insignia) counted for infinitely more than the individual candidate;[35] the qualifications of individual Nazi candidates on the party lists did not bear examination, but then, they were not examined. Above all, Hitler brought *magic;* he grasped—as no other contemporary German politician grasped—the role of the irrational factor in human existence, and offered escape from the agonies of individual choice and the troubles of the Depression into some undefined collective salvation and the pursuit of 'alien' scapegoats.

The Nazis were no longer an obscure group of anti-semites parading in para-military gear. They were an important party in the Reichstag, which was used as a platform for virulent attacks on democratic politicians. But Brüning, with the grudging support of the social democrats, retained a Reichstag majority for his cabinet—although he was drawn to rely increasingly on Article 48 to push his financial measures through.

The systematic violence used by both Nazis and communists at political meetings drove the government to apply repressive legal measures. In the spring of 1932, the government ordered the immediate dissolution of the SS and the SA; the defence minister, Groener, did not consider the communist *Reichs-*

banner sufficiently dangerous to be worth banning. In the summer of the same year, *all* political gatherings were banned throughout Germany for a period of three weeks. Although the courts martial of 1920 were not revived, a decree of 9 August 1932 set up courts that were entitled to act according to summary procedure to deal with cases of terrorism. It should be noted, however, that this response came relatively late in the day. Chancellor Brüning (1930-2) had grave reservations about responding in force to nationalist violence, and may have believed that the presence of the Nazis in the background was a useful bargaining counter in dealing with the Allied powers. His successors, Papen and Schleicher, were both ultra-conservatives who hoped to be able to use Nazi support in the Reichstag. One of Papen's first acts was to revoke the ban on private armies by a decree issued on 15 June 1932. After mid-1932, as Dr Watkins notes, 'no really consistent and wholehearted effort was ever made to use the resources of Article 48 against the national socialists. This fact alone would suffice to explain the failure of constitutionalists in dealing with the problem of civil violence in Germany.'[36]

The unresolved, and finally tragic, dilemma of the Weimar Republic was that a strong executive is essential in the face of a totalitarian threat, but the powers ascribed to it are open to abuse. Government by emergency decree helped to discredit the Weimar constitution without providing sufficient defences against the Nazis in the 1930s. A device that was central to the survival of the Republic against the failed insurrections of the 1920s (and that provided Stresemann with a means for acting quickly to promote financial recovery in the wake of the Great Inflation) became a tool for conservative dictatorship under Papen and Schleicher—a tool that quickly slipped from their fumbling hands to be seized upon by Hitler.

Yet the responsibility for the demise of the Republic rests with the 'wooden titan', President Hindenburg, more than with the system of emergency powers. It was through those emergency powers, after all, that Chancellor Brüning managed to steer Germany through the worst phase of the Depression. Brüning could lay claim to a parliamentary majority, but the Reichstag was in recess during much of his nineteen months in office, and the social democrats, who lent him reluctant support, would not join a government that insisted on making ends meet (through cutbacks in public spending) rather than in inflating its way out of the Depression. But Brüning lost Hindenburg's confidence when he set out to expropriate and redistribute neglected agricultural estates in East Prussia, the president's own stamping-ground, and was driven to tender his resignation on 30 May 1932. The exceptional powers that had hitherto been used with the more or less grudging support of the Reichstag were now being used by the president in a brief experiment in authoritarian rule.

By dissolving the Reichstag, Hindenburg gave the new chancellor, Papen, and his cabinet of conservative aristocrats three months of untrammelled authority. But the results of the subsequent elections on 31 July gave the Nazis, for the first time, a plurality of the votes (38 per cent) and made them the biggest party in the Reichstag (with 230 seats). The nationalists got 6 per cent, the communists 15 per cent. There was no longer a constitutionalist majority in parliament—and no working majority for any potential government except an alliance of incompatibles. The possibility of ruling by emergency decree, furthermore, made it unnecessary to seek some kind of parliamentary basis for government—and that it was not what Papen and his friends of the *Herrenklub* were seeking anyway. They proceeded, under Article 48, to stage a mini-coup in Prussia: they ousted the social democrats from the state government and installed a federal commissioner. This was the first move in a gambit that was apparently intended to substitute a conservative authoritarian system for the Weimar constitution. Hindenburg was basically in sympathy. But Papen was too inept to bring about what he designed. As the French ambassador put it, 'there is something about Papen that prevents either his friends or his enemies from taking him seriously; he bears the stamp of frivolity, he is not a personality of the first rank. . . If he succeeds in an undertaking, he is very pleased, if he fails it doesn't bother him.'[37] Through his own ineptitude, he allowed a vote of confidence to take place in the Reichstag that was lost by a margin that must surely be unique for a government functioning under a democratic constitution: by 42 to 512 votes. Papen was to find his real historical role as the man who welded together the alliance of conservative and revolutionary nationalism in which the nostalgics for 'the old Germany' were to fall victims to the carriers of the modern totalitarian idea.

The failure of German conservatism and the intellectual corruptibility of its proponents, taken together with the authentic and widespread appeal of a strident nationalism, are clues to Hitler's triumph. It had something to do with the conservatives' contempt for the little man from Austria who, with his untutored manners, Charlie Chaplin moustache and neurotic silences in 'polite company' (interspersed with fervent monologues) seemed to them almost a comic figure. It had even more to do with their failure to comprehend the nature of a totalitarian mass movement; with the traditional ruling class, the army, the police and the civil service behind them, they were confident of turning the poacher into an assistant gamekeeper. This blind spot is not peculiar to conservatives of an authoritarian bent dealing with fascists, be it noted. The parallel today is with social democrats who are similarly blind to the perils of cooperating with (and legitimising) communists. The men who helped to legitimise the Austrian corporal by lending him the symbols of the Second Reich were later to awaken, like Schacht, to complain, 'Dear lady, we have fallen into the hands of criminals, how could I have suspected that?'[38]

New elections in November showed that the Nazis had begun to lose ground; their vote slipped back by two per cent. Was the tide beginning to turn? There no longer seemed to be any imminent prospect of a Nazi majority in parliament. But the last Chancellors of Germany represented no one except the President and the restricted military, aristocratic and industrial circles that probably found their political expression in Hugenburg's National Party. Both Papen and Schleicher, his successor, proposed a permanent form of dictatorship in order to dispense with the 'political question'. When Papen raised this shortly before his resignation, Schleicher (always pursuing his own interest) argued that it would mean a civil war in which the Reichswehr could not keep order against competitive threats from the Nazis and the communists. When Schleicher proposed it in January 1933, Papen was already playing his role as a mediator for Hitler.[39]

So Hitler was summoned on 30 January and a new era began. But not quite yet. The new cabinet, with Hitler as Chancellor, contained only two other Nazis, together with eight old-style conservatives. But the Nazis controlled the federal interior ministry and the Prussian state interior ministry, and Hitler was not planning to play the game by the old rules. He had insisted on new elections in March, and the climate was rapidly prepared. 'Unreliable' police chiefs were purged; 50,000 SA, SS and Stahlhelm men brought in as 'auxiliary police'; and a controlled election campaign commenced that was the most violent in German history—by official admission, fifty-five people were killed, and most of them were not Nazis. Then there was the little matter of the Reichstag fire on 27 February, which was used to justify the immediate suppression of the communist and socialist press.

The constitutional provisions designed for the defence of the Republic were used to bring about its meticulous destruction. Communist meetings were banned; a social democrat rally due to be held on the same day as an elaborate state funeral for a stormtrooper who had been shot was also banned; the SA was assigned in the guise of a special police force to stand guard over *all* electoral meetings in the run-up to the new elections on 5 March. An emergency decree forbade the press to criticise the government. Police protection was withdrawn from opposition groups in the face of brutal attacks by Nazi thugs. It was all apparently legal.

The elections gave the Nazis forty-four per cent of the vote—enough, with the support of the nationalists, to govern with a parliamentary majority, but a long way short of the two-thirds of the vote needed to pass a new enabling law to redefine the origins and purposes of exceptional powers. But Hitler had not entered the Chancery to rule through the institutions of bourgeois democracy. The problem was simplified by the arrest of the entire communist delegation to the Reichstag, before the first sitting, on charges connected with the Reichstag fire. The culmination of the Nazi coup was the famous Enabling Act of 23 March 1933, passed by 441 votes to 94, which handed over absolute powers to the new regime. Such a measure required not just a two-thirds majority; but a two-thirds *attendance* by Reichstag deputies. The Nazi seizure of power, it would seem, was perfectly constitutional. If anyone had doubts, there was no longer any legal authority with the capacity—let alone the courage—to investigate them.

It is worth mentioning that Engelbert Dollfuss' brief

experiment in authoritarian rule in Austria (1932-4) bore some resemblance to the Nazi seizure of power. He assumed his chancellorship against the background of military defeat, the loss of empire, and a rapid inflation that had demoralised the middle class; and within a political system where proportional representation resulted, as in Weimar Germany, in weak coalition government in which the position of the social democrats—as an overtly Marxist party—was, at the best, ambiguous. (The social democrat leader, Otto Bauer, made it plain that, while he did not subscribe to violent revolutionary methods, he regarded the parliamentary system as a passing phase on the road to socialism.) Dollfuss used a wartime Enabling Law to seize full powers during a period of parliamentary confusion in 1933, but grossly misunderstood the purposes of the German Nazis and their sympathisers in the Austrian Heimwehr, and ultimately fell victim to Hitler's designs for *Anschluss.* [40]

Weimar Germany and, to a lesser extent, Austria, were notable cases of the successful exploitation of pseudo-legal methods by right-wing anti-democratic movements before 1939. In the post-1945 world, it has been established that the totalitarian left can be equally successful in employing the same techniques—and is making significant progress in long-established democracies where traditions of civility and limited government have until recently been much more deeply rooted than in the shaky societies of central Europe between the two world wars. This may be partly due to the same incomprehension of the aims and methods of a totalitarian movement that was pathetically apparent in the Berlin or Vienna of the early 1930s—and to the fact that, as Philip Selznick notes, 'under conditions of political combat, those who have no firm values of their own become the instruments of the values of others'. [41] The same principle was applied in Prague and in Santiago as in Hitler's Berlin: 'the outer shell of the law-based state was preserved until the total state had grown and matured under its protection.' [42] We have already seen enough to substantiate one of the opening propositions of this book: that democracy is a means rather than an end, and that the mechanism itself is multivalent.

8
The Prague Model

> It should be stressed that in their actions against
> democracies the totalitarian regimes were always offen-
> sive and were consistent in their mutual support; the
> democratic regimes were not consistent in this respect and
> at critical moments in their difficult fight they deserted
> and betrayed each other. *Eduard Benes*

The way that a bloodless revolution was organised in Prague in
1948 is the classic case of the seizure of power by a communist
movement working within the existing institutions. It is also a
model, in Marxist language, of the creation of a situation of
'dual power' as the prelude to revolution—a situation, that is,
where power is no longer a monopoly of the organs of the state,
but is matched by a parallel apparatus controlled by the
revolutionaries. Reflecting on the lessons of the Bolshevik
Revolution, Trotsky wrote that 'the historic preparation of a
revolution brings about in the pre-revolutionary period a
situation in which the class which is called to realise the new
social system, although not yet master of the country, has
actually concentrated in its hands a significant share of the
state power, while the official apparatus of the government is in
the hands of the old lords. This is the initial dual power in any
revolution'.[1]

In Czechoslovakia, however, the communists, as the
dominant partners in the governing coalition, were able to use
the 'official apparatus of the government' as well as their own
mass organisation and clandestine network as a means to their
definitive takeover. The key to their success was the
combination of government action, or 'pressure from above',
with the creation of new power-bases such as 'action
committees' and factory militias to apply 'pressure from
below'.[2] The other striking feature of the Prague coup was its
pseudo-legality. As I have argued in discussing the advance of
fascism in the 1920s and 1930s, an anti-democratic movement
in an advanced society is required to observe some of the

constitutional niceties. In Czechoslovakia, President Benes played the same reluctant role as King Victor Emmanuel before him in Italy. He helped to legitimise a *fait accompli,* and this in turn, helped to deter many of the people who might otherwise have decided to resist.

What happened in 1948 must of course be seen as part of a longer historical process that began with the abandonment of Czechoslovakia by Hitler's appeasers at Munich in 1938 and the subsequent dismemberment and occupation of the country by the Nazis. After 1939, Czechoslovakia inevitably produced its own generation of quislings, and the communists were subsequently able to use the charge of 'collaborator' to discredit conservatives and secure the banning of right-wing parties. Ironically, the communists' own credentials as resistance heroes hardly bore close examination. Before Hitler invaded Russia, the communists played no direct part in the resistance; indeed, the evidence suggests that there was widespread cooperation with the Gestapo. In his reports to Berlin, the Nazi Minister-Protector, K. H. Frank, 'stated more than once that the communist movement was of no danger, because it was not only controlled, but to a certain extent directed, by the Gestapo'.[3]

The framework for Czechoslovakia's brief post-war experiment in democracy was partly determined by the role of the Soviet army in its liberation. Under the Teheran agreement concluded between Churchill, Roosevelt and Stalin in November 1943, Czechoslovakia was defined as part of the Red Army's theatre of operations. The Czechs were unlucky in their liberators; the Russians failed to support the Slovak uprising in 1944 and were slow to support the Prague uprising in 1945. The Russians carried off a slice of eastern Czechoslovakia (the area known as Sub-Carpathian Ruthenia) and the troops engaged in systematic looting of many areas. All the same, a potent propaganda myth had been created. And the background threat of Soviet military intervention overshadowed the subsequent course of events. Although France, Britain and America were prepared to speak out, belatedly, against the installation of a 'disguised dictatorship' in Prague, Czech democrats never had any real confidence that their friends abroad would help them in the event of a Soviet invasion.

On 4 April 1945—more than a month before the liberation of Prague—a Czech coalition government was set up under Russian auspices in the eastern town of Kosice. The communists, with six ministers, were the dominant force in this 'National Front', although the nominal prime minister was Zdenek Fierlinger, a 'sleeper' in the Social Democratic Party who was to play a decisive role in bringing about the coup. Elections were eventually held in May 1946. The communists (who had never been able to attract more than 10 per cent of the votes before the war) now emerged as the strongest party, with 38 per cent of the votes and 114 seats out of 300 in the House of Deputies.

The communists' new-found electoral popularity was not unrelated to the fact that they already controlled the ministries of the interior and information—in other words, the police and government propaganda. It also appears that the names of more than 250,000 people were removed from the electoral rolls on various (and usually unsubstantiated) charges of 'collaboration'. Although many of the people who were denied their electoral rights on this pretext were subsequently able to clear themselves, they had lost their votes.[4]

Having produced a popular mandate of sorts, the communists now moved rapidly to consolidate their power. A new cabinet was set up with the communist leader, Klement Gottwald, as Prime Minister. Nine of the twenty-six ministers were communist. As before, the communists' control of the police and of government propaganda was decisive, but they used the resources of lesser ministries (such as agriculture and internal commerce) with consummate skill. The communist under-secretary for foreign affairs, Dr Vladimir Clementis, was able to undercut the popular non-party foreign minister, Jan Masaryk. The crucial ministry of defence remained in the hands of a nominally independent soldier, General Ludwik Swoboda, who had spent the war years in Russia and was to take charge of the neutralisation of the armed forces in the run-up to the coup. At the same time, the communists tightened their grip over the trade union federation, the URO.

The stage was now set. The developments over the next two years demonstrated, as the communist ideologue Jan Kozak later put it, 'that it was possible to transform parliament from an organ of the bourgeoisie . . . into a direct instrument for the victory of the socialist revolution'.[5] The condition for this revolutionary use of parliament, as Kozak also noted, was the use of government agencies to suppress 'counter-revolutionary' elements and the simultaneous building-up of extra-parliamentary centres of power. 'Linking and systematic combination of parliamentary and non-parliamentary actions has always been the fundamental principle of revolutionary tactics in making use of parliament'. In the last analysis, the communist takeover—although masked by legalistic forms—depended on the effective threat of force.

Rifts between the non-Marxists in the ruling coalition ensured that the communists never lost control of parliament. Indeed, it can be said in retrospect that liberal pacifism was what presented them with their most important opportunities. Even a relatively enlightened social democrat like Vaclav Major could say late in the day that it was necessary to 'declare war against the fear of Bolshevism and forbid the formation of any anti-communist front whatsoever'.[6] President Benes consistently failed to give any clear lead, and must be held responsible for allowing the communists to occupy the all-important interior ministry at the very outset. Benes intimidated and then scalded by Hitler in 1938, seemed to believe in the possibility of democratic coexistence with communism. In pursuit of that mirage, he agreed to a series of concessions that at last put paid to any hopes of democracy in Czechoslovakia. As in the 1920s and 1930s, it was the debating-society tactics of the liberals in the face of a determined totalitarian threat that supplied the conditions for the collapse of democracy.

The communists operated on several fronts after May 1946. On the economic front, their tactics were designed to isolate Czechoslovakia from its traditional trading partners in Western Europe and to destroy the private sector inside the country. Politically, the party embarked on a systematic attempt to discredit its rivals through classic methods of defamation and the use of the Reichstag fire technique. The civil service was purged and the police were brought under direct party control. At the same time, the party established a parallel administration throughout the country through mass organisations and parallel armed forces, in the shape of armed militias. The non-Marxist parties remained frozen in a state of semi-paralysis, partly because their leaders failed to grasp the nature of the organisational weapon in the hands of the Communist Party, which was prepared to exploit the institutions of a parliamentary democracy—but always worked according to a separate set of priorities dictated by its own general staff.

The economic isolation of Czechoslovakia from the West was central to the Communist Party's strategy, as well as to Stalin's plans for 'industrial mobilisation'. It was Soviet pressure, supported by the Prime Minister, Klement Gottwald, that compelled the government to reject Marshall aid and to sign a new commercial agreement with Russia in 1947. This agreement, which resulted in Russian grain shipments (to make up for a poor harvest) in return for Czech industrial goods, was represented in communist propaganda as a humanitarian gesture by Stalin, but was in fact conceived on strictly commercial lines that favoured the Russians. The important thing, from the communist viewpoint, was to close Czechoslovakia's 'window on the west'.

Internally, the confiscation of private industry and a far-reaching programme of land redistribution were seen as means of cutting away the social base of political opposition. Under pressure from communist-run peasant commissions and party propaganda, parliament voted through a new agricultural reform law in July 1946. This provided for the redistribution by lot of all estates over fifty hectares and of all investment property. The state takeover of industry began with the confiscation of Nazi war industries and the nationalisation decrees of October 1945; by the beginning of 1947, the government had direct control of sixty-two per cent of Czech industry. These formal measures were combined with the harassment of 'social reactionaries' by communist flying squads—some of them camouflaged as official inspectors. The ministry of agriculture, for example, sent out 'Special Food Commissions' in 1947 to confiscate stocks of grain and punish 'hoarders'. Later that year, inspectors from the communist-run ministry of internal trade announced that they had unearthed an extensive black market in textiles—which provided a pretext for the confiscation of virtually the entire private textile business and the setting-up of state distribution centres.

The economic travails of Czechoslovakia between 1946 and 1948 were attributed by the party's *agitprop* men to the nefarious work of saboteurs and profiteers. Policy failures that might have served to destroy the credibility of the government were thus explained away, and the ensuing search for scapegoats was another means of striking at anti-communists. Thus in 1947, the communists proposed to pay for a new food subsidy by a 'millionaires levy'—a punitive wealth tax of five per cent on 'fortunes' amounting to more than $16,000. This bill was rejected by parliament, but the communist press and the party's front organisations throughout the country made great play with the claim that the 'bourgeois' parties were stealing the bread from starving children in order to defend the interests of an oligarchic clique. The party organ *Rude Pravo* published the names of all the ministers who voted against the measure and fulminated that 'All these gentlemen were elected by our people in the honest belief that they have subscribed to the programme of the National Front. However, by their attitude they demonstrated to the broad masses of workers, peasants, office workers and tradesmen who elected them that they protect millionaires, speculators, industrialists, land-owners and merchants.'[7] It was not the first time that the politics of envy had been used by an anti-democratic movement to divert attention from the real causes of economic hardship.

The communists used other kinds of smear tactics against their rivals. The charge of 'collaboration' with the Nazis was endlessly rehearsed, despite the vulnerability of a number of prominent communists on this score; it transpired for example, that Josef Fucik, a member of the party executive, had written a sixty-page document for the Gestapo on his contacts after his arrest in 1942.[8] It is probably necessary to recall only the most egregious example of this kind of communist disinformation: the character assassination campaign waged against Professor Vladimir Krajina, the secretary-general of the National Socialist Party—whose name should not be taken to imply any affinity with its German namesake. The Czech National Socialist Party, and Krajina himself, were on the other side of the barricades. Krajina was one of the heroes of the Czech resistance, whose radio links with London and whose network of informers in the German intelligence services allowed him to give early warning of Hitler's planned invasion of Russia. His family suffered considerably at the hands of the Nazis: his brother was executed, his wife despatched to Ravensbruck, and Krajina himself was captured and tortured by the Gestapo in 1943, apparently after a tip-off from Czech communists. Nevertheless, his revelations of how the communists were making use of ex-Gestapo sources in order to tarnish the reputations of rivals or subject them to blackmail induced the party to choose him as a target. They made use of Frank, the former Protector of Czechoslovakia, as a 'witness' against Krajina, but, in a face-to-face confrontation, he retracted his charges. The communist official responsible for the rigged inquiry was relieved of his post, but promptly entrusted with a new post in the information ministry.[9] It should be added that others were not as fortunate as Krajina, who had the decisiveness and the sheer guts to defend himself against methods that left some of his colleagues gaping.

To systematic defamation, the communists in Czechoslovakia added the time-honoured Reichstag fire technique. Again, one notable example will have to suffice. In September 1947, explosive devices were sent to three government ministers (Masaryk, Zenkl and Drtina) disguised as gift packages of perfume. The Communist Party's secretary-general, Rudolf Slansky, promptly alleged—on the basis of no evidence whatsoever—that the whole business was a National Socialist plot. A leisurely inquiry by the communist-run interior ministry then began, and got nowhere. It was a separate inquiry masterminded by Professor Krajina and employing the resources of the socialist-run ministry of justice that began to uncover some interesting evidence. It eventually established (i) that the boxes containing the bombs had been manufactured by a communist carpenter (who confessed); (ii) that the local Communist Party headquarters in Olomouc had given him the job; (iii) that the explosives were packed by a communist deputy, Jaroslav Jura-Sosnar, who was arrested; and (iv) that the party leadership in Prague must have been aware of the whole conspiracy. It did not pass unnoticed that large arms caches, including stockpiles of heavy machine-guns, were found in party premises in the course of Krajina's investigations.

As these examples show, the use of slander and *agents provocateurs* did not always work. The efforts of the communists to put their men into key posts in the administration were more effective in the long run. The case of the police is the most interesting, since the communisation of the police brought about the final confrontation with the democratic parties—on ground where it was probably impossible for them to win. After the Red Army occupation, the communists set up new police bodies—mobile units and a special branch—politically committed to themselves. By February 1948, as the National Socialist minister, Drtina, disclosed in a tense cabinet meeting, that five of the nine senior police chiefs were communists, and the party had just secured the substitution of its own militants for eight district commissioners. Control of the police was even more important than in most circumstances, given the relative disorganisation of the armed forces. But the colonisation of the army was pursued simultaneously under the auspices of the defence minister, General Swoboda and his chief of staff, General Bocek. Both were crypto-communists, and the nucleus of their post-war army was drawn from the forces that had trained with them in Russia. Command posts were reserved for 'anti-fascists' and the communists were able early in 1946, to substitute their own man for the nonpartisan chief of military intelligence, General Bartik. (His successor, Captain Pokorny, later distinguished himself by claiming, on the basis of his interrogations of ex-Gestapo chiefs, that the non-communist resistance had been controlled by the Nazis.)

By such stratagems, the communists remoulded the security apparatus of the state in their own image. But, true to their doctrine of class struggle and the example of the workers' and soldiers' councils in revolutionary Russia, they set about arming their supporters in farms and factories as well. The party worked through the institutions of the 'bourgeois' state; but it worked outside it as well. The ministries of defence and the interior, and local party headquarters, distributed arms to workers in nationalised plants on the pretext of defending them against vengeful former owners or brigands; these workers were then organised into a network of local militias that was a critical deterrent to democractic resistance to the coup. As Kozak recalls, 'in February 1948, when the preparations for a counter-revolutionary conspiracy by the bourgeoisie were uncovered, strong armed people's militias were formed. In the last instance it was the arming of the working class which took away the bourgeoisie's liking for an armed conflict.'

Physical force was combined with the constant show of force, through political strikes and demonstrations, and the staging of elaborate workers' and peasants' congresses where party leaders vied with each other in dropping spine-chilling threats about their plans for those who stood against them.

The crunch came on the eve of elections which the communists, despite all their gains, had little reason to welcome. The elections were scheduled for May 1948. An opinion poll conducted in January by an organisation sponsored by the information ministry (which the party controlled) showed that the communist share of the vote was likely to fall by eight to ten per cent. That same month, ballots in high schools and universities had shown an overwhelming swing against the party among students. So that the clash over the control of the police that erupted in February was not badly timed from the communist point of view; anything that might serve to defer the elections, or to alter the basis on which they were to be held, would suit the party's interests. The only question was whether, this time round, the non-Marxist parties would manage to mount a united and effective campaign.

The cabinet, as already noted, was drawn from four parties as well as the communists. (It also included two non-party ministers.) Three of those parties—the National Socialists and the smaller Catholic People's and Slovak Democratic Parties— were wholly convinced by 1948 of the need to curb the steady extension of communist power. The unknown factor throughout the whole period was the position of the social democrats. The fellow-travelling social democrat leader, Fierlinger, had been deposed from his job as secretary-general at a special conference in November 1947, but he remained a very powerful figure within the party. In view of subsequent events, the description of Fierlinger by his political enemies as 'the gravedigger of Czech democracy' seems warranted. While Fierlinger's own position was clearly dictated by personal ambition and communist influence, it was supported by the naiveté of other social democrats who went on believing till the end in the possibility of peaceful cohabitation with a totalitarian party.

It was perhaps symptomatic of the well-intentioned

insouciance of the Czech democrats that their belated effort to halt the communists took the form of a purely negative gesture: resignation. The crisis began on 13 February 1948, when a majority in the cabinet voted to suspend the recent appointment of eight communist police commissioners pending a full inquiry. The communist interior minister, Vaclav Nosek, simply stalled, pleading illness to explain his absence from a subsequent cabinet meeting. The national socialists took the lead in pressing for the resignation of all non-communist members of the government if the cabinet decision was not carried into effect. It appears that they were encouraged in this by President Benes.[10] It also appears, however, that the president never contemplated the possibility of using the army to remove the eight police officers—perhaps because he was convinced that this would provoke the intervention of the communist armed militias, and doubtful about whether Swoboda or his troops would obey orders. The social democrats, meanwhile, debated the pros and cons of resigning and finally, swayed by the Fierlinger faction, decided against. So that only a minority of the cabinet (twelve of twenty-five ministers) resigned on 20 February. It was a dramatic gesture, certainly, but the communists were subsequently able to argue that the constitutional right of the government (which still had a parliamentary majority) to remain in office was unbroken.

The democrats now tried, far too late in the day, to mobilise public opinion. The national socialist paper, *Svobodne Slovo,* had come out with a slashing article on 19 February, entitled 'We will not tolerate a police state' that for the first time gave full information to the public on what had been happening inside the police. But broadcasting was firmly in the control of the communists, who moved armed guards into the main radio building. And there was never any question of who controlled the streets. The democrats' neglect of mass organisation could not be compensated for by spontaneous effusions at this stage. The communists moved rapidly. The new police shock units were moved into Prague. On 22 February, Gottwald addressed a huge rally of factory councils, calling on the president to accept the democratic ministers' resignations. The following day, the offices of the National Socialist Party and of opposition newspapers were taken over by the police, and a spokesman for the ministry of the interior claimed that documentation of plans for a 'reactionary coup' had been uncovered. A 'Central Action Committee' was set up under the communist union leader, Zapotocky, with the task of coordinating the takeover of local authorities by local action committees. The Social Democratic Party was also rewarded for its lack of solidarity with the other non-Marxist parties: its headquarters were also invaded, and Fierlinger appeared to take over the building.

For five days, President Benes swung back and forth like a pendulum, uncertain whether to accept the resignations, doubtful about whether some new coalition could be cobbled together. On 25 February, he finally made up his mind. He accepted both the resignations and the communists' list of a new set of cabinet members. The new government contained twelve communists, four fellow-travelling social democrats, five renegades from other non-communist parties, a forlorn representative of a tiny group known as the Slovak Freedom Party, and two non-party men—Swoboda and Masaryk, who stayed on as foreign minister.

All that awaited Czechoslovakia now was systematic integration into the Soviet bloc and the methodical elimination of those opposed to communist rule who had failed to flee the country. Those who had walked, unwillingly, with the communists thus far along the way vanished in quick succession: Masaryk was found dead after an unexplained fall from his window in the foreign ministry on 3 March; Benes resigned 'for health reasons' on 6 June, and died three months later; the Social Democratic Party was swallowed up. The elections that were held in May worked according to the improved rules of people's democracy: the voters were given the choice between the official list and a blank voting form. The day was not far off when Czechoslovakia would meet with the final betrayal—the reception of its new-look parliamentarians as honoured guests in London.

Why was there almost no resistance (except a few courageous, but hopeless, student demonstrations) to the communist coup in Prague? Some of the answers must by now be obvious. The communists had the guns, and they had the kind of disciplined mass organisations that the other parties lacked. They had control of broadcasting. After the resignations on 20 February, they were able to extend their control over the sections of the administration that had so far eluded them. They had the background presence of the Red Army—at the height of the crisis, *Pravda* made some ominous rumblings. They had the confidence that the Western powers would make no move to interfere with their aims in a part of central Europe that had been assigned to someone else's sphere of influence twice in a decade.

Finally, of course, the communists were able to make great play with the illusion of legality. The government set up on 25 February was nominated by the President of the Republic and approved by a docile parliament. Only parliament itself had the legal power to throw out the communist prime minister, Gottwald, and it did not exercise it. One could hardly look for a better demonstration of Engels' proposition that 'the irony of world history turns everything upside down. We, the "revolutionists", the "overthrowers"—we are thriving far better on legal methods than on illegal methods and overthrow. The parties of order, as they call themselves, are perishing under the legal conditions created by themselves.'[10]

The Prague coup was rubber-stamped, but it can hardly be understood as an act of parliament. The general lesson that Jan Kozak draws from it is that although 'the bourgeoisie has never yielded its power by a simple act of parliament . . . it may be deprived of its power at an opportune moment without an armed uprising and civil war—by the force of consistently acting revolutionary masses led by the revolutionary workers' party, supporting their representatives in the parliament and transforming the parliament into an active revolutionary assembly'.[11] As a previous quotation has already made clear, Kozak, addressing his words to a closed circle of party activists in Prague, had no intention of masking the fact that the crux of the matter in 1948 was the threat of force. Parliament became a 'revolutionary' body—at least in the sense of conferring a kind of legitimacy on revolution—precisely because it was overshadowed by the mass organisation of the Communist Party and the force at its disposal.

But parliament was also an instrument of revolution in its own right, underwriting an economic programme aimed at 'depriving the bourgeoisie of its power' and serving as a convenient propaganda forum—'a mirror showing the working masses the class interests and conflicts in bourgeois society in their nakedness'. Take away the conditions that were unique to Czechoslovakia—the role of the Red Army, the border with Russia—and you are left with a model that can readily be applied to other situations. Its relevance is obvious in the light of events in Portugal, where the Communist Party is led by a man who spent fourteen years in exile in Prague.

9

Lessons from Chile

We reached those last days when we could endure neither
our vices nor their remedies.   *Livy*

Chile has supplied martyrs and rallying cries for the left in the
1970s as Spain supplied them in the 1930s. Left-wing
demonstrators in the streets of Lisbon or Rome have made the
most famous slogan of Chile's Marxists—*El pueblo unido jamas
será vencido**—their own. In Britain, even two years after the
coup, the Chile Solidarity Campaign (directed by the
communist son of a former minister) and similar groups were
still drawing significant numbers of trade unionists, students
and party activists to study-sessions in pubs and local halls all
over the country; the cry 'Remember Chile' could still induce
socialist ministers and communists to make nostalgic speeches
from the same platforms. The hundreds of political exiles from
Chile who had gained entry to Britain, including veteran
guerrillas from the Uruguayan Tupamaros and Brazilian and
Bolivian groups, as well as the Chilean Movement of the
Revolutionary Left (Mir)—were available to contribute
first-hand impressions and technical advice.

What happened in Chile made a splendid addition to the
hagiography of the left. The subsequent propaganda barrage
was remarkably effective in masking the full truth of Allende's
overthrow, and so a major defeat for the Marxists in Chile was
transformed into a psychological victory for Marxists
elsewhere. Chile's lesson, we are told, is that the enemy is on
the right. The propaganda helped to isolate the new military
regime in Santiago from the outside world, adding to the
crippling balance of payments problem inherited from
Allende—although I would readily admit that the political
objections to aid and investment for Chile from western liberals
might soon have been dissipated but for the mistakes of the
new military regime and the crimes of some of those who have
acted in its name.

*The people, united, will never be defeated.

But the continuing importance of the 'Marxist experiment' in Chile concerns the tactical lessons which may be drawn from it. They are an important point of departure for left-wing activists throughout Europe today. The Marxists in Chile came within a hair's-breadth of seizing total power in Chile over the three years following Allende's success in the 1970 presidential elections—in which his share of the vote was slightly less than that of the Nazi party in the Reichstag elections of July 1932. Allende, like Hitler or Gottwald, was able to attempt a pseudo-legal revolution. On the economic front, his government was able to extend an already vast area of state control[1] and to skew the effects of accelerating inflation in order to protect its own working-class constituency, while inflicting severe hardship on the middle class and driving small companies and independent newspapers into bankruptcy. On the political front, Allende was able to manipulate the far-reaching powers of the presidency and the initial divisions among his opponents in order to override Congress (where the opposition was always in a majority) and the Supreme Court. It seemed, until quite late in the day, that force was also on his side. The left not only disposed of workers' militias and terrorist bands; it seemed to have been able to neutralise the army, with the help of a group of sympathetic officers, and notably General Carlos Prats. And yet the whole structure crashed to the ground in the matter of a few hours when the armed forces—under new leadership—executed their carefully-planned coup on 11 September 1973.

So the would-be Allendes elsewhere are left to ask: What went wrong? No serious revolutionary analyst of the Chilean coup believes for a moment the propaganda myth that Allende was brought down by the Central Intelligence Agency. Of course the CIA was involved. But the extent of its support for the opposition to Allende was very limited. All that has been reliably established[2] is that the CIA was authorised to spend a total of eight million dollars between 1970 and August 1973, initially in the effort to block Allende's election and later in the hope of 'destabilising' the Popular Unity government. It is not a great sum of money compared with the amounts supplied by both the Americans and the Russians for clandestine operations elsewhere, with the millions spent by the British in the anti-Bolshevik cause after 1917, or with the $650 million that the Soviets made available to the Allende regime in various ways. The beneficiaries of the CIA's miserly largesse included three opposition newspapers (*El Mercurio, La Prensa* and *La Tribund*); radio stations, political parties; and the organisers of the 'national strikes'—spearheaded by the leaders of the truck-drivers' federation—who played a key role in rallying the opposition to Allende in 1972 and 1973, and in fuelling the economic crisis that contributed to his downfall.

It has *not* been established, however, that there was any direct American involvement in the preparations for the coup. There may well have been contingency plans, but that is not the same thing at all. A great deal was made by some commentators of the fact that the American naval mission in Valparaiso was supposed to have kept in close touch with the admirals there; it would hardly have been doing its job if it had not. A great deal was also made of the fact that a US naval squadron due to take part in joint exercises (Operation Unitas) with the Chilean navy around the time of the coup was diverted. This may indeed suggest that someone tipped off the Americans that the coup was about to take place, but foreknowledge is not the same thing as conspiracy—and very different from *fabrication*, which is what many commentators actually claimed to have taken place.

The idea that the coup against Allende was fabricated by the CIA is not only not borne out by the evidence (which must in any case be weighed against the evidence of a remarkable degree of covert Soviet and Cuban involvement) but reflects a remarkably simplistic view of how politics work. It is ironic that many of those who seek to minimise the evidence of communist intentions in Chile by asserting that history can never be explained by 'conspiracy theories' end up by resorting to a much cruder kind of conspiracy theory in order to explain how the counter-revolution came about. Of course there were conspiracies on both sides: you cannot make either a revolution or a counter-revolution without conspiracy. But the point that needs stressing is that the coup did not take place in a vacuum; it could not have succeeded if there was not already widespread support for military intervention. We have already seen that public support, or public apathy, is a precondition for the *coup d'état* anywhere. How much more so in a society as highly mobilised and as politically sophisticated as Chile in

1973! That sea-change in public opinion, that apparent readiness of a large part of a democratic electorate to welcome the armed forces as saviours in conditions of total breakdown, is what needs to be explained—together with the remaining capacity of the military to act against a Marxist regime that had had three years to entrench itself in power.

I have dissected the history of the Allende regime and the way that the coup was put together elsewhere.[3] It is the tactical lessons to be drawn from Allende's failure that interest me here. The Soviet analysts, and notably Boris Ponomarev, the Secretary to the Central Committee of the CPSU responsible for the non-ruling Communist Parties, have supplied a useful handhold on the subject. The Russians had little to say about the Chile coup in its immediate aftermath, apart from ritual denunciations of the 'fascist' General Pinochet. But more recently, they have been analysing Allende's failure in a series of speeches and articles that are clearly designed as rather more than an academic exercise. It is possible to abstract four key field-instructions for future Allendes from the analyses published by Ponomarev and a number of leading Soviet academicians, including Professor A. Sobolev, in 1974.[4]

The first concerns the need to expand state control over the whole economy even faster than Allende managed to do it in Chile. As Ponomarev puts it, once a Marxist-inclined government assumes power, the economy becomes 'the main battlefield for the victory of the revolution'. Next, and equally important in his view, is the need 'to deprive the class enemy of the mass information and propaganda media as soon as possible'. As we shall see, the survival of a powerful opposition press and radio network in Chile was crucial to Allende's final defeat: it is scarcely an exaggeration to say that this was the nerve-centre of the political opposition to Marxism.

Thirdly, the Soviet analysts stress the need to build up 'extra-parliamentary power bases'—although they are also critical of the revolutionary 'adventurism' of ultra-left groups which, in their view, can trigger off a right-wing reaction before the government is ready to deal with it. Sobolev says that the Marxists in Chile should have done more to establish 'all-embracing mass organisations' on the model of the Soviets in Russia in 1917. Although the need to set up armed workers' groups is not explicitly discussed, the underlying aim is clearly to ensure that, when the inevitable confrontation with the dying middle class comes about, the revolution will be equipped to win it.

Finally, the Russians maintain that the enduring lesson of Chile is that a showdown between the 'popular masses' and the 'reactionaries' is *inevitable* in a pre-revolutionary period. They do not dismiss the possibility that through an effective show of strength—perhaps the threat of a revolutionary general strike—the 'exploiter classes' might be cowed into submission. But in the last analysis, the armed forces will have to be dealt with, and the task of the next Allende will be to ensure that they have been effectively neutralised. Allende was on the road to doing that, but he did not move fast enough.

The next Allende, one presumes, would have various options, including (i) a thorough purge of 'unreliable' elements in the officer corps at an early stage; (ii) the gradual cutback of manpower levels and military expenditure to the point where the armed forces would be reduced to a position of marginal importance in any serious internal crisis; and (iii) the creation of independent politically-controlled armed groups—mobile police, workers' militias, or para-military brigades—that would end the monopoly of force that the armed services are normally supposed to enjoy. Such possibilities are certainly being studied closely by the Marxist left elsewhere.

Of course, there is nothing very novel about the Soviet guidelines; they are based on principles familiar to every practitioner of Marxist revolution. In fact, the Marxists in Chile followed them fairly scrupulously. It is open to doubt whether Allende might have survived if, by moving faster than he did, he had provoked a confrontation earlier on. His government was always divided over tactics, with one faction (led by the Moscow-line communists) urging the need for political caution in order to reassure the army and the middle class while pushing steadily forward on the economic front, while another faction (led by left-wing socialists) urged the need to push forward faster on all fronts in order to bring about a showdown while the opposition was still confused. Outside the ranks of the Popular Unity government, the revolutionaries of the Mir insisted that civil war was the only solution and organised the violent takeover of farms and factories. The President's own position was always equivocal. A weak man, notoriously fond of wine, women and fine tailoring, and addicted to the new-found pleasures of office, he bobbed about among his many advisers like a cork in the stream. He was intellectually closest, perhaps, to the Moscow-line communists. Yet his youthful Trotskyism remained a constant thread, and there were many revolutionary romantics in his immediate family— his sister Laura and his nephew, Andrés Pascal, the MIR leader. He surrounded himself with *miristas* (who formed his private bodyguard and intelligence service) and with revolutionary gangsters like 'Coco' Paredes, the sometime chief of the Chilean Criminal Investigation Department, who showed him how to use the automatic rifle he received as a gift from his friend Fidel Castro. The Cuban influence—particularly in the person of Luis Fernández de Oña, Allende's son-in-law and a leading figure in the Cuban intelligence service, the DGI—became increasingly important.

There is little doubt in my mind that, at the last, Allende was ready to organise his own *coup d'état* to consolidate his failing power. Whatever his personal attributes (those characteristics of the *bon viveur* that so reassured the most unlikely visitors during his early period in office) Allende always remained a revolutionary Marxist whose conception of 'democracy' and 'legality' were radically at odds with the constitution that enabled him to take power. The choice between the 'peaceful way', *la via pacifica* and revolutionary violence, *la vía armada*, was therefore only a choice of means. The end remained constant. That this was not perceived by Allende's liberal admirers abroad is a tribute to how Lenin and Trotsky (let alone the speeches and writings of the Chilean president and his supporters) are apparently hardly read at all, or only as fiction. Any serious revolutionary knows that revolution is about one thing, and one thing only—power. The Marxists in Chile captured the presidency through an election. It remained to take total power—and for this, a coup, whether or not camouflaged in legal forms, was essential.

Let us explore the territory that the Marxists in Chile were able to gain in those four areas specified by Ponomarev and his colleagues: in the control of the economy and the media, in the creation of mass organisations and in the kennelling of the armed forces. Their handling of the economy should really be studied under two headings—nationalisation and crisis management. State takeovers, and the redistribution of land and income, were designed to change the whole balance of power within Chilean society and bring about the eventual dictatorship of the proletariat. There was nothing secret about that. Allende's first minister of economy declared soon after taking office that 'state control is designed to destroy the economic bases of imperialism and the ruling class by putting an end to the private ownership of the means of production'.[5] The point was made crystal-clear in an internal document of the Socialist Party that was made public early in 1972. In this *Informe Político*, the leaders of Allende's own party reaffirmed their commitment to 'the highest form of socialism, communism'. The most relevant part of the document read as follows:

> The bourgeois state in Chile will not serve as a basis for socialism, and it is necessary to destroy it. To build socialism, the Chilean workers should use their political domination over the middle class to seize total power and gradually expropriate all private capital. This is what is called the dictatorship of the proletariat. . . .
> We understand that, in the last instance, the power of the middle class resides in its economic power. . . . It is possible for the government to destroy the bases of the capitalist system of production. By creating and expanding the public sector at the expense of the imperialist enterprises and the monopolistic bourgeoisie, we can take their economic power away from them.[6]

The Allende government carefully declined to define just how far nationalisation was supposed to go; it transpired that there were to be no limits at all. The goal, as the socialist document makes as plain as a warning flare, was power, not efficiency; the government itself admitted that the losses of the state-run corporations exceeded one billion dollars in 1972.[7] The methods used were often openly illegal.

But the government was also able to make effective use of a legal device dredged out of the statute books by Allende's exceptionally artful legal adviser, Eduardo Novoa. This provided for state intervention 'in all basic industries which do not conform to operational norms which are freely laid down by the administrative authorities'. Under the cover of this decree-law, state managers, or *interventores*, were assigned to take over businesses on the most threadbare pretexts—often involving supposed non-fulfilment of 'production quotas' or the announcement of 'unjustified' redundancies. Situations rapidly developed in which militant trade union groups occupied factories or paralysed production, and then appealed to the government to appoint an *interventor*—who would often enough spend his time trying to produce evidence of the owners' 'incompetence' in order to justify definitive expropriation. The use of this law in Chile has greatly interested the left elsewhere; there have been proposals from the Labour left in Britain, for example, for a new Bill to make state intervention mandatory when jobs in private industry are at risk. The other means for crushing the private sector in Chile—through the arbitrary fixing of prices and wages, for instance—are familiar enough.

The process of state takeover in industry and the subsequent decline in production (partly due to the flight of managers and technicians) contributed to Chile's mounting economic crisis. The collapse of local agricultural production in the wake of the land collectivisation programme was even more disastrous. The government resorted to the printing-press to cover the soaring budgetary deficit; according to Central Bank figures, the money supply was expanded by 120 per cent in 1971 and by 171 per cent in 1972. Naturally, inflation accelerated out of control: over the twelve months up to the coup, prices rose by more than 350 per cent, and over the whole of 1973, the increase was more than 600 per cent.

Unable to cover the costs of vital imports, the Allende government resorted to a draconian system of controls and to rationing. Local committees—the 'Japs' (or *juntas de abastecimiento y precios*)—were set up to police officially-determined price levels and to denounce 'hoarders'. They were mostly controlled by local communist cells. Meanwhile, the government sought scapegoats for the crisis in the famous 'invisible blockade' that the Americans were supposed to be organising, and in 'economic sabotage' carried out by the Chilean middle class.

Now I would not wish to suggest that the economic collapse in Chile was entirely due to the designs of the Marxists in power; there is too much evidence of the sheer incompetence of those who set themselves up as economic planners. But it is important to note, as we have observed in other situations, that what seems to be a nerve-shattering crisis to ordinary people may look like a major opportunity to a revolutionary movement. This could not be made clearer than in a remarkable statement by Carlos Matus, another of Allende's economic ministers, in an interview with the West German weekly *Der Spiegel* early in 1973. He said that 'if one goes by conventional economic criteria, we are, in effect, in a state of crisis. If, for example, the previous government had found itself in our economic situation that would have been the end of it. *But what is a crisis for others, is for us the solution.*' [My emphasis]. It is easy enough to see what he meant. An economic crisis provides a socialist government with the pretext to seize more and more sweeping powers in the interests of national survival. It is curious to observe how such a crisis, even when it clearly results from excessive state intervention, is used to justify still more intervention. In Chile, it supplied a pretext to impose the most sinister form of political control of all—control through the stomach.

By the same token, the Chilean inflation was used as a political tool. It washed away the savings and investments of the middle class, and bankrupted companies which were forced to respect wholly unrealistic pricing regulations. But the social groups regarded as politically loyal to the regime were insulated from this holocaust that was sweeping away what was left of civility in Chilean society. Middle-class housewives were reduced to buying shoes from the smart shops of Providencia in the morning in order to sell them back for a higher price in the afternoon. Gold, foreign currency and goods for barter became the only reliable forms of exchange. But while black marketeers made their killings (often enough with the complicity of crooked officials) and small businesses put up their shutters, the socialist state was always ready to invent more jobs for the boys; the number of state employees more than doubled under Allende. Wage levels in certain sectors were pushed far above price rises in the first period of the regime—although it proved incapable of cushioning even its favoured working-class constituency in the long run, when shortages of most essential consumer goods became universal and the pricing system gave rise to an uncontrollable black market. Inflation not only exacerbated the class war in Chile; it was used by a Marxist regime as a means of waging it. The natural result was a middle-class revolt which led housewives and respectable professional men to employ the tactics of trade union militants and, when those failed, to welcome a military coup.

Allende's calculation was always that the system of prices and incomes controls that were used to destroy private industry would also bring about the closure of the opposition newspapers—in combination with the wrecking activities of union militants. The survival of the opposition press over three taxing years was a tribute to the loyalty of journalists and employees, the resolution of proprietors and shareholders and the covert financial support that was channelled in both from Chilean enterprises and from abroad—in that order. The Marxist campaign against the press would have been much easier, of course, if strong left-wing printers' and journalists' unions had been able to impose a different editorial policy on editors and proprietors. But there was no closed shop in *El Mercurio* or *La Prensa*. Direct censorship could hardly be applied without exposing the totalitarian aims of the Marxists in government, so they were reduced to indirect methods, including a campaign to close down the only independent source of newsprint in the country. These might well have proved effective in the end, but as it turned out, Allende did not have time enough. The opposition press was able to mount a series of highly effective attacks on the government, which was infuriated by the disclosure of confidential documents such as the socialist *Informe* quoted earlier. Hence Mr Ponomarev's concern that future Allendes must move faster to muzzle the press: counsel that was immediately applied by the communists in Portugal after the Caetano regime was overthrown.

What about those extra-parliamentary power bases? On the eve of the congressional elections in March 1973, Carlos Altamirano, the leader of the socialist left, pointed out that 'revolutions are not made with votes'.[8] It was the socialist left and its allies, rather than the communists, who set out to create a situation of *dual power* in Chile after Allende's electoral victory that would create the bases for a Bolshevik-style *coup d'état*. The left could count, from the beginning, on its traditional hold over the trade union conference (CUT)—

although it lost ground to the Christian Democrats in subsequent polls. But new organisations were developed as the crisis sharpened. On the extreme left, the MIR and some socialists prepared for armed insurrection. In working-class suburbs and state-run industries, 'communal commandos' were set up and coordinated through the *cordones industriales.* 'The concept, character and aims' of these new organisations, according to one of the publications they spawned, 'are such as to prepare the working class and direct it towards taking power; at the same time, this struggle means combating the dangerous reformist and bureaucratic deviations that appear in the workers' movement, as well as combatting the resistance of the bourgeoisie to the conequest of POWER.'[9] Para-military groups were organised in key service industries including gas, electricity, posts and telegraphs and the water supply. They were linked together by two-way radio and telex—after all, technology has progressed since the workers' soviets were set up in pre-Bolshevik Russia. 'Departments of direct action' with the job of organising street rallies, factory occupations and para-military training were set up in enterprises like the state construction firm, Cormu, with the blessing of their managers.

There was no lack of foreign experts on hand to help in such preparations. Russians, Cubans, Czechs and East Germans as well as veteran guerrillas from failed revolutions elsewhere in Latin America, were all allowed access to state-run industries in key areas like the Cordón de Cerillos in Santiago. Tupamaros toured the slum suburbs in propaganda teams and set up a rural base in the north of Chile under the leadership of Raul Bidegain Greissig. A Brazilian revolutionary, Sergio de Moraes, moved into the state-run Madeco refrigerator plant and organised the manufacturers of 'people's tanks'—armour-plated fork-lift trucks. One of the more egregious cases involved the activities of the twenty-man Russian team (which included eight technicians and twelve Red Army officers) that was assigned to help run a Russian-built plant for the manufacture of prefabricated housing in El Belloto, near Valparaiso. After normal working hours, the army officers drilled carefully-chosen squads of workers in urban guerrilla tactics. Such goings-on were a frequent source of debate within the cabinet, especially after the introduction of military ministers late in 1972, but there is no doubt that they took place with Allende's blessing. I was told by a senior naval officer at the time that, in the midst of a dispute with his military ministers in January 1973, Allende exclaimed that, if they ever decided to turn against him, he would 'take refuge in the Cordón de Cerillos, and you will never get me out'. It was of course an empty threat. There was no serious armed resistance to the coup—partly, of course, because most of the Marxist leaders took the rational decision to seek safety immediately in prepared safe houses or foreign embassies; partly because a converted fork-lift truck is no match for a tank.

Perhaps the threat of a general strike and of systematic industrial sabotage would have been more convincing. But there was no one, it seemed, to give the order; the workers were divided, the middle class (which had participated in two nation-wide strikes) was with the junta, and few of the people who mourned the Allende regime were prepared to face soldiers who were ready to shoot. Perhaps the coup might have turned into a civil war if the armed forces themselves had split, and if power in Chile had been more dispersed geographically— the only towns that really mattered in a coup were Santiago, Valparaiso and, to a much lesser extent, Concepción. But the armed forces marched together.

The history of Allende's love-hate relationship with the military is too complex to be recounted here. He may have believed, until the very end, that it was possible to bring about a social revolution in Chile with the complicity of the army—although he always recognised the navy, which emerged as the driving force behind the coup, as a potential enemy. The murder of a constitutionalist army commander, General Schneider, shortly before Allende took office (apparently at the hands of the right but in conditions that remain mysterious) helped the new president to appeal to the apolitical traditions of the army. He also offered a more tangible appeal, in the form of increased salaries and social status. There were moments when the Popular Unity government seemed to be engaged in a full-time courtship of the men in uniform.

The point that needs to be underlined is that it was Allende himself, in the attempt to set the armed forces against his middle-class opponents, who drew the military into politics. The military agreed to join the cabinet in November 1972, in the aftermath of the first 'national strike'. From this time onwards, they were to find themselves saddled with partial responsibility for the disastrous economic policy of the government and for a series of controversial decisions—including the decision to set up a de facto system of rationing—that were sometimes taken without consultation.

For an entirely different reason—because of a new law on the control of arms passed by Congress at the instigation of the Christian democrats—the armed forces were also increasingly committed to an internal policing role. Military intelligence became fully apprised of the situation in the industrial suburbs and the guerrilla bases in the south, and there were a series of clashes with left-wing extremists when troops were brought in to confiscate arms caches. Thus on the one hand, the service chiefs found themselves compromised with the policies of a Marxist government, while on the other hand, the armed forces found themselves dealing with private armies loyal to that government.

Allende could have attempted to neutralise the armed forces by reducing manpower levels, while simultaneously sponsoring the growth of countervailing forces in the form of the *cordones industriales,* the para-military groups, and the riot police (who were thoroughly purged and placed under leftist control). But he was either over-confident about the conversion of his commanders to the revolution, or frightened of provoking a reaction too soon. No doubt for the same reasons, he never attempted a purge of the officer corps. He was exceedingly fortunate in his army commander, General Carlos Prats, who was largely sympathetic to the aims of the Popular Unity government and was flattered by communist leaders like Luís Figueroa with hints that they would make him their presidential candidate on a national unity platform when the next elections came round. But it would be wrong to think of the men who were finally persuaded to move against Allende as 'unreconstructed' right-wingers, whatever their subsequent policies and allegiances. The distinctive features of the Chilean coup are, first, that the trigger was an immediate threat to the military themselves, in the form of a plan—approved by Altamirano and other government leaders—for a naval mutiny in Valparaiso and reports of a further plan for a Marxist *coup d'état* in Santiago. In this, the Chile coup resembled many others: it was when the revolution entered the barracks that the soldiers decided to act. Second, there is a basic distinction between a coup that is made by generals and a coup made by colonels—or captains. This was a generals' coup, and they were able, as it transpired, to count on unquestioning obedience from their subordinates further down the chain of command. Allende's sympathisers in the high command had already been dispensed with or were swiftly brushed aside. Third, the coup took place against a backdrop of economic collapse and the conspirators were satisfied that it could be justified in quasi-legal terms by rulings of the Supreme Court and a large majority in Congress that Allende was governing 'unconstitutionally and illegally'; finally, General Pinochet, Admiral Merino, General Leigh and the others were no longer political novices. The armed forces had been dragged into politics by Allende; the education of a section of the officer corps was rounded off by contact with opposition politicians—especially the group of young economists who prepared the junta's economic programme well in advance of the coup.

Chile's coup was far from bloodless. There was resistance in several parts of Santiago, and bitter fighting around the Technical University and in the Cordón de Cerillos. But the trade union left and the 'communal commandos' proved to be paper tigers in the path of the tanks. The dangerous things, as Trotsky said, are extremely simple. The workers were not committed to the Allende regime as a class, as left-wing propaganda made out; indeed, the Christian Democrats controlled the trade union headquarters in Santiago. And those who might have contemplated trying to organise a general strike had to contend with the fact that the Chilean army was fully prepared to shoot.

The threat of a general strike may be effective even against an army that is prepared to shoot; that is the lesson that has often been drawn from the failure of the Kapp putsch in Germany in 1920. But a general strike requires a general staff of its own, and a sufficient following to paralyse vital services. The success of the coup in Chile depended less on the capture of the symbols of state power—the presidential palace and the ministries—than on the rapid elimination or flight of the possible leaders of a revolutionary strike, and on the precautions taken by the military to guarantee control of power, water and communications.

With the overthrow and suicide of Allende, Chile drifted out into a constitutional limbo and a degree of international isolation from which it showed no signs of returning two years after the coup. The junta's subsequent economic failure and record of repression is not my concern here, although it raised serious doubts about the long-term stability of a regime that began as a holding operation and rapidly turned into a novel, and bleak, way of life. The cost of the counter-revolution in Chile was still undoubtedly less, life for life, dollar for dollar (in relation to the population and resources of the country) than the cost of communist revolution wherever it has taken place—in Russia, in Czechoslovakia, in China, in Korea, in Cuba or North Vietnam.

But the lesson to be drawn from Chile is not just that the revolution could not withstand the armed forces when they finally decided to act. It is that *the revolution withstood everything else.* The policies of the Marxist regime provoked a bitter reaction at every level of Chilean society. It produced housewives' demonstrations—the women of Santiago, indeed, were the first to resist openly. It produced a sea-change in student opinion that enabled right-wing and Christian Democrat groups to capture control of student unions that had hitherto been fiefdoms of the Marxist left. It produced a powerful upsurge of middle-class militancy and the creation of new types of trade unions (the *gremios*) to defend the interests of the social groups that were worst-hit by inflation. It produced the two 'national strikes', in October–November 1972 and August 1973, which failed to bring the country's economy to a complete standstill (as their organisers had threatened) but proved that the industrial trade unions were not the only groups that could organise effective strike action. It produced 'patriotic declarations' from retired military men, and, towards the end, it produced right-wing violence—from dispossessed farmers in the south and from the neo-fascist Patria y Libertad movement.

All these forms of 'direct action' were related to the fact that the regime steam-rollered its way over the opposition of a majority in both houses of Congress, the courts, and the Contraloría, or auditor-general's office, which was supposed to determine the propriety (or otherwise) of the government's financial measures. Allende and his supporters were never able to command majority support in Chile. If they had, they might have been able to provide a genuine mandate for their executive actions in the form of a referendum on new constitutional proposals. As things were, Allende brought on a constitutional crisis of momentous proportions, in which he simply chose to ignore Congress and the Supreme Court, as well as what was going on in the streets.

If the right to resist tyranny means anything, it can surely be claimed that it applied to the Chilean middle class, whose leaders seemed to have exhausted the peaceful means of opposing Allende. The Marxist left has been more honest about this than Allende's liberal admirers, drawing the conclusion, quite simply, that the middle class was bound to fight. Chile's tragedy is that the political system, when manipulated by a revolutionary government, no longer provided the means for *mediating* and *containing* this fundamental conflict. The banks of the river could not hold the flood.

What expedient was left to those who felt that a thirty-six per cent plurality of the votes in 1970 was an insufficient mandate for social revolution? Yet Allende might have managed to have left that question unanswered if the government itself had not gone over to *la via armada*. Two days before the coup, the general secretary of the Socialist Party declared 'you attack a reactionary coup by staging a coup against the coup, not by conciliating seditious people . . . You do not combat it with dialogue, but with the force of the people, with its industrial commandos, its peasants' councils.'[10] In the same speech, he admitted attending clandestine meetings with naval petty officers and other ranks.

It will be endlessly debated on the Marxist left whether Altamirano was right; whether the failure of the revolution in Chile was due to the fact that Allende hesitated for too long about organising a 'coup against the coup'. A Gallup poll was held in Chile early in 1975. It was commissioned by the junta, but was apparently conducted according to the normal rigorous standards of the Gallup organisation. It showed that over sixty-five per cent of those interviewed approved of the coup; a much lower percentage (the figure was not published) approved of subsequent economic and social policies. Of course, you can never trust the polls, especially one held in a climate of fear. But if, as might be argued from other evidence, only a third of the electorate of a highly politicised country was prepared to go all the way with a government bent on revolution, then confrontation, in the form of a civil war, a right-wing coup or a Bolshevik-style coup was inevitable— unless the regime was prepared to abandon some of its original goals. There was certainly no hope for democracy in a situation where the will of the majority could not be translated into an effective brake on the ambitions of a revolutionary elite.

10

The Portuguese Way

'Then how does the popular leader start to turn into a
tyrant? Isn't it, clearly, when he starts doing what we hear
about in the story of the shrine of Zeus Lykaeus in
Arcadia?'
'What is the story?'
'That the man who tastes a single piece of flesh, mingled in
with the rest of the sacrifice, is fated to become a wolf.'

Plato

The early course of the Portuguese revolution provided some
fresh lessons in communist tactics and in how the majority,
even in a backward society, can be organised to resist them. The
communists' bid to turn Portugal into the Cuba of Western
Europe gave rise, late in 1975, to a tremendous wave of popular
resistance; what remained to be decided, at the time of writing,
was whether the communists would be able to mount a
successful comeback or be forced to make way for either a
genuine experiment in representative government or an
authoritarian counter-revolution.

As a result of the events that followed the overthrow of the
Caetano regime on 25 April 1974, the western Mediterranean
became the focal point of the ideological conflict in Europe.
The advance of the Marxist left in Lisbon can hardly be
interpreted as another example of the collapse of democracy:
Portugal passed from one form of dictatorship to another. But
Portugal is directly relevant to the themes of this book because
the tactics employed by the Marxists and the anti-Marxists
there have a more general application and their eventual success
(or failure) will influence communist strategy towards the West
in general.

This is the only recent European example of successful
communist infiltration into the armed forces. This was not a
primary explanation for the coup against Caetano. The Armed
Forces Movement (AFM) originally coalesced around professional grievances, involving such matters as the conditions of
promotion and pay levels for career and conscript officers. The

experience of a protracted colonial war had the same radicalising effect on draftees that was visible among American soldiers in Vietnam. The prime movers on 25 April were certainly men who had studied politics; many of them, even at this stage, would cheerfully have accepted the label of 'Marxist'. A significant number had joined the army as career officers in the late 1950s, when recruitment was opened to lower-income families and the officer corps began to lose its aristocratic character. Since then, they had engaged in long political discussions with younger conscript officers who had come fresh from university.

These were men who did not share the traditional soldierly distrust of communism but were not, for the most part, communists themselves. They were moved by a woolly idealism compounded, in the case of some naval officers, by Maoism rather than Moscow-line communism. Their ideas were fluid and unsystematic—which was to make them, in the end, the easy victims of the vendors of ideological patent-medicines.

There was a hard-core communist element within the AFM from the very beginning, and in the medium term it was this group that proved to be the main beneficiary of the coup. The AFM worked in close liaison with the communists, and with other opposition groups, in the months prior to the coup. It is of some interest to recall that the communists, apparently acting on advice from Moscow, had called a halt to the campaign of urban terrorism waged by their military wing, the Armed Revolutionary Action (ARA) in 1973—in the belief, subsequently proved correct, that more promising lines of action were about to be opened up. One of the most important meetings held by the military conspirators took place later that year. On the morning of Sunday, 9 September 1973, 136 Portuguese officers in civilian clothes gathered in the ruins of the ancient Temple of Diana at Evora. Most of these men were captains and majors; only one, a certain Colonel Vasco Gonçalves, was an officer of field rank. They were the nucleus of the AFM. At Evora, they received details of their final rendezvous. It was a remote farm on the slopes of the Monte do Sobral, owned by a member of the Central Committee of the Portuguese Communist Party. It seems that the link man in the exercise was a conscript lieutenant who had joined the Communist Party while studying medicine at university.[1]

Political enemies of Colonel (now Brigadier) Vasco Gonçalves, prime minister between June 1974 and 29 August 1975, allege that he has long been a secret member of the Communist Party—card number 1062. The accusation has been made by a number of prominent exiles, including Major Sanches Osorio, formerly minister of information under President Spínola. Similar charges have been levelled at other key leaders of the AFM who subsequently figured on the far left of the movement—at several members of the seven-man Coordinating Commission, at Captain Costa Martins, who later became minister of labour and strongly supported the communist plan for the trade unions, at Colonel Varela Gomes, who surfaced after the coup as a key man in intelligence (in the so-called 5th division of the general staff) and the editor of the *Bulletin* of the AFM (whose style was usually indistinguishable from that of the communist paper *Avante*).* It is impossible to substantiate most of these charges. The truth is no doubt to be found among the dossiers of the former secret police, but the relevant material appears to have been shrewdly whisked away by the communists after the coup.

In any case, the debate about whether Captain X or Colonel Y is a card-carrying communist is basically sterile. What matters is the fact that, as events subsequently proved, a key element in the AFM marched in step with the Party and that Alvaro Cunhal, the communist leader, was undoubtedly the civilian politician with most influence over the movement as a whole. Officers like Brigadier Vasco Gonçalves—as other military ministers privately confessed to me at the time—were so closely aligned with Cunhal in the crucial cabinet debates that, as one ex-minister put it, 'it was difficult to remember afterwards which of them had said what.' Before taking any important administrative decision, Gonçalves always insisted on consulting Cunhal, which was to lead to tension with other equally left-wing, but less docile, leaders of the AFM. For example, Brigadier (formerly Major) Otelo Saraiva de Carvalho, the key operational commander in the coup and subsequently one of the strong men of the regime, told me of an argument he had

---

*Varela Gomes, who was arrested for his part in the 'Beja plot' of 1961, shared a cell with Communist Party leaders in the early 1960s and was publicly praised by Alvaro Cunhal in his book *Rumo à Victoria* a decade before the coup.

had with Gonçalves in April 1975 over the arrest of five communist militants who had attacked a group of Maoists with iron bars. Gonçalves wanted to talk the matter over with Cunhal before taking any action; Carvalho (frequently referred to, like Fidel Castro, by his first name) insisted on enforcing his own rules.

But let us begin with the situation on 25 April 1974. A conservative dictatorship (with a thin corporatist overlay) that had lasted for nearly half a century had been abruptly overthrown. The dreaded secret police—formerly called the Pide, recently renamed the DGS—had been locked up in their own jails, or forced to flee the country, or were still on the run from howling mobs. Their antiquated surveillance and interrogation equipment had been placed on public display. The new government was headed by President Antonio de Spínola, the former deputy chief of staff and military commander in Guinea-Bissau whose book, *Portugal e o futuro*,[2] which put the case for cautious devolution in the African provinces, had helped to bring about the crisis of the Caetano regime. Yet Spínola's appointment came as a surprise to some of the organisers of the coup; Otelo was later to say that he was unaware that Spínola, was to be made president until his face bobbed up on the television screen. General Francisco da Costa Gomes, the former chief of staff, and a man who stood some distance to the left of Spínola had been the choice of the Marxist captains. They regarded Spínola as a man who had contributed nothing to the coup. The communists, for their part, recognised him as a man of deeply conservative leanings who would never willingly tolerate social revolution in Portugal. At the same time, his appointment helped to allay the doubts of many moderates and conservatives in the country and the armed forces and prevented any immediate reaction to the coup. It also reassured many western observers that the AFM's promises of an evolution towards democracy would be respected and that a Portuguese withdrawal from Africa would not take place without some attempt to take account of the views of the local inhabitants themselves.

But it rapidly became plain that Spínola was not in control of the revolution to which he had lent his name. Over the following months, he was consistently outmanoeuvred. In the cabinet crisis in June, when the prime minister, Senhor Palma

Carlos, resigned, Spínola was compelled to accept the AFM's choice of a successor—Vasco Gonçalves—in place of his own choice, Colonel Almeida Bruno, who was a close comrade from his time in Guinea-Bissau. As the AFM established new command structures and the communists developed their own apparatus, it became clear that the president himself would be reduced to a figurehead. Brigadier Otelo took over a new operational headquarters—the Continental Operations Command (Copcon)—which was to be responsible for internal security operations. Although only three units (the Parachute Battalion, the 11th Commandos and the Fusileiros) were directly assigned to it, they contained the best troops in metropolitan Portugal, and Otelo had the right to call upon other units in 'defence of the revolution'.

The Communist front movement, the MDP (which began as an umbrella organisation for various left-wing groups and later presented itself in the elections as an independent party) seized control of local authorities throughout the country. The communist trade union federation, the Intersindical, appropriated the funds of individual trade unions; it was later formally recognised as the *only* federation in the country.

Simultaneously, the communists set out to apply the lessons of the Prague coup. Since Alvaro Cunhal had spent fourteen years in exile in Prague it is no coincidence that his tactics—including the use of the Reichstag fire technique—were so often reminiscent of those we have considered in a previous chapter. At least four features of the Prague coup were exactly copied in Portugal. The first was the communist use of character assassination and blackmail techniques. In both situations, the communists made exorbitant use of allegations of collaboration with the fascists. The most notorious example in Prague was the attempt to blacken the reputation of Professor Krajina; in Portugal, the communists took over Pide's dossiers immediately after the coup, and pilfered whatever it pleased them to take (or photocopy). This material was later deployed effectively. For example, in their efforts to discredit Dr Miller Guerra, now a leading socialist, the communists dredged up the fact that he belonged to the para-military Portuguese Legion for a few months back in the 1930s.

Senior Spanish intelligence sources added a more disturbing allegation. They claimed that the communists were holding a police dossier on one of the most prominent socialist leaders, which purportedly showed that he was paid (with cheques drawn on the Banco de Portugal and mailed to Paris) for giving information on communist activities to the authorities. Whether it is forged or not, a skilled propagandist can wield such material to devastating effect in the context of a Marxist-controlled press. The communists used the same methods to turn many civil servants into pliant tools.

Second, the communists in Portugal, as in Prague before, seized control of much of the intelligence apparatus. The bugging devices left over from the old regime were supposedly left under lock and key, but there were reports that the Party has removed quite a number of them. Senior officers talked frankly in private about the fact that their own lines were tapped and that the communists had agents at every major switchboard in Lisbon who regularly taped and summarised 'interesting' conversations. The AFM received regular intelligence digests based on these sources from Party headquarters. The situation differed from Czechoslovakia in the sense that the police as such were not under direct Party control, while the para-military National Republican Guard was feared by the Left as a predominantly conservative force.

Third, in Portugal, as in Prague, the security forces lost the monopoly of force. There were various armed groups in the country, including former terrorist outfits like LUAR and the Brigadas Revolucionarias. But the Communist Party was the real force to be reckoned with. I discovered definite evidence early in 1975 that it had been arming itself on a bigger scale than most people—even those who saw armed militias swing into action last September—had imagined. A senior staff officer admitted that the communists had removed some 40,000 guns from the arsenal of the para-military Portuguese Legion immediately after the coup. He was not prepared to confirm or deny further reports of Soviet gun-running, via the freighters and fishing trawlers that are now bobbing up along the coast with significant regularity. But it was plain that, when the barricades went up again, the communists would be armed—and they made no secret of that after the coup attempt on 11 March.

For reasons that are later discussed, the 'Prague scenario' did not work according to plan in Portugal. But it is important to

observe that the armed forces, by the end of the first year of the
revolution, were by no means the only force to contend with in
any serious armed confrontation. Indeed, as it eventually
transpired, the breakdown of discipline and the rapid
expansion of the communist network among other ranks
created a situation in which even radical left-wing officers (let
alone moderates) could not be sure that their men would obey
orders. Some leaders of the AFM, such as Brigadier Otelo, saw
the armed groups as a support rather than a threat (as 'the
reserve of the revolution') and talked of forming a new
para-military force from them.

Finally, in Portugal, as in Prague, the Reichstag fire
technique was used as the pretext to carry the revolution
forward and purge enemies. This seems to be at least a partial
explanation for how two great watersheds—28 September
1974 and 11 March 1975—were passed. In September, a
planned 'rally of the silent majority' in support of President
Spínola was seized upon as evidence of a right-wing coup
attempt. This was used as the pretext for locking up prominent
conservatives and ousting General Spínola's friends from the
high command and the cabinet. After the three key
conservatives in the high command—General Galvão de Melo,
General Diogo Neto and General Silveiro Marques—were
pushed out, Spínola was left with only two options: to step
down, or to lend his name to a Marxist-dominated government
that, in his view, was leading Portugal into 'a new kind of
slavery'.

His friend and chief of staff, General Costa Gomes, replaced
him as president. Costa Gomes had always stood some way to
the left of Spínola; he opposed the African wars from the very
beginning, in 1961, and took part that year in an abortive coup
against Salazar.

Brigadier Otelo subsequently claimed that there was a
'reactionary' plot against the government.[3] But the only
evidence produced at that stage was a rifle with a telescopic
sight said to have been found in a vacant apartment across the
road from the prime minister's house (which seemed
suspiciously like a plant); a batch of pamphlets put out by
something calling itself the Portuguese Action Movement; and
a few guns allegedly picked up in cars belonging to people
planning to attend the rally of the 'silent majority' in support

of Spínola that was banned after left-wing objections.

More interesting are accounts that Spínola was planning a pre-emptive strike and that he tried to place the prime minister, Brigadier Vasco Gonçalves, and other left-wing officers under house arrest at the start of the weekend. It is clear that the right was reorganising in Portugal, despite constant harassment from the left (including a ban imposed on the Portuguese Nationalist Party earlier in September and the virtual left-wing monopoly of the news media). There had been a constant buzz of rumour from Madrid that the right was planning 'something' in Lisbon—and given the state of the economy, the tightening grip of the Marxist parties over all aspects of public life, and the handover to the guerillas as in Guinea-Bissau and Mozambique, it would be remarkable if this were not the case. But the left struck first, and hardest.

Its great leap forward, however, came in March 1975. This subsequent right-wing plot came at a suspiciously opportune moment—after a cabinet clash that had almost driven the socialists to resign in protest at the acceptance of a communist plan to establish a monolithic trade union federation. (This was watered down as part of a compromise, but the communist proposals were eventually implemented in full.) The events of 11 March interrupted a gradual process by which the moderates in the AFM and the country as a whole had seemed to be at last taking back the initiative from the communists. It is necessary to look behind the surface of what happened that day.

The initial report of the official commission of inquiry (presided over by Admiral Rosa Coutinho) described the putsch on 11 March as 'the culmination of a gigantic campaign against the infant Portuguese democracy by the forces of national and international capital, the financial and industrial haute bourgeoisie and their allies'.[4] Great play was made of the allegation that the 'climate' for the coup had been prepared by 'alarmist' warnings issued by the socialists and the PPD, which came under particular fire for having published an interview with Spínola in January in which he defended the idea of 'socialism with liberty'. The report concluded that the lessons to be drawn from the events of 11 March were that the 'cleaning-up' (*saneamento*) of the armed forces had to be carried further and that special attention should be paid to strengthening 'mass organisations' which could 'impose adequate discipline' in places of work throughout the country. The Communist Party—if the report is to be believed—had again proved itself as 'the principle civilian enemy of the counter-revolutionaries'.

But the report was remarkably vague on the origins of the coup attempt. It claimed that some of the conspirators had close links with 'civil and military personnel of various embassies, with some political parties and with certain elements of high finance'—but their identities were not specified. This bald, undocumented assertion may well have been thrown out in order to clear the way for further 'investigations' designed to discredit political leaders in Lisbon who were considered too strong to be touched at this stage. As for the contacts with various embassies, Brigadier Carvalho had warned the American ambassador on the day of the putsch that he had better get out and that his safety could not be guaranteed. But when I asked Otelo (on the day the report was published) whether he had any evidence of covert American operations in Portugal, he confessed that none was available.

So what are we to make of the events of 11 March? Was this simply an act of criminal irresponsibility by a handful of military bunglers associated with Spínola? There are three reasons for suspecting that there was a bit more to it than that. The first is that, despite his political ineptitude, Spínola had shown himself to be a capable and imaginative military commander in Africa and it is hard to believe that he can have thought that he had the makings of a coup with the pathetic forces that he was able to mobilise on 11 March. Second, the timing of the coup attempt was even harder to explain, since it took place during the run-up to elections that were expected to be a humiliation for the Communist Party. Finally, there are one or two factual indications that left-wing *agents provocateurs* may have been at work.

You do not, of course, set out to overthrow a government at 11.50 in the morning; nor do you have the makings of a coup if your forces consist of a couple of antiquated training planes, a few armed civilians, and a handful of muddle-headed paratroopers who refuse to fight when a left-wing mob implores them to lay down their weapons. The coup attempt was almost incredibly incompetent, and it only begins to make sense if Spínola was led to believe that other units had pledged their support. The mysterious but ubiquitous Captain Maia (the man who negotiated Caetano's surrender in the original coup) may have played some part in this. At any rate, it appears that (i) Spínola was expecting the 11th Commandos (commanded by another of his subalterns in Guinea-Bissau, Major Jaime Neves), the cadets at the cavalry school at Santarem[5] and the National Republican Guard (whose headquarters was briefly taken over) to take part in the coup; and (ii) that Otelo's headquarters at Copcon was kept fully informed of everything that the conspirators were doing. Although there is insufficient evidence to support the claim that the whole affair was a put-up job, it looks very much as if some interested parties in Lisbon allowed the plot to go ahead; the same people may actually have encouraged Spínola to think that it would succeed by conveying false assurances to his house at Massama.

This impression is reinforced by several rumours that were floating around in the days before the putsch. The conspirators were moved to act, it transpires, by reports that an 'Easter massacre' was being prepared by the left. According to one variant of this story, the LUAR guerrilla group was planning the massacre of five hundred officers and a thousand civilians; the people on the black list were to be tracked down and killed on 13 March. There are differing accounts of where this report originated. The evidence of the official commission is itself contradictory on this score. It says at one point that a certain Lieutenant Rolo brought the news back from Madrid (where he had allegedly been in contact with Spanish intelligence sources) on 10 March; further down, the text of the report says that the story was already circulating among conservative civilians on 8 March. The rumour was of course highly suspect; the possibility remains that it was floated by *agents provocateurs* in order to goad the circle around Spínola into making a premature move.

Panic rumours about right-wing plotting were being circulated by the extreme left in the days before the coup attempt. A particularly interesting report was published in the evening paper *A Capital* during the preceding week. This paper, hitherto regarded as relatively responsible, devoted a lot of space to an extraordinary story lifted from the pages of an obscure left-wing West German student publication called

Extra. The original report, which the authors claimed to be based on Syrian intelligence sources, was built around the idea that neither the Americans nor the West Germans would be prepared to permit the Portuguese to deny the use of the Lajes airbase in the Azores to the American air force. The West Germans' interest in this was supposedly to ensure that their country would not be the only one used by the Americans in mounting a future emergency air-lift to Israel. For this reason they were alleged to be playing a critical backstage role in providing financial and other support to the Portuguese socialists. They were also claimed to be working hand-in-glove with the CIA in a plot to oust the communists and left-wing AFM leaders including Otelo.

This story, denied by everyone who was supposedly involved, was symptomatic of the way a climate of intoxication was generated in the days before the putsch. The *Extra* story was attributed by some observers to the work of the KGB's 'disinformation' department, working in collusion with East German intelligence.[6] That is another so far undocumented allegation. But the excitement that was generated created an ideal backdrop for the extraordinary speech delivered by Alvaro Cunhal on 9 March, in which he declared that he had proof of 'a new grand offensive by the reaction with the aim of producing a change in the political situation in the near future'. Cunhal must have passed on his 'evidence' to someone, since there are reports from the Algarve that printed leaflets denouncing the coup attempt were being circulated at 11 a.m. on 11 March—a full hour before it actually started.

But the circumstantial evidence is perhaps less convincing than the *cui bono* argument: 'who stood to gain?' The question remains why anyone in his right mind should have decided to move in March 1975. After a series of lurches to the left, the pendulum in Portugal had at least started to swing back the other way. The most dramatic sign of this was the fact that elections for some lower-level councils of the AFM in the week before the coup attempt resulted in striking reverses for the left. The elections that took place were for the artillery (*Arma da Artilheria*) and cavalry (*Arma da Cavalharia*) councils of the army—elected bodies responsible for 'advising' the director of each arm. In the polls for the artillery council, three leading left-wingers were defeated: Brigadier Otelo, Colonel Manuel

Charais (a key figure on the Coordinating Committee of the AFM) and Major Melo Antunes. The man elected director of the artillery council was Brigadier Orlando Costa, commander of the Coimbra military region and a close friend of General Spínola. Those polls confirmed previous reports that a reaction against the pro-communists in the government was developing within the AFM itself, and that the movement was closely identified with Spínola.

Shortly before, the debate over the government's economic plan had resulted in another victory for the moderates. The plan announced late in February was much less radical than had been expected; in particular, it ruled out the idea of nationalising the banks and insurance houses and provided important guarantees for foreign investors.

Finally, despite the systematic disruption of democratic rallies by left-wing mobs (culminating in the wrecking of a mass meeting organised by the PPD in Setubal on 7 March) there were many reasons for thinking that the elections for a constituent assembly—which were then scheduled for 12 April, only a month away—would result in a rout for the Marxist left. The communists' own opinion polls had shown them that they would be lucky to get even ten per cent of the votes. It appeared that only the left had anything to gain by sabotaging the elections: the important thing for everyone else was that they should go ahead as scheduled, and that the ballot should be honest.

Seen against this background, the events of 11 March look like the combination of right-wing stupidity and left-wing cunning. Perhaps the historians will conclude that this was Portugal's Reichstag fire—or one of a series of Reichstag fires. At any rate, its effects were far-reaching. A situation was created in which the left had a free hand to carry forward the purge of potential rivals in the officer corps and the administration, to steamroll through a radical new economic programme and to dictate its own terms for the ballot and the country's future constitutional system. The beauty of it was that Portugal's allies in Nato were reduced to making baffled clucking noises in the background: had it not been shown that it was the supposed 'moderates', and not the communists, who were the enemies of democracy in Portugal?

The AFM's next steps supplied a partial answer to that

question. On the evening of the putsch most of the complicated machinery of the AFM was scrapped and a body described as the Supreme Revolutionary Council was set up in its place. This was a Portuguese version of the Committee of Public Safety: its powers were apparently limitless and it immediately initiated the great terror in Lisbon, locking up businessmen for such horrendous crimes as lending money to 'social reactionaries' and for unspecified forms of 'economic sabotage'. The twenty-four members of this Council—all military men—were mostly on the extreme left of the AFM. At the insistence of Admiral Crespo, the high commissioner in Mozambique, however, the Council was subsequently expanded to include himself, Major Vitor Alves, Major Melo Antunes and one other 'moderate'; the fact that these men now figured as 'moderates' in the AFM gives some indication of how far leftward the whole spectrum had moved.

The Council could write its own laws. The first was the decree ordering the state takeover of banks and insurance companies, which reversed the policy laid down in the three-year economic plan unveiled at the end of February. The political effects of this move were bound to be far-reaching. President Costa Gomes described the decree ordering the takeover of the fourteen private Portuguese banks as 'the most revolutionary law ever promulgated in this country'. Independent newspapers and opposition parties now had to apply to communist-run trade union committees for credit. The response seemed unlikely to be charitable. The same applied to private businessmen who, if not already driven out of the country as 'traitors' or bankrupted by the combination of a price freeze and soaring labour costs, now found themselves in a situation where they might be unable to borrow, since the top priority was to subsidise the losses of state-run firms.

The promised elections eventually went ahead, on the first anniversary of the coup against Caetano. They were honest and comparatively orderly elections which did register the strength of the non-communist majority in Portugal: the real victors were the socialists, with 38 per cent of the vote, and the PPD with 26.4 per cent. The communists trailed behind with 12.5 per cent, and their front movement, the MDP managed to scrape just over 4 per cent. The only party to the right of the ruling coalition, the Social Democratic Centre (CDS), won 7.6

per cent, with most of its votes coming from the conservative northern provinces. The various fringe left-wing groups—which had exercised quite disproportionate influence over some members of the Supreme Revolutionary Council—were wiped out. Another seven per cent of the electorate turned in blank votes, although AFM spokesmen had suggested to the voters that a blank ballot paper would be interpreted as a vote against the existing party system and in favour of a more representative system based on the radical military movement. The left-wing minister of information, Commander Correia Jesuino, had actually predicted that forty per cent of the electorate would turn in blank ballot papers.

The comparative failure of the CDS was perhaps the most surprising feature of the election—although its score had been privately predicted, to within a few percentage points, by its gentle and intellectual leader, Professor Diogo Freitas do Amaral. The CDS, after all, could be represented as the only genuine *alternative* to the existing regime.* It was also the only party whose leaders talked about the economic situation in a practical way in the course of the campaign, which was generally remarkable only for windy rhetorical outbursts and the presence of a permanent mob in the Lisbon streets. It could appeal to the deep conservatism of the smallholders of the North and make further capital from its intimate links with the Church—which, in a country of peasants where half the adult population is unable, for all practical purposes, to read or write, should have counted for something. Yet it trailed far behind the Communist Party in the final results.

This poor showing was related to the fact that the CDS was excluded from the media over the whole period up to the formal opening of the electoral campaign and that its rallies were systematically broken up—to the point where some meetings took place semi-clandestinely, and the party's leaders were reduced to sleeping in different houses every night and to watching the election results from a secret retreat on the outskirts of Lisbon. There was also the phenomenon of tactical voting, familiar among more sophisticated electorates: PPD sources admitted that their party had pulled in 6 to 7 per cent

*Major Sanches Osorio's Christian Democratic Party was banned after 11 March, and the small monarchist party (PPM) had espoused a largely socialist ideology.

more of the votes than they had expected and that this was probably due to the feeling that a vote for an opposition party would be wasted.

In any event, the poor showing of the CDS meant that the political initiative still rested with the non-communist parties of government. It was up to them to show whether they had the courage and the tactical skill to seize the opportunities that had now presented themselves—to show whether, in fact, the election amounted to anything more than a glorified public opinion poll. It must be borne in mind that the elections had been largely deprived of meaning by the steps that had been taken by the AFM after 11 March—above all, the 'pact' that the parties were obliged to enter into. The terms of the pact made it plain that the Supreme Revolutionary Council would remain the prime element in any future constitution, responsible to no one but itself and the shade of Karl Marx. In technical terms, all the election had achieved was the choice of 260 people to sit in a sort of glorified debating society and mull over the marginal questions.

But the scarcely-camouflaged displeasure of AFM left-wingers at the results showed that of course it meant more than that: it had provided a kind of mandate, if Soares and Balsemão were willing to use it. They could now press for a cabinet reshuffle to produce a more representative government. They could press for local elections to replace the MDP admin-istrations which had taken over by *fait accompli*; failing those elections, they could organise the occupation of the local authorities themselves—as some moderates in the AFM thought they should do. They could use the constituent assembly itself as a forum to ventilate many of those touchy issues that were never mentioned in the Lisbon press.

But these opportunities appeared to be lost a month after the election. The AFM left no one in doubt that it meant to carry on down its own road, and the communists (by excluding the socialists from the May Day rally) made it equally plain that what they lost in a ballot they could make up by their power in the streets. The continuing strength of the communists in Lisbon was related not only to their organisation and tactical skill, as already studied, but to the crucial fact that they were the only major civilian movement that gave total support to the AFM's drift into permanent military dictatorship. At every point, it was the communists who were there, flattering the praetorians (among whom the familiar addiction to power was becoming daily more compelling) with the notion that they should continue their rule indefinitely. The democratic parties—however far to the left they stood and however timidly they approached the soldiers—were always saying, in effect, that there must be a transition back to civilian rule and that elections should be taken seriously. There was reason to fear, a year after the revolution began, that this advice was highly unpalatable to a majority of men in the Supreme Revolutionary Council. This was not just a problem of the aims of the communists (in or out of uniform) but of the strange marriage of convenience that bound them to that larger group in the AFM who were perhaps best regarded as brigands.

I was forcibly struck at the time by the 'Cuban' atmosphere that surrounded many of the key figures in the AFM; the style of the new regime is perhaps best characterised as early *barbudo*. I went out to see Brigadier Otelo in the military governor's palace in Lisbon one evening just before the elections. The guards at the gate were all playing handball. In the guardroom across the courtyard, more soldiers (in various combinations of civilian and military attire) were absorbed in a French television serial based on an Alexandre Dumas novel which showed dukes in powdered wigs cavorting across the screen. On the wall was one of the legion of freshly-printed AFM posters. This one was designed to show the correct military appearance in Year One of the Revolution. On the left were sketches of soldier-hippies with hair flowing down over their shoulders and beards of truly prophetic dimensions in grubby and unpressed uniforms. These were labelled 'Mal'. On the right were sketches of soldiers with hair edging over their collars, long side-whiskers and somewhat shorter beards, labelled 'Bem'. It was not quite my idea of military appearance, but then, the Portuguese army is not quite a conventional army.

After a three-hour wait (during which I shared the antechamber with a crowd of civilians who had come to consult Otelo on all sorts of domestic problems) I was ushered in to see the Brigadier, a little after midnight. It was one of the most strikingly 'latin' features of the revolution: no one in a responsible post seemed to sleep—the nights were given over to endless talk. It was a revealing conversation, in which Otelo spoke of his admiration of the 'rich human experience' of Cuba (he was shortly to go there). We spoke for some time about Otelo's attacks on the Americans and on the US Ambassador in Lisbon, Frank Carlucci. He said that it was an insult to Portugal that the Americans had picked a well-known CIA operative with a Latin American background for the Portugal job. I asked if he had any evidence of covert American operations in Portugal. He admitted that he had none. Then I asked why—whether or not his allegations about Carlucci were true—no mention was ever made of the presence in Lisbon of Mr Kalinin, the Soviet Ambassador, and a well-known KGB operative who was formerly based in Cuba.

'He is very discreet', said Otelo, 'and anyway the press doesn't mention him. The people aren't concerned about him.' I could hardly refrain from pointing out that, in Lisbon today, what is said in the press is not entirely unrelated to what the government wants it to say. Otelo's reply was to ask why I was 'obsessed' with Russia. 'Good things come from Russia', he declared.

'For example?'

'Well, they send these cultural missions. The ballet girls and so on. I have never seen such good shows in my life.'

This is not an entirely unfair example of the relative political sophistication of a key leader of the AFM. What is saddening about a man like Otelo, who has considerable human charm, is his complete ignorance about his own country's constitutional history and his equally complete indifference to the democratic experience of other western countries. He says quite complacently that he is 'not impressed' by the British democratic experience, for example. The model is always being sought somewhere in the third world, in some more or less incompetent dictatorship—in Cuba, or Peru, or Algeria.

Given this kind of attitude, it seemed probable that Portugal would follow the Cuban path: a fluid and, if the AFM remained in power, romantic revolutionary movement will eventually be completely colonised by Moscow-line communism. Portugal is already the victim of economic circumstances that could result in this gradual, Cuban-style satellisation by the Soviet bloc. It has ditched the mineral wealth of Angola, the habits of frugal housekeeping that amassed the foreign reserves it is now gobbling up, and even the attractions of cheap labour and peaceful beaches. The soldiers returning from Africa—who were rapidly demobilised—created a large pool of unemployed. Inflation was running at over thirty-five per cent in 1974 mainly because of the reckless expansion of the monetary supply. (And yet the president of the Central Bank could say that monetary restraint was no longer necessary.) After the March decrees the smashing-up of private enterprise was accelerated. And no doubt the best and the brightest of the UN development experts will turn up before long to complete the collapse of the economy by urging gross government overspending to mop up unemployment, and the savage redistribution of wealth and incomes as a means of 'expanding the internal market'.

If it carries on down this road, Portugal could easily become the economic hostage of whatever power is willing to bail it out. Western bankers and governments are unlikely to queue up to do so before some reassurances—concerning both the management of the economy and the political future of the country—are given; and it is certainly not too soon to imagine the government auctioning off military facilities in the Azores and, indeed, in southern Portugal.

The covert Soviet role in Portugal which pre-dated the overthrow of Caetano steadily increased afterwards. A third of the members of the Soviet embassy (with a listed staff of about seventy) were believed by western intelligence sources to be KGB agents. This does not take account of the large number of 'technicians' and 'trade officials' posted to Lisbon, and of the activities of the East Europeans and the Cubans; the Cuban *Dirección General de Inteligencia* (DGI) which is supervised by a KGB controller in Havana,[7] was believed to have been especially successful in cultivating the Portuguese military.

From the time of the elections, the political conflict in Portugal narrowed into an ideological tussle between the orthodox communists and the New Left—some of whose leaders were urging the AFM to ban all political parties and to set up a network of Cuban-style revolutionary committees as a link between radical soldiers and the people. The socialists tried vainly to translate their electoral success into political power. Instead, the socialist paper *República* was seized by communist printers and eventually closed down on the orders of the

Supreme Revolutionary Council. The socialists were finally driven to resign from the government early in July, creating a situation that was eerily reminiscent of Prague in February 1948.

Mario Soares, the socialist leader, had earlier complained to the French press that 'if you are not a communist in Portugal today, then you are a reactionary and an enemy of the people'. It was a sad post-mortem on what many people had once conceived to be Portugal's democratic experiment. The uncertainty that remained was related to the breakdown of discipline and the normal command hierarchies in the armed forces, which created a situation in which (in the view of some observers) a thousand trained men who had chosen their targets well might be able to mount a coup-within-the-coup.

But a sea-change came over Portugal in the summer of 1975. The Communists in government were now seen to be dangerously isolated, and their efforts to set up a united front with the fringe groups on the revolutionary left (through the Unitary Revolutionary Front, founded on August 25th) came to nothing. The prime minister, Vasco Gonçalves, was opposed by all the democratic parties and by four-fifths of the officers of the AFM. Despite continuing support from President Costa Gomes—whose total and now—public commitment to the Communists in government prolonged a crisis that appeared to be dragging the country into a potentially bloody civil war—Vasco Gonçalves was finally replaced on 29 August, when he was nominated as chief of staff of the armed forces. The air force and a majority of army officers blankly refused to accept his new appointment, which may well have been intended as the prelude to a new series of purges of anti-Communists, and Vasco Gonçalves was finally pushed into retirement a week later.

With the removal of Vasco Gonçalves, the way was clear for a tactical compromise between the Communists and the non-Communist left—notably the Socialist Party and the group of AFM radicals identified with Major Melo Antunes, Brigadier Charais and Brigadier Pezarat Correia, the commanders of the central and southern military regions. But it was increasingly unlikely that a tactical compromise of this type would offer any sufficient solutions for Portugal's immense economic and social problems, or any lasting basis for genuine democracy.

And behind the governmental crises being played out in Lisbon and Tancos (the air force base where the final decision was taken to drop Vasco Gonçalves) a broader struggle for power was being waged in Portugal in relation to which the internecine feuds within the AFM looked more and more marginal, if not altogether irrelevant.

In late July and early August, there were the first unmistakeable tremors of a new political earthquake in Portugal. In small towns across the north, the offices of the Communist Party and its sister-movement, the MDP, were put to the torch by angry mobs of Catholics. The Church (which in Portugal has never succumbed to those notions of 'Christian-Marxist dialogue' that are fashionable in other latin countries) broke its silence, and prelates like the bishops of Braga and Leiria rose to denounce atheistic Communism. The local organisers of the democratic parties—the Socialists, the PPD, the CDS, the PPM—began to wage the 'battle for the streets' as the Communists had taught them.

With the emergence of the Portuguese Liberation Army (ELP) and similar right-wing guerrilla groups well-organised for battle, and the return of tens of thousands of refugees from Angola who had no reason to love a government which they blamed for civil war and the loss of their livelihoods, the way seemed to be opening up for a far-reaching counter-revolution in Portugal. The 'Angolan factor' alone—the return of 365,000 white settlers by 11 November, when the territory was scheduled to achieve independence—was enough to transform the whole balance of social power in Portugal, a country with only nine million people. The Communists in Lisbon correctly perceived the airlift of refugees (at the rate of some 4,000 a day by September) as a direct challenge to their own political survival.

The groundswell of anti-Communism in Portugal late in 1975 held out the possibility, not merely that Alvaro Cunhal's party would be driven from power, but that the country would at last enter into a genuine experiment in pluralism, both political and economic. But a well-organised and, in this case, well-armed Communist party has never been known to give up power willingly, and the risk remained of a bloody confrontation in which any remaining hope of democracy would be extinguished, and possibly of an attempt at a pre-emptive 'night of the long knives' by the Marxist militas. The effects of a worsening crisis that had been initially muted by the existence of the huge foreign currency reserves bequeathed by the old regime (which could be said, in a real sense, to have paid for the Portuguese revolution) also supplied arguments for a temporary' phase of conservative dictatorship.

Whoever the ultimate beneficiary of Portugal's erratic revolution proves to be, it shook the sleep from the eyes of many liberals and social democrats in Western Europe who had come to accept Communism as a party *comme les autres*. The pro-Communist mob outside the Belem palace on 27 August chanted, *'Morte a CIA. Abaixe a social-democracia'*. ('Death to the CIA. Down with social democracy.') The bedraggled set of camp-followers (like Mrs Judith Hart MP) who turned up in Lisbon in the guise of members of democratic parties to praise the 'democratic' aims of Vasco Gonçalves and his friends were clearly seen for what they were.

This chapter remains open to the future. What can be said, by way of conclusion, is that if any hope that representative government can be made to work in Portugal has now dawned, it is because the great majority have learned what it means through the experience of Communist proto-dictatorship, and managed to find leadership and organisation before it was too late. But not many societies live to survive this kind of apprenticeship. If Portugal does survive it, the Portuguese are unlikely to deal charitably with their former task-masters.

11

The Limits of Tolerance

Any man who seeks to overthrow a state based on law is guilty of the greatest crime of which a man is capable. He becomes the common enemy of all mankind and must be treated as such. *John Locke*

'The whole post-fascist period is one of clear and present danger. Consequently, true pacification requires the withdrawal of tolerance before the deed, at the stage of communication in word, print and picture. Such extreme suspension of the right of free speech and free assembly is indeed justified only if the whole of society is in extreme danger. I maintain that our society is in such an emergency situation, and that it has become the normal state of affairs.'[1]

Who is the author of this remarkably lucid statement? He is clearly no great friend of a free press, or perhaps of freedom in any form. He clearly knows what kind of society he wants, and is ready to apply systematic repression ('the withdrawal of tolerance before the deed') to those who think differently. But for the somewhat abstract language in which he chooses to express himself, one might be tempted to guess that the author was an uncompromising reactionary.

He is, in fact, Herbert Marcuse, the doyen of the New Left, who encourages his disciples to fight the 'repressive tolerance' of a liberal society with a 'partisan tolerance' that will eventually silence rival opinion. In his quarrel with the kind of society that allows him to write and publish what he pleases, Marcuse has posed a central problem for the defenders of that society: what are the limits of tolerance? Up to what point should we tolerate *intolerant* movements and ideologies? Up to what point should we be prepared to extend those rights of free speech and free assembly (which Marcuse would like to deny to people with whom he happens to disagree) to totalitarian groups that aim at the overthrow of democracy?

Classical liberal thinking offers no adequate guidelines—

perhaps because this is a dilemma that the classical liberals, pursuing their debates in a clublike atmosphere, had not fully had to face. The most celebrated statement of liberal doctrine on tolerance is John Stuart Mill's essay *On Liberty*. Mill was deeply concerned with the problem that has recurred throughout this book: the need to defend the individual against 'the tyranny of prevailing opinion'. To this end, he formulated a famous definition of the one reason that, in his view, entitled the state or society as a whole to apply coercion (legal, physical or moral) to the individual: 'the sole end for which mankind are warranted, individually or collectively, in interfering with the liberty of action of any of their number, is self-protection . . . The only purpose for which power can rightfully be exercised over any member of a civilised society, against his will, is to prevent harm to others. His own good, either physical or moral, is not a sufficient warrant.'[2] From this general principle, he proceeded to argue the case for complete freedom of thought and expression. To prevent the expression of unpalatable ideas, in Mill's view, was to assume infallibility. And even if the censors were right in their own beliefs, they would reduce them to mere bigotry by suppressing the discipline of lively discussion that is essential to 'a real understanding of moral and human subjects.[3] What is true of philosophy is true also of politics, where the basic tension will always be between a party of order and a party of change: it is through the open give-and-take between them that each will be given its due.

All this is relevant today, but hardly serves as a practical guide. Mill was applying the doctrine of *laissez-faire* to ideas: let them contend in the market-place, and reason will triumph. The trouble with this approach is that it gravely underrates man's need for certainties and something even more fundamental: the extent to which man *apprehends* rather than comprehends the truth. The attack on Mill's philosophy of tolerance in his own day came from conservative thinkers who belonged to an older, and more permanent tradition, who believed that the state had a fundamental moral duty to lead and educate the citizen, rather than adopt a neutral posture while he chose between contending beliefs. J. F. Stephen, Mill's most systematic critic, offered the view that 'all government has and must of necessity have a moral basis, and the connection between morals and religion is so intimate that this implies a religious basis as well.'[4] Stephen believed that most people were incapable of discriminating between different ideas on a rational basis and that it was unlikely that society would ever reach the Utopian phase in which important matters would be determined by rational discussion. Mill had underrated the necessity for social coercion and the danger of alienation and a destructive scepticism when the state failed to provide a moral lead. In Stephen's view, social intolerance, far from being an evil, was one of the bonds that knit society together.

Mill and Stephen are the exponents of the two sides in a debate from which the truth can emerge only dialectically: through the synthesis of what each is saying. The terms of their argument (and its religious focus) have a somewhat archaic ring today. These were men who were not familiar with a situation in which universities and organs of opinion could be usurped by Marxist cliques—although Stephen, profoundly sceptical about the way that freedom could be abused in a permissive society, would have been less surprised than Mill to observe these recent developments. But even Mill would surely have modified his argument if he had found that his market-place of opinions was ceasing to be a market-place in any sense.

A society cannot be neutral between its life and its death—between those, for example, who are ready to work within the limits of a democratic system, and those who are working for its overthrow. Mill's inadequacy in this respect is shared by many contemporary liberals who seem to regard the world of politics as a glorified debating society. In their commitment to respecting all ideas as sacrosanct, they have often failed to organise the effective defence of their own philosophy. The noble but now threadbare statement of faith: 'I may disagree with your opinion, but I would die for your right to say it', loses meaning if the man addressed is proposing to kill the speaker. It is not just a question of what we will tolerate, but of what we will *defend*.

Where Stephen was surely right was in his conviction that a society cannot hold together without a public philosophy that embraces positive as well as negative values: a consensus involving the ends as well as the limits of politics. In a democratic society, this consensus may be remarkably inclusive. But tolerance reaches further. It encompasses groups (communists, fascists etcetera) that are openly anti-democratic but are able to exploit the liberties and the political opportunities afforded to them by a free society. Tolerance towards such groups, however, cannot be infinitely elastic. How far it may be stretched or circumscribed will depend on historical circumstances; above all, on the immediacy of the threat that such movements are seen to pose to democratic institutions and on whether or not they resort to violence and other illegal methods.

The trouble is that if the opportunities for a totalitarian threat to grow are left open for too long, a democratic government may find it literally impossible to act. No doubt most people (excluding a few gentlemen now in Argentina or the French Foreign Legion) would agree that it would have been a good thing for democracy if the National Socialist Party had been banned under the Weimar Republic. But it is not all that easy to see how this would have worked out in practice. To begin with, the Nazis were by no means the only movement in Weimar Germany that was hostile to the constitution. They were not alone in practising street violence and setting up strong-arm squads. There was a whole congeries of right-wing groups and para-military militias, and there was a strong Communist Party which had recently experimented in insurrectionary tactics. Even-handed justice would have demanded that in banning the National Socialist Party, the government should have acted at the same time against all other movements that were guilty of the crimes attributed to the Nazis. In the Weimar situation, this would have meant asking a weak and divided group of centre and centre-left politicians, unsure of their army, to take action against powerful and dynamic groups on both flanks.

But the argument that the Nazis should have been banned does not rest so much on the dreadful things that they did on the road to power as on the dreadful things they did afterwards—which is to say that the argument is really that they should have been banned because they were successful. Yet the key to their success is that they were able to exploit the political openings that the Weimar system of democracy offered to them. This was an anti-democratic movement which assumed power by democratic means.

It is just one of the many cases studied in this book where a totalitarian movement successfully cultivated pseudo-legitimacy within a democratic context. There are things that the Weimar democrats could have attempted in the effort to curb their enemies: they could, for example, have made a more determined effort to retain a monopoly of force in the hands of the state by disarming the Freikorps and the veterans' associations. They could have chosen a different electoral mechanism; it has been suggested that if Germany had had constituency voting instead of a system of proportional representation, the social democrats would have won 186 (instead of 143) seats in the crucial Reichstag elections of September 1930, and that the Nazis would have won only 48 (instead of 107).[5] But these are the sterile 'ifs' of history. It was not the electoral system that produced Hitler. The consensus was too weak, the experience of liberal democracy too novel, the economic problems too catastrophic in Weimar Germany to have made it possible for the democrats to have taken decisive measures against their enemies. If they had tried, they might well have brought down in revolution what was to be brought down anyway through the workings of the system itself.

Leaving the specific problem of Nazi Germany, it is clearly not open to a liberal government consistent in its own beliefs to prosecute ideas or to ban political movements on the grounds that they subscribe to an anti-democratic ideology. A government that behaved this way would be open to many of the same charges that it levelled at its opponents. Furthermore, its action might only serve to drive the menace underground and even to endow it with a romantic halo—and ready-made martyrs—that would add to, rather than detract from, its popular appeal. This was one of the reasons for doubt about the measure adopted by the French government in 1973, after violent street demonstrations, when the Trotskyist Ligue Communiste and the extreme right-wing movement Ordre Nouveau were both banned on the grounds that they constituted a threat to public security. Neither movement, of course, was really dissolved: their cell-structures remained intact, and Ordre Nouveau promptly re-emerged under a new name. The justification for such a move is obvious only in a situation of internal war (which can, and should, be legally defined): it was arguably intolerable, for example, that until the end of 1974 the IRA was able to function—and raise funds—as a political movement in Britain while simultaneously waging open war on the British Army in Northern Ireland.

The full measure of this problem becomes apparent when one remembers that the powerful Communist Parties of France and Italy are only an election (or, in the Italian case, a backroom bargain) away from assuming power in Chilean-style coalitions and that both have long been accepted as legitimate and even democratic movements by large bodies of electors. They cannot be banned by a democratic government on the grounds that they might be successful; indeed, as their chances of returning to government increase, their leaders can reasonably argue that this is proof that they represent a popular force of considerable magnitude with as much right to present itself as democratic as anyone else. We are back with the dilemma of the democrats in Weimar or Chile in 1970: what do you do if your enemies decide to play by your rules and beat you according to them?

I would like to propose one general principle: that, in the interests of their own survival, liberal democrats should never lose sight of the fact that totalitarian movements in their societies are being allowed to operate *on sufferance*. There must be no relaxation of the drive to expose their real aims and tactics and, indeed, their entire organisational structure. We have already observed some of the basic organisational differences between a totalitarian movement and a conventional political party: the movement will always operate on three distinct levels—through the legal party, through front organisations and through the clandestine apparatus. Each must be recognised and tackled in its own terms. Ideas move the world, certainly, but no one can come to terms with the present challenges to democracy if he ignores the uses of the organisational weapon. It is because Mr Mill never had to come to terms with that, that his views on tolerance seem so Utopian today.

If we can agree that anti-democratic movements should be tolerated only on sufferance, then we can also agree that there are things that they should not be allowed to do and opportunities that they should not be allowed to exploit. Members of such movements should not, for example, be allowed to occupy positions in the civil service. Nor should they be allowed to propound their ideologies in the classroom. If they are permitted to present their political views through a state broadcasting system, then it should at least be made plain to the audience that this is not professional reporting, but a partisan statement.

Education is an egregious example in Britain of an area where government—while expanding its control over schooling at a pace which has appalled those who believe in an independent system—has simultaneously disregarded its duty to ensure that the schooling it provides will be *liberal* in the broadest sense of the word. Other countries provide safeguards against the propaganda activities of political extremists masquerading as schoolteachers, by one of two devices: (i) by requiring teachers to sign a pledge to the effect that they will not promote their political views in the classroom; or (ii) by denying access to employment to the members of organisations 'hostile to the constitution' on the grounds that state teachers are civil servants like, say, employees of the Home Office or the Ministry of Defence. The pledge is used in America; the ban is enforceable under West German law, although rarely employed. Britain has neither.

It does not even have provision for central regulation of school curricula, although there is scope for this through the deployment of Her Majesty's Inspectors of Schools (first appointed by Lord John Russell in the early nineteenth century) whose functions have been allowed to atrophy. The initiative rests with school boards of governors and local authorities, which have been shown by a number of notorious recent incidents to have neglected their responsibilities. One or two will have to suffice.

Early in 1975, an interesting discussion pamphlet was distributed to fourth-year students at the large Holland Park Comprehensive in West London. It was entitled *Law and Order* and was written (in a barely literate style) by a teacher at the school as background for a 'social education' project. It was distinguished, first, by its description of the legal system and, second, by its criticisms of the police. According to the anonymous author, 'it would be tempting to say that the courts are there to provide justice. This is not true.' Law, it would appear, is largely concerned with the defence of property and is applied by a police force that 'favours the rich'. The main

reason why the police adopt this social attitude is apparently
plain stupidity:

> There are no qualifications at all to join the police, except
> that you have to be taller than five foot eight inches and
> physically fit. There is an entrance exam which you would
> have to be really silly to fail. So to a person with not much
> chance at anything else, the police force represents a job
> with prestige, responsibility, an attractive ammount [sic] of
> power (In what other job do you START by telling people
> what to do?) good chances of promotion, which is quite well
> paid and would be considered by most people to be a 'step
> up' the social ladder. Such a man is not going to stand by and
> let an oppertunity [sic] pass . . .

Another factor, the pupils are told, is the brain-washing that
policemen, like soldiers, are made to undergo in order to
practise complete obedience.

> It is extremely difficult for a person to work with
> enthusiasm for too long, doing things that he does not
> approve or beleive [sic] in. So with the policeman it is not a
> case of his own ideas against the people that he works for.
> The question is: how do you get all those men to beleive
> [sic] in the same things? . . . It is done in the same way that
> every armed force does it: all the things that make a man
> seem an individual, the things that make him seem different
> from all the others, are taken away. First his name is replaced
> by a number then the way in which he looks is made the
> same as all the others by cutting his hair and providing the
> same uniform. Any forces training school will only allow
> you to bring a few of your own things with you, so you are
> no longer surrounded by the things that express your likes
> and dislikes . . .

Finally, the policeman is detached from his old neigh-
bourhood and friends; the police 'loose [sic] contact with their
freinds [sic], even those who would be willing to know a
policeman, and with that they loose [sic] contact with any
variety or difference in ideas.'
    Plenty of food for thought here. The last page of the Holland
Park pamphlet suggests a few 'things to write and talk about'.
The suggestions give a fair idea of just what kind of social

studies project was being launched. Pupils are invited to consider propositions such as 'There's one law for the rich and another for the poor' or 'Anyone who gives information to the police about a criminal is an informer and deserves to be beaten up.' Another question reads:

> People no longer think of the policeman as the freindly [sic] bobby. They think of him as a 'bleedin copper'. Do you think that the publics' [sic] attitude to the police has changed? If so why do you think this is?

Finally, pupils are asked to describe their rights if stopped and searched by the police or placed under arrest.

Quite apart from anything else, this document, bristling with elementary spelling mistakes and other schoolboy howlers, could hardly be described as a model of the prose-writer's art; it is extraordinary for that reason alone that the headmaster of a large school was prepared to allow it to be distributed to 360 boys and girls. I am drawn to wonder how the author of *Law and Order* would have fared in that police entrance exam that he thought you would have to be 'really silly' to fail. But the most disturbing aspect is the pamphlet's crude anti-police bias and the kindergarten Marxism implicit in its discussion of the supposed class basis of British justice. Its whole tone seems calculated to exacerbate the problems of communication between the police and the community in the racially tense areas of Notting Hill from which some of the school's pupils were drawn. The only consoling footnote to be added is that, in a typically English way, local police officers who later visited the Holland Park Comprehensive to address the 'social education' course appear to have defused the explosive elements in the document through direct contact and discussion.

It did not entirely escape attention that the wife of the then Labour Secretary of State for Industry, Mr Benn, was a member of the Board of Governors of Holland Park Comprehensive, and that a large body of its pupils were trooped out to listen to the speech he made during the May Day rally in Trafalgar Square in 1975.

I have quoted this example at some length because it is a good illustration of how some militant teachers in Britain have been allowed to distort the purposes of education and import their own dogmas into school curricula. There are more dramatic examples to be found. Two recent ones are the decision of the Birmingham local education authorities to include Marxism on the religious studies syllabus, and the efforts of Trotskyist school-teachers to distribute propaganda leaflets (often devoted to foreign issues such as Vietnam or Chile) in schools in north London.

But it must be emphasised that, in an open society, it is the responsibility of the community as a whole—not merely that of governments acting through police powers and statute law—to apply the necessary controls. You cannot legislate in such a society, for example, to prevent the proprietor of a great liberal newspaper from employing Trotskyists and agreeing—without any legal compulsion being applied to him—to institute a closed shop for journalists that could give the militants eventual control of his journal's editorial policy. You cannot legislate in such a society to prevent the arch-capitalist proprietor of a great popular publishing house from appointing and tolerating editors who will turn it into a library of neo-Marxist literature. There is no want of examples of how many of the people with a vested interest in the survival of a capitalist system have, consciously or unconsciously, acceded to its undermining.

I would like to suggest the following general conclusions as guidelines for a democratic society that is confronted with totalitarian enemies:

1 No man should be punished for his beliefs, which should be allowed free expression except where such expression violates normal criminal law—for example, the laws of libel or laws forbidding incitement to violence.

2 But no democratic state is under a fundamental obligation to tolerate *parties or organisations* that aim at overthrowing the constitution and achieving absolute rule. Nor is it morally obliged to grant them equality with democratic parties before the law.

3 An organisation that declares its intention to seize absolute power has, *morally speaking,* placed itself outside the law and cannot claim its protection. From this perspective, it is immaterial whether it operates illegally or under the cloak of pseudo-legality, since its

purposes remain constant.

4 Such organisations can therefore be tolerated only *on sufferance,* and appropriate legal and administrative curbs must be maintained on their scope for manoeuvre.

5 Such curbs might be viewed as part of a strategy of *civilised intolerance* which would presumably be acceptable to democrats of all persuasions so long as the following principle was observed: that if all political groups working within the law are free to use certain channels, there can be no objection to barring certain other channels to all of them.

6 But it is also the responsibility of a liberal democracy to defend its own ideals and traditions through the promotion of the public philosophy as it has been defined in this book—that is, not as a partisan doctrine, but as a transcendent body of beliefs about the values and purposes of a free society. De Tocqueville doubted 'whether man can support at the same time complete religious independence and entire public freedom. And I am inclined to think, that if faith be wanting in him, he must serve, and if he be free, he must believe.'[6] The purpose of education should be moral as well as vocational, and a system that aspires to be 'value-free' about the relative merits of a liberal democracy and a totalitarian order, or (worse still) tolerates the propagation of totalitarian ideas in the classroom is bringing about its own downfall. The same applies to state-controlled broadcasting media.

It will be observed that I am in no way suggesting the suppression of communist or other anti-democratic literature. I believe with Milton that the 'scanning of error' may be necessary to the 'confirmation of truth'. 'What wisdom can there be to choose, what continence to forbear, without the knowledge of evil?'[7] What I am suggesting is that the freedom of the individual is possible only in a society that prevents some of its members from usurping the freedom of others. The brain-washing and 'thought reforming' regimes of the communist world have no doubt about their right to be *systematically* intolerant of dissident ideas and to impose total ideological conformity on their subject populations. In the ideological conflict that is now being waged, our chances of survival are reduced if democrats do not accept the need for *selective* intolerance, based on stated regulations, and for the moral education of their young.

12
Violence and the State

I wanted to show the bourgeoisie that their pleasures would no longer be complete, that their insolent triumphs would be disturbed, that their golden calf would tremble violently on its pedestal, until the final shock would cast it down in mud and blood.

Emile Henry (anarchist bomber) Paris, 1893

The first duty of the state is to establish a monopoly of legitimate violence and to secure the enforcement of law throughout the whole of its territory. When the state is not *seen* to be fulfilling this basic function, in the face of a serious and sustained upsurge of violence—either criminal or political—we can be sure of one thing: that sooner or later, ordinary citizens will either take the law into their own hands or will be disposed to support a new form of government better equipped to deal with the threat. Once the state is seen to have lost its monopoly of force, it will prove to be increasingly difficult to prevent successive groups from intruding upon it. This is surely one of the lessons of the British experience in Northern Ireland, and of several Latin American democracies (notably Uruguay and Argentina today) which, through their failure to suppress political violence, have engendered a situation in which private vigilantes step into the breach and in which the widespread demand for 'strong government' may produce a military or authoritarian takeover.

A sustained campaign of political violence is profoundly subversive of democracy. I would agree that Britain is not in imminent danger of finding its institutions overthrown because of a fresh spate of anarchist terrorism, a new IRA bombing campaign, or the sporadic attacks of 'ideological mercenaries' like the Palestinian commandos and their auxiliaries. West Germany was not brought to its knees by the Baader-Meinhof gang and its successors, and the effect of the Weathermen, the Symbionese Liberation Army and their imitators in the United

States can be rated, in political and military terms, as no more than a pinprick. The anarchist bombings in Paris in 1892-4 did not bring down the Third Republic in France, despite its already shaky condition. But it would be dangerous to assume from such examples that political violence will fail to have the same corrosive effects that were evident in central Europe after 1918, Uruguay and Argentina or Northern Ireland today, in societies that are generally assumed to be more cohesive and where sympathy for revolutionary violence would appear to be more limited.

Political violence needs to be viewed as part of a continuum: as the razor-edge of those broader processes of subversion and alienation that are sapping the foundations of Western societies. Terrorism is an overt form of internal warfare, just as the techniques of subversion already described are covert forms of internal warfare. Paul Wilkinson puts it well in a recent book when he declares that 'terrorism is the most flagrant form of defiance of the rule of law. It challenges government's prerogative of the monopoly of armed force within the state. Terrorists attempt to replace the laws of the state by their own laws of the gun and the kangaroo court. It is therefore vital for government to act speedily and forcefully against them and, above all, to preserve their power to govern.'[1] It can hardly be said strongly enough that those who plant bombs or plan assassinations are making *war* on society. Whatever justifications may be contrived for this type of violence in a non-democratic state, none of them apply in a society that allows the means for peaceful change.

Thus 'sociological' attempts to come to terms with the social motivation of terrorists in the West and to identify the 'just grievances' that they represent will be found to lead us down a blind alley. The conquest of political violence is the signal achievement of modern democratic societies, and those who challenge it with force are endangering a political culture that is infinitely more precious than any of the causes that they may claim to represent. There is thus a fundamental responsibility for democratic governments to respond with whatever force is necessary to deal with a specific terrorist threat.

I would agree, again, that the force employed should be *minimal,* but only in the sense that it should be the minimum force that is *necessary.* Determining exactly what this will mean in a particular situation will involve taking account of popular response, and popular demands, as well as of an exact evaluation of the threat. The danger of over-responding has been frequently discussed. The danger of under-responding, which is less often pointed out, is equally great. The danger is apparent—to take an example from the world of common crime—when a lenient judge hands down a suspended sentence to a rapist who has assaulted two housewives at knife-point, and had actually returned to the home of the first with a friend, presumably to assault her again. This happened recently, in a notorious case in Britain, where the judge's decision was based on the argument that the assailant had been undergoing severe emotional problems and had been unable to restrain his sexual impulses. This was hardly an argument that was likely to appeal to his victims, one of whom had felt compelled to move house in order to avoid a possible second attack. It was an argument, on the other hand, that seemed bound to persuade other would-be rapists that the law was on their side, and to persuade the families of victims that the only way to exact satisfactory retribution was to take the law into their own hands.

This may seem alarmist; but the human desire for 'an eye for an eye' is only held in check by the conviction that justice exists and will be properly meted out—and of course, by long habits of civility and non-violence. That conviction that justice will be applied is at risk when criminals or terrorists are seen to be evading it through the inefficiency or exaggerated leniency of the policing and legal authorities. You then have the conditions for the 'death wish' style of vigilante action, for political counter-violence and so for the disintegration of the common rule of law which, as we have seen, is fundamental to the survival of liberal democracy. I wish that the sociologists who give so much attention to the sources of political or criminal violence would give equal attention to the roots of counter-violence: to the symbiotic link between the rise of Protestant vigilante groups in Ulster and the widespread feeling that the IRA was not being tackled head-on, for example, or between the successful career of the Ejército Revolucionario del Pueblo (ERP) and its sister-groups in Argentina (one of which exacted a ransom of $50 million in June 1975) and the emergence of a right-wing vigilante group, the Alianza Anticomunista Argentina.

Political violence in Western societies is used for a variety of purposes. Short-term goals may include publicity, fund-raising, the extortion of political or social concessions (for example, agreement from a company to re-employ men who have been laid off), the demoralisation of the legally constituted authorities, or sheer psychological gratification. Longer-term goals may include regional secession, violent insurrection or—in the case of *agents provocateurs,* who make frequent appearances in the annals of terrorism—the creation of a pretext for an authoritarian *coup d'état.* All serious terrorists understand the corrosive effects of violence and the dilemma that it poses for a democratic government. Left-wing terrorists, following the strategy defined by the failed Brazilian guerrilla theorist, Carlos Marighella[2] hope to create a 'pre-revolutionary' situation in which society will become polarised between two extremes. If the government reacts strongly, according to this thesis, it will alienate moderates and create extra sympathy for the revolutionary cause. If it reacts feebly, it will still lose out, finding itself under attack from both the right and the left.

Terrorist groups in Western societies belong to one of the following categories:

1 *Marxist revolutionary groups.* These are characterised by their adherence to a coherent Marxist ideology—Communist, Maoist, Trotskyist or some modish combination of the three. It should be noted that, although orthodox Communist parties in Western Europe have eschewed terrorist methods, for the obvious reason that there is more to be gained, in the short-term, through peaceful subversion, there is a significant body of evidence on Soviet support for political violence. It is sufficient to mention the allegations of the West German interior minister in May 1975 on covert Russian support for terrorist groups, including the Italian *Brigate Rossi,* which was borne out by a secret intelligence report that was publicised in Rome about the same time.[3]

2 *Secessionist groups.* Minority nationalist groups depend on the support of a minority of ethnic, religious or linguistic minorities at odds with the majority community. Secessionist movements in Europe include the IRA (Provisional and Official) in Northern Ireland; the

Breton Liberation Front (FLB) in Brittany; the Jura Liberation Movement in Switzerland; the Basque ETA (V Assembly) group and the Catalan Liberation Front (FAC) in Spain, and a number of less well-organised groups in Corsica, Scotland, Wales and other areas that have generated claims to regional independence.

3 *Anarchist groups.* Traditional anarchist philosophy continues to inspire some revolutionary groups in southern Europe, and notably in Spain, where the Iberian Liberation Movement (MIL) has been involved in terrorist actions. The term 'anarchist' is used more loosely to describe ideologically incoherent groups such as the Baader-Meinhof gang in West Germany, the Angry Brigade in Britain, and side-shows such as the 'We Must Do Something' commune in France, which has staged bombings of foreign corporations.

4 *Neo-fascist and extreme right-wing groups.* Italy is the only notable contemporary example in Western Europe, although such groups remain active in the Hispanic world (including Spain) sometimes with covert backing from local security forces.

5 *Pathological groups and individuals.* Most of the aircraft hi-jackers in the United States during the rash of 'skyjackings' in the early 1970s belong to this category. But there are also groups—including the Red Star Army in Japan and the Symbionese Liberation Army in America—where the revolution is apparently conceived as a way of life rather than a coherent political cause. Here the prevailing motivation seems to be related to personal inadequacy or white middle-class guilt feelings rather than to ideology or specific social grievances.

6 *Ideological mercenaries.* This is not so much a separate type as a distinct mode of behaviour: the export of a violent revolutionary cause across state frontiers. The Palestinians and the Japanese Red Army pioneered this type of transnational terrorism, and there is now some evidence to suggest that Latin American groups may follow suit.

I do not propose to examine any of these groups, or the recent evolution of terrorist tactics, in detail here. There is now a body of literature on the subject, including the report of the

Institute for the Study of Conflict on *The New Dimensions of Security* in Europe and the author's own *Urban Guerrillas,* which the interested reader may consult. What needs to be noted is the ever-expanding range of targets for terrorism. Indiscriminate bombings of the kind committed by the IRA in Britain (as well as in Ulster) or by fringe anarchist and neo-fascist groups in Italy, place every man, woman and child in the front line. The range of targets for selective terrorism includes many private individuals as well as government officials and members of the security forces: businessmen are popular targets, because of the established readiness of their companies to pay blood-money.[4] The legal system is another obvious target; in West Berlin in November 1974, a magistrate was killed in retaliation for the death of a member of the Baader-Meinhof gang who had been on hunger strike. The situation in Argentina, where the intimidation and harassment of judges and their families has made it virtually impossible to obtain an honest verdict in any 'sensitive' case, gives some idea of how far this can lead.[5] The further terrorists cast their nets, the more urgent the requirement for the government to respond, and be *seen* to respond, effectively.

I wish to confine myself here to stating some of the basic principles, and modalities of counter-action. We cannot begin without sloughing off what should now be seen as a delusion: the notion that a serious terrorist campaign is, by definition, the product of social oppression and legitimate grievances that can only be dealt with by far-reaching social reforms. I am not suggesting that there is no such thing as deprivation, and indeed the sense of *relative* deprivation is usually found to be the psychological motor of serious social upheavals. What I would insist on, however, is that in a society that allows for peaceful change and the free expression of opinion, armed revolutionaries cannot be accepted as spokesmen for legitimate pressure groups. Our intellectual pacifism extends, in many instances, to the argument that political violence is merely the symptom of a social malaise that must be tackled at source and that a policy of straightforward anti-terrorist action is no better than sticking a plaster on an ulcer. Violence could, perhaps, be described as a means of bringing about 'necessary' social change in situations *where all other roads are blocked;* the Soviet Union would be an excellent example. But the argument does not apply in situations where other roads are open—even in situations where a minority group has difficulty in asserting its views. It is significant that those who support the need to assert 'minority rights' through the gun and the bomb in the case of a 'socially deprived' black minority or a group that supports the reunification of Ireland would not extend the principle to other minority groups that might feel similarly at odds with a democratic majority—for example, landowners whose property is confiscated, or small businessmen and shopkeepers whose ability to keep their businesses 'in the family' is destroyed by a tax on capital transfers.

A young American radical said in 1968 that 'the whole ability to function as a revolutionary . . . depends upon the ability to depersonalise your enemy.'[6] In other words, label the enemy as 'imperialism' or 'capitalism' and bomb away. We must be careful not to do the same, but equally careful not to err on the side of excessive 'humanisation' of the practitioners of violence. The personal background and the ideological claims of a terrorist are secondary to the fact that he is waging war on society. In a democratic country, he is waging war on a kind of society whose prime attribute, perhaps, is that it minimises the use of force as a political weapon, by governments as well as citizens. A democratic government therefore should never be seen to *reward* terrorism (or the use of other forms of physical coercion) by granting political concessions. Nor should it be seen, through negotiations with terrorists, to endorse their claims to represent a legitimate bargaining partner. Such behaviour can only lend credibility to the terrorists' propaganda claims and encourage others to borrow their methods.

The response to political violence in a given situation will hinge upon the government's estimate of the threat and on the prevailing state of public opinion. The battle is primarily a battle for minds. Since the overwhelming majority of the population in Western democratic societies is opposed to the use of violence for political ends, the burden on governments will be less to demonstrate the need for action against terrorism than to justify the specific measures that are adopted. The kind of political debate that will subsequently ensue will frequently revolve around allegations of excessive brutality on the part of the security forces and of an unwarranted intrusion on civil liberties.

A whole literature on this theme was produced by critics of the British army's operations in Northern Ireland, alleging 'torture', brutality in the conduct of searches, and the killing of innocent civilians. It was supplemented by complaints lodged by bodies such as the National Council for Civil Liberties alleging the violation of civil liberties in the course of police searches conducted in the aftermath of the IRA bombing raids in Britain. Such complaints—to those who have witnessed the remarkable restraint and self-discipline of the British army in Northern Ireland at close quarters—will often appear like the outburst of the man who protested that his carpets were being ruined while the fire brigade doused his house in an effort to prevent it burning to the ground. But it must also be recognised that such complaints are inevitable, not merely (and perhaps not least) as a result of honest doubts about the use of public force, but as a result of systematic black propaganda designed to discredit the security forces and undermine their morale. There are daily examples of such black propaganda concerning the Northern Ireland campaign.

The onus is therefore on the government to mount an effective educational campaign to create full public awareness of the need for exceptional measures to deal with an exceptional situation; to bring home the risks and stresses of a soldier's (or policeman's) life in a situation of entrenched terrorist violence; and to provide similar instruction in the methods used by the terrorists themselves. A democratic government must know how to wage psychological warfare as effectively as its enemies—with the important distinction that a democratic government is required to tell the truth. It is significant that in the war of words that was fought over Northern Ireland, cases of sensory deprivation applied to detainees in 1972 were still being wielded as examples of indiscriminate 'torture' three years later[7] while incidents such as the regular 'knee-capping' of those who declined to follow IRA orders were treated as routine incidents unworthy of much attention in many British newspapers—not to mention the papers read by the IRA's major financial patrons in the United States.*

*The standard form of 'knee-capping' was to fire a bullet through the back of the victim's knee. A variant was to drive an electric drill through it.

So long as the menace seems remote, or the terrorist network appears to be confined to a handful of psychopaths or New Left romantics, the government's response will be halting and slow. It took the deaths of twenty-one people in the Birmingham bombing at the end of 1974 to induce the British Home Secretary to take steps that many professional observers had long considered essential: the banning of the IRA and of propaganda and fund-raising in support of it; the tightening of controls on movement between England and Ireland; broader powers of police detention, and the formation of an anti-IRA police unit organised at national level. These measures put an end to the confusing situation in which a terrorist movement that had been at war with the Northern Ireland authorities for nearly five years was still able to parade openly, collect money, and publish its propaganda in Britain. But it might well be argued that they failed to provide Britain with the *permanent* structures for controlling political violence that many other Western democracies have found it necessary to devise. In particular, they did not alter the fact that, in the absence of a specially trained and equipped counter-terrorist force, the army will have to take immediate responsibility for internal security in the event of any major upsurge in urban guerrilla warfare in Britain.

Britain's remarkable tradition of non-violence, as described in an engaging (but now, unfortunately, somewhat nostalgic) book by T. A. Critchley, broke down in the early 1970s.[8] The growth of political violence over this period was, of course, largely related to Northern Ireland. But it cannot necessarily be dismissed as transient for this reason. In the first place, the destinies of Britain and Ireland are indissolubly linked— whatever political settlement is finally reached for Ulster. There was a growing, and dangerous tendency among some British politicians—notably in the Labour camp—in the mid-1970s to shrug off responsibility for Northern Ireland. Not a few people were apparently prepared to adopt the ultimate counsel of despair; let's withdraw the troops and let the Irish sort things out for themselves. The result of withdrawal would probably be civil war across the whole of Ireland, with the emergence of a right-wing Protestant regime in Ulster and, quite conceivably, the collapse of democratic politics in Eire and the emergence there of a left-wing government heavily influenced by the Marxist element in the Official IRA.

The war between North and South could hardly fail to concern the British, whatever their determination to slump into an ever-increasing insularity. And the war would be likely to pursue them to their own doors, not just in the form of revenge bombings and killings in Britain, and gang warfare within the large Irish immigrant community, but in the form of imitative terrorism. The IRA has already found would-be imitators in Scotland; the demonstration effect of British withdrawal from Northern Ireland would almost certainly produce a powerful upsurge of secessionist and revolutionary violence elsewhere. Quite apart from that, the British government's decision to flout the wishes of the majority in Ulster to such an extent (if the decision were actually taken) would hardly enhance the reputation of British democracy, and would leave an exceedingly sour taste in the mouths of those who had been assigned to fight a war on this closest frontier for principles that the government no longer appeared to share.

But my argument about the erosion of the British tradition of non-violence goes beyond this. The tradition was related to that far-reaching consensus about the goals and limits of politics that has been seen to be breaking down, to the prevention of private coercion in all forms, and to the old but enduring Anglo-Saxon attitude that the defence of the community was the duty of the community as a whole. It was this last attitude that explains the hereditary British distrust for standing armies and police professionals, and its roots stretch back to the Anglo-Saxon system of tithings and to Henry II's Assize of Arms in 1181, which made it obligatory for every able-bodied man to keep arms in the defence of the commonweal. The medieval understanding that peacekeeping is the responsibility of the whole community is still embedded in the collective psyche of the British, however anachronistic it may appear in the context of an unarmed community facing professional killers. Of more recent derivation, but equally fundamental, is the tradition of a limited response to domestic upheaval. There is no better demonstration of the contrast between the British and the Continental traditions than the differing response to the turbulence of 1848, the 'year of revolution'. While order was maintained, or overthrown in Paris and Berlin at the point of the bayonet, the 30,000 demonstrators who turned out on Kennington Common were peacefully dispersed after being confronted with six times as many Special Constables—specially-recruited civilian volunteers. The soldiers were kept carefully hidden from view behind the trees.

The tradition of restraint and the exceptionally close bond between the police and the public should not be thoughtlessly sacrificed to the need to respond forcefully to a terrorist group that may be seen, in retrospect, to have posed only a negligible or transient threat to social stability. But the modern terrorist must be dealt with by professionals, as the British government became aware during an earlier spate of Irish 'troubles', when it set up the Special Branch (originally described as the 'Special Irish Branch') in 1884. Techniques have evolved a long way since then, and I would argue the need to institute (i) a permanent counter-terrorist force (whose usefulness was fully demonstrated by the performance of the special Dutch unit at Scheveningen jail on 31 October 1974); its members might well be seconded from the army; and (ii) the need for centralised coordination of counter-terrorist planning and the accumulation of all relevant data under a new government committee or department, directly responsible to the Prime Minister.[9]

To revert to my basic theme: We have seen how a protracted campaign of political violence will increase the image of 'ungovernability' even in a sophisticated society. In combination with other factors—including economic stagnation, high inflation, and publicised cases of serious corruption among senior members of the government—political terrorism brought about the collapse of Uruguay, one of the most stable democracies in Latin America. We cannot afford to neglect the lessons of this catalytic effect of terrorism on democratic institutions farther afield.

13

The Need for the 'People's Veto'

*To restore a commonplace truth to its first uncommon
lustre, you need only translate it into action.*

Samuel Taylor Coleridge

The great English constitutional lawyer, A. V. Dicey, declared
at the end of the last century that 'the referendum is the
people's veto'—a necessary brake on the whims of parliamentary assemblies. His was a fairly solitary voice in England at that
stage. Even in 1975, when the Labour Government broke with
tradition by resorting to a referendum on British membership
of the European Economic Community, the prevailing view
among political commentators still seemed to be that the use of
this device was a serious affront to parliamentary sovereignty,
and that it certainly should not be used again. It was ironic that
many prominent Conservatives were now inclined to talk this
way, since historically the Tories were the prime advocates of
the referendum in twentieth-century Britain—in 1911, during
the constitutional crisis over the power of the House of Lords,
and in the 1930s, during the debate over Empire Free Trade.

It is my view that the familiar arguments against the use of
the referendum are misconceived and that the referendum on
the EEC should not be regarded as an exceptional case but as a
timely precedent for tackling equally urgent problems. The
referendum should now be studied as a means of reasserting the
views of the majority.

The critics of the referendum usually deploy three standard
types of argument. The first is that the referendum is a tool of
would-be dictators, the weapon of Hitlers and Louis
Napoleons. The second is that direct democracy of this kind
runs contrary to the basic principle of representative
government—that the representatives should be able to exercise
their own judgement. Finally, it is argued that the attempt to
fit the referendum into a long-established political system like
that of Britain creates a host of technical problems which are

too laborious to be worth solving. Let us look briefly at each of
these propositions.

It is perfectly true, to begin with, that the referendum has
been favoured by European dictators—but not all of them.
Hitler used it; Mussolini and Franco did not. But throughout
modern European history, the referendum has been used as a
means of legitimising dictatorial powers rather than creating
them. It was the vote of the Reichstag on 23 March 1933, that
gave Hitler total power, not the referendum which was used to
confirm his succession as president after Hindenburg's death
the following year. Later, he used the referendum to display
popular support for his expansionist ambitions.

France, where the phenomenon of 'totalitarian democracy'
was first observed, is a better example of the use of direct
voting to establish absolute power. The first Napoleon was
made a life consul by referendum in 1799. His great nephew,
Louis Napoleon, legitimised his *coup d'état* by another
referendum in 1851, in which the French people voted by 7½
million votes to 650,000 to confirm his dictatorial powers. (He
used the plebiscite on four later occasions before 1870.) More
recently, General de Gaulle carried on the tradition by using
the referendum to provide a personal mandate, transcending
the *régime des partis* which he so greatly despised, and to solve
his problem of decolonisation in Algeria. But de Gaulle's own
career demonstrated that a political leader who tries to live by
the referendum—in the context of a democratic system—can
also die by it. He felt obliged to resign after losing the
referendum on the reform of the senate which he had insisted
on holding in 1969, in the aftermath of the tremendous
upheavals the previous year.

But the fact that the two Napoleons, Hitler and de
Gaulle—three dictators and one very singular charismatic
leader—used the referendum for their political purposes does
not substantiate the common assertion that the referendum is
'the instrument of would-be dictators'. From the evidence of
this century, it could just as well be said that parliament, or a
presidential election, is the instrument of would-be dictators.
Hitler, Gottwald and Allende were all the products—or at any
rate, the exploiters—of the electoral process. On the other
hand, as Philip Goodhart points out in a valuable recent work[1]
the referendum is regularly used to settle a whole range of

issues, ranging from constitutional amendments to licensing laws or local rates, in many of the countries that are regarded as exemplary democracies: in Switzerland, Australia, Canada and the United States.

So there are already considerable grounds for misgivings about that second standard argument against the referendum: that it undermines parliamentary sovereignty. Those who argue this way are often really saying: you can trust parliament, but not the people. Lord Curzon, arguing against the suggested use of the referendum to settle the question of Home Rule for Ireland in 1894, put this quite candidly[2] when he declared that 'in the interests of good government any proposal should be deprecated that is likely to tempt the electorate to believe in its own infallibility'. The assumption is that the electorate is not qualified to determine what is in its own interest and that if it were set free to do so, the result would be the rule of passion and prejudice. Representative democracy, according to this school, depends upon the 'senatorial' discretion of a political elite. We have already examined some of the fallacies of this elitist view of democracy.

It is a curious thing that in Britain—at least until the Common Market became a major issue—it was the left rather than the right that most vehemently opposed the use of the referendum. It was precisely those political leaders who always invoked the people's will in order to justify their actions who seemed most frightened of actually consulting it. Thus Clifford Sharp, a Fabian and the first editor of the *New Statesman,* was one of the most fervent polemicists against the proposed use of the referendum in 1911. Clement Attlee brusquely dismissed all thought of using the device when he took government in 1945.

The socialist calculation was clearly that it would be easier to capture Parliament than to win the hearts and minds of the British people on specific issues. This was no doubt compounded with the view that the role of a socialist government was to 'educate' the people in its own conception of social morality, whether they liked it or not. One of the few leading socialists to depart from this doctrine on principle (and not just for tactical reasons involving the EEC) was Mr Anthony Wedgwood Benn. In his 'white-hot technology' days in 1968, Mr Benn foresaw an approaching science-fiction era in which people would be involved in a kind of non-stop referendum by pushing buttons on their television sets. He enthused about the mandate that Labour could obtain through the referendum for sweeping social reforms. It would be interesting to see whether Mr Benn would be prepared to submit his more recent policies to the test of a referendum. At any rate, his early enthusiasm did not catch fire with the left in general.

The reason is obvious enough. Many people on the left are well aware that a referendum is likely to reflect the conservative instincts of the community at large rather than the radical ideology of a minority in power. Since it is, furthermore, a form of voting in which the electors are asked to make up their minds on an issue instead of a party—and in which the composition of the government is not normally at stake—that radical minority cannot rely on partisan loyalty or dislike of the 'other lot' of politicians to see it through. The referendum is likely to express the desire for continuity rather than rapid change, and the sovereignty of 'settled opinion' over radical proposals.

Thus in Britain the referendum could and should be used as a means of upholding those long-standing traditions and individual liberties that can at present be swept aside by a majority of one or two votes in a single assembly and as the people's veto on unrepresentative or irresponsible legislators. Parliamentary sovereignty is a great and noble phrase, but the absence of constitutional curbs on the power vested in the House of Commons is one of the two great problems of British democracy today. (The other, of course, is the abdication of authority by that otherwise almost omnipotent body over the industrial trade unions.)

Deciding on the guidelines for the use of the referendum does present a large number of technical difficulties. Is the holding of a referendum to depend always, as it now does in Britain, on a majority vote in the House of Commons—or could it also be brought about on the petition of, say, two hundred Members of Parliament, or a million voters? Should the referendum remain a purely consultative device, or should it in some cases be allowed to overrule a parliamentary decision? Are there particular issues—proposed changes in the constitution, for example—that should always involve consulting the people through a referendum, and how could these be specified in Britain, which has no written constitution? What safeguards could be provided to ensure that disingenuous drafting of the question to be put to the people did not help to determine the result? And how much is it all going to cost?

I shall not attempt to answer these questions fully. It is surely important to ensure that the decision to resort to the referendum does not rest exclusively with the government of the day. Otherwise, we are left with the same problem as before: the power of a transient parliamentary majority to do (or not do) almost anything it likes. There is the further danger that if the referendum is to be solely the tool of government, it could be used at some future stage (through Machiavellian drafting and one-sided official propaganda) in the attempt to engineer a spurious mandate for authoritarian measures. Some countries make it possible for a referendum to be held on the petition of a prescribed number of electors: the requisite number of signatures is very low indeed in Switzerland and some states in the USA. My own feeling is that if a very large number of electors want to express their views on a specific issue, they should be allowed to do so and that this kind of public involvement is not unhealthy for democracy—quite the reverse. Just how large that 'large number' should be is open to dispute; given the good-natured tendency of many Englishmen to set their signatures to almost any bit of paper that is thrust in front of them, I would suggest that it would be at least a million. The national referendum should remain an exceptional device; but the referendum could also be used on a whole range of local issues—for example, the spread of comprehensive schooling.

Many people will immediately object that any plebiscitary initiative coming from outside Parliament is even more dangerous than one coming from within it. My answer to that goes back to the earlier discussion about the nature of ends and means in a democracy. It is not a particular voting system that makes or breaks a democratic society or makes it a worthwhile place to live in. It is the capacity (or incapacity) of that society's institutions to mediate political differences and the willingness of its leaders to observe the conditions for a free society. The Swiss have referenda on all sorts of things all the time, and this has not so far resulted in a savage assault on private property or the rise of anti-democratic leaders. Britain has done less well without ever sniffing at a referendum—apart from deciding when the Scots and the Welsh should be allowed to drink—until the socialists decided that the people should choose whether to stay in the EEC.

Should the results of a referendum be binding on parliament, or not? I think that there is a strong case for maintaining the purely consultative character of the referendum—its moral impact will be enough—except if it is to be used in resolving a constitutional crisis along the lines suggested below. The abiding problem with the referendum is that it must always present a simple yes/no option and is therefore singularly unsuited to the presentation of complex issues. As Morley, a great Liberal critic of the referendum, put it, 'we all know that draughtsman's English is not the English of Bunyan, Defoe or Swift'. But with a parliamentary commission to watch over the drafting of referenda, I think that the way the question is put is not a central problem: what is far more likely to exercise those who are suspicious of the device in the first place is the very idea that certain matters (hanging or immigration, for example) might be submitted for the people as a whole to decide on. The question of cost is also surely secondary. If the referendum were to be made possible by public petition, the initial cost would rest with those trying to gather signatures. Limits to public expenditure on referenda would certainly need to be prescribed.

But these technical problems do not add up to a case against the *principle* of using the referendum, which is what concerns me here. More pertinent to that is the question of when the referendum would be used. If a referendum could be called on the private initiative of a certain number of electors or MPs, there is no doubt that there would be a strong demand for it to be used to tackle a number of 'gut' issues, ranging from licensing hours and capital punishment to immigration and autonomy for Scotland and Wales. Even if the decision is left to a parliamentary majority, the use of the referendum on the EEC and perhaps now on other issues can be expected to create a ground-swell of opinion in favour of its wider application which MPs may find it difficult to ignore. But there are three crucial areas where I think that the referendum may be found a useful, if not indispensable, device: in the attempt to impose limits for government, in the attempt to bring trade unions within the law; and in the attempt to establish a 'people's veto' over administrative decisions at a local level—especially rate levels and schooling. Let us explore these three areas in turn.

First, the question of limits for governments. The Conservatives brought up the question of the referendum in 1910–11, during the constitutional crisis which resulted in the powers of the House of Lords being severely pruned. The suggestion was then that any Bill approved by the Commons but defeated in the Lords should be submitted to a popular referendum. In the final debate, Arthur Balfour declared that 'in the Referendum lies our hope of getting the sort of constitutional security which every other country but our own enjoys'. The general principle that was at issue then is still what concerns us today: how do you impose restraints on the lower house if the powers of the upper house have been largely shorn away; if there is no written constitution to uphold the rights of the citizen, and no constitutional court to decide if they have been violated by new legislation?[3]

Oliver Cromwell, who might be thought to have understood something about parliaments, said that, 'In every Government there must be somewhat fundamental, somewhat like a Magna Charter, which should be standing, be unalterable. . . . That parliaments should not make themselves perpetual is a fundamental. Of what assurance is a law to prevent so great an evil, if it lie in the same legislature to un-law it again.' But Cromwell rejected the suggestion of those of his supporters who presented the Assembly of the People Bill in 1647, which recommended the use of the referendum to safeguard specified rights.

Early custodians of the common law in England, like Sir Edward Coke, maintained that it was the duty of judges to stand watch over the legislation of parliaments, and to throw out whatever statute laws could not be reconciled with the customary laws of England. But this position was soon abandoned, and, as we have seen, the English constitution as well as individual liberties is curiously vulnerable today—in the absence of a supreme court or a sufficiently specific, and modern, Bill of Rights—to the whims of a majority in the House of Commons.

The ancient Athenians entrusted total powers to an

assembly (composed, it should be remembered, of whatever citizens cared to turn out) which was actually persuaded in 411 BC to vote to abolish democracy. But the Athenians acknowledged at least one restraint: the unique device known as the *graphe paranomon*. This allowed for a man who brought an 'illegal proposal' before the assembly, and was accused for so doing by one of his peers, to be put on trial even if his suggestion had become law. Perhaps in this institution one can detect the ancestor of the modern constitutional court—with the all-important difference that, like everything in Athenian democracy, it was manned by ordinary citizens, not professional judges.

Athenian democracy, for all the obvious differences, had one thing in common with its British descendant: in the last analysis, the survival of the constitution depended on the good sense and the spirit of community (of *koinonia*) of the citizenry as a whole. Take those away, in conditions of economic disaster and military decline, and you were left with no checks on the emotions of an assembly that could vote itself out of existence, and no checks on the passions of popular courts that could condemn Socrates and Anaxagoras for impiety. It has probably always been the same, however carefully wise law-givers have tried to circumscribe the will of the majority, as expressed by parliaments, by fencing it around with paper constitutions and the apparatus of a supreme court. Despite the absence of such checks, British democracy has proved more stable than its relations on the Continent. But the duration of full parliamentary democracy in Britain (as defined by universal adult suffrage) has been less than half a century, and it would be rash to conclude that safeguards that have not been needed over this brief span of recent history are not needed now. When the sense of *koinonia* breaks down, as the Athenians found, the untrammelled power of an assembly can be a perilous thing—and we do not even have the *graphe paranomon*.

There is growing interest in the possible use of two particular safeguards: a new Bill of Rights and a supreme court to examine the constitutionality of parliamentary votes, and with power to invalidate them. Britain has two celebrated bills of rights: the Magna Carta, which spelled out, in embryonic form, the principle of habeas corpus; and the Bill of Rights of 1689, which asserted the sovereignty of parliament over the monarch and enshrined the principle of parliamentary privilege.

The classic argument against any new attempt to defend general principles through a constitutional document was fielded by Dicey, who maintained that 'where the right to individual freedom is a right deduced from the principles of the constitution, the idea readily occurs that the right is capable of being suspended or taken away.' He contrasted this danger with the benign situation he thought to be prevailing in Britain, where the right to individual freedom was 'inherent in the ordinary law of the land' and so could not be hastily swept away.[4]

But Dicey's view now resembles that of a legal Arcadia. Individual freedom, and much else, is at risk because, as one distinguished jurist puts it, common law 'cannot resist the will, however frightened and prejudiced it may be, of Parliament.'[5] In this situation, the whole concept of law is changing abruptly. England has until recently been unique for carrying on the medieval conception of 'liberties under the law'—a tradition in which law is seen as a body of general principles and innate rules that precedes legislators and serves as a curb on all power. Our times, however, are characterised by the 'loss of belief in a justice independent of personal interest'.[6] In the hands of socialist legislators, the law ceases to be a 'purpose-free' restraint upon all and becomes a means of coercion applied to political targets. The idea of the rule of law over all is replaced by the false grail of 'distributive justice'—legislation weighted in favour of the chosen constituency of those in temporary control of parliament.

In this situation, there is a clear and urgent need for a new Bill of Rights to codify those traditional liberties under the law that are being swamped by the tide of socialist legislation. I would certainly include on the list the right *not* to belong to a trade union as a condition of employment, the right to own and bequeath property, and the right to individual choice in important areas of social life such as health and education— what some constitutional thinkers describe as 'secondary liberties' but which are fundamental to the survival of a liberal democracy. There is bound to be intense debate about just what a bill of this kind should contain, and just what can be classified as a basic 'right'. One recent advocate[7] of a new Bill of Rights for Britain lists the following 'fundamental liberties': the right to personal security [in deference to which, for example, he would propose to limit police powers to search]; the right for beneficiaries of the Welfare State to appeal against adverse administrative decisions and challenge the bases on which they are made; the right to freedom from discrimination, racial, sexual or religious. I have some grave reservations about his list, and the way he defines economic privileges (in the case of the social services) as fundamental rights. He defends as basic rights some things that I do not regard as rights at all, and leaves out others—such as the ones I mentioned above—that liberal democrats would regard as absolutely central.

We live in times when it is widely assumed that society is required to assure 'a life of dignity and well-being' to all its citizens. Few people would dispute the social duty to provide limited security (that is, security against physical privation) but, as I argued earlier, to extend this into the argument that society has the further responsibility of guaranteeing an assured standard of living to everyone is to adopt a position that is at odds with the values and goals of a free society.

My point here is that any Bill of Rights would be worthless unless enforceable—which supplies the argument not just for a supreme court, but for entrenched provisions. On certain issues, parliament would not be allowed to proceed without a large majority; Lord Justice Salmon has suggested three-quarters of the votes. But provision might be made for a referendum to be held if the government, short of the requisite majority, remained determined to forge ahead.

The problem of how to harness parliamentary power is related to the problem of how to harness trade union power to parliament—the second area where the referendum could be extremely useful. Dicey complained after the passage of the Trade Disputes Act in 1906 that Parliament had created, in the legal immunities conferred on the trade union movement, a privileged body exempt from the ordinary law of the land. His judgement stands today, after the repeal of the Tories' Industrial Relations Act.

Some radical suggestions for dealing with trade unions have been floated in the aftermath of a Conservative electoral defeat that was generally attributed to a miners' strike. One of the most recent comes from Mr Brendon Sewill, a former adviser to

the Conservative Chancellor of the Exchequer, Mr Barber.[8]
'The only long-term solution' he maintains, 'is to limit the right
to strike'. He suggests a legal amendment to outlaw 'strikes
against the community (or strikes which exploit monopoly
power). Strikes against the rule of Parliament could also be
outlawed, as indeed they were from 1927 to 1946.' He accepts
that such an amendment would inevitably result in the jailing
of strike leaders, who would inevitably provide martyrs for the
trade union movement as a whole, like the 'Pentonville Five'
and the 'Shrewsbury Two' before them. The confrontation
that would then ensue could be very bitter indeed. It could not
be won, as Mr Sewill concedes, if the new law were imposed 'by
an unloved government on an unwilling people.'

His suggested amendment is not in itself a solution, and it
should be differently worded. But I am fairly certain about two
things. The first is that some attempt must be made to bring
trade unions within the law and to curb restrictive practices.
The second is that any such attempt will mean confrontation,
and it would be preferable to show that the attempt to reassert
the rule of law was supported, not just by a parliamentary
majority, but by society as a whole (as it almost certainly
would be). The obvious way to produce such a mandate is
through the referendum.

The fact that apart from the brief hiatus of the Industrial
Relations Act, the legal immunities of the trade unions have
remained largely untouched since 1906, could be taken as one
sign that those who organise effectively in Britain can override
the feelings of an entire community that is rarely given the
chance (or rarely seeks the chance) to register its view of issues,
as opposed to parties. If it were given that chance, things might
work out rather differently. It is worth recalling something that
Ludwig von Mises, a great systematic critic of socialism, once
said on this score: 'This is surely clear: that should there ever be
a thorough discussion upon the right of the workers in vital
industries to strike, the whole theory of trade unionism and
compulsory strikes would soon collapse and strike-breaking
associations . . . would receive the applause which today goes
to the strikers.'[9]

But the referendum is not just for use at a national level, or in
dealing with nationwide crises. Even reduced to the status of an
organised local opinion poll, the referendum could be used to

restore initiative to the community as a whole—when it comes, for example, to determining the level of local rates (and hence the extent of local government spending) or the absorption of grammar schools into the comprehensive system. It is not the head-counting itself, so much as the whole approach to political life, that is now at stake. However much, or little, the instrument of the referendum is used in the future, it seems that a number of the ailments of British society could be healed by the growth of what can possibly best be described as 'referendum-mindedness'. Apathy and lack of public participation in politics have been regarded by many thinkers who were (rightly) suspicious of the excesses of 'mass democracy' as preconditions for the survival of a free society.

But recent experience in Britain has suggested that the fact that so many vital decisions have been left to competing teams of 'professionals' has hastened, rather than curbed, some of the worst tendencies—tendencies, moreover, that appear to run counter to the instincts of the great majority. I am thinking, in particular, of 'progressive' education; the tepid response to terrorism, and the ever-burgeoning scope of state intervention in the economy, coupled with the sprawling advance of the Welfare State. We should now ask the exponents of the 'people's will' to let the people choose. Remember what Tacitus said about the way that the Teutonic tribal assemblies operated: 'On small matters the Few decide, on great matters the Many.' Too many great matters have been left to the Few.

The question, in the end, comes back to one of the underlying conditions for democracy which was summarised well by Lord Hailsham when he wrote that 'there are moments in a free society when a more general consensus is required to achieve a radical change without violence'—a more general consensus, that is, than a majority in one house of parliament. To suggest that Britain's political institutions are not well-designed to do this is not to attack the system of parliamentary democracy but to be deeply concerned about the prospects for the democratic society as a whole. If the 'full-hearted consent of the people' was necessary for British membership of the Common Market, it is equally necessary for other far-reaching changes through legislation which affect the whole structure of British society.

14
In Defence of Liberty

> We belong to an age in the proportion in which we feel
> capable of accepting its dilemma and arraying ourselves
> for battle on one side or the other of the trench it has dug.
> For the process of living is, in a very real sense, an
> enlistment under certain standards and a preparation for
> battle. *Vivere militare est,* Seneca used to say, with the
> proud gesture of a legionary.   *Jose Ortega y Gasset*

The time has come to attempt some kind of reckoning. I have
not tried to encompass, in these few pages, all of the problems
that weigh down upon our present consciousness, and the
reader may be disappointed to find neither an analysis of the
shift in world resources (and in relative financial stability)
brought about by the oil producers' cartel, nor a discourse on
the sources of world monetary disorder—nor, for that matter,
an inquiry into the effects of the Watergate affair on the
American constitution, or of how the judgement of the
Allahabad court on Mrs Gandhi's electoral peccadilloes
inspired her to dismantle India's semi-democracy.

Nor have we come to grips with the fragility of Western
Europe's 'blocked' democracies—France and Italy—where a
genuine alternation of power would seem to depend, under the
existing party systems, on a return to government by the local
communist parties. Yet the results of the regional elections in
Italy in June 1975, when Enrico Berlinguer's Communist Party
won a third of the votes and came within two per cent of
overtaking the Christian Democrats, who had held power for 27
years, showed that Europe may be very close to having
first-hand experience of the 'Santiago model' in action.

A country-by-country survey would show that the prospects
for liberal democracy, outside north-western Europe, North
America and Australasia, are fairly dismal, and the rising
external threat of Soviet military power places even northern
Europe under the cloud of possible 'Finlandisation'. But this
book was not designed as an almanac, still less as a score-card of

the relative chances of survival and adaptation of the various contemporary democratic systems. All the same, it may be worth glancing rapidly across the map to see where genuinely representative governments remain. I will exclude from the list those countries (including India and Mexico as well as Tanzania and Zambia) which are governed under a *de facto* or *de jure* one-party system. In Europe, the situation is somewhat better than in 1939, when the only democracies were Britain, Eire, France, Belgium, Holland, Norway, Sweden, Denmark and Switzerland. The countries since restored to the list are: Italy, Greece, Austria and half of Germany.

In Africa, new forms of authoritarian rule have replaced the former colonial governments in nearly all countries; South Africa and Rhodesia, of course, maintain representative governments on the basis of a minority franchise comparable in its extent (though of course not its racial basis) to that of Britain in 1866, when there were 1.2 million people registered to vote in a total population of some 23 million. The Middle East has not taken kindly to Western models of representative government—with the exception of Israel (to some extent a European export) and the extremely precarious exception of the Lebanon, where power is shared out between the different religious groups according to a quota system, but where communal tension and the presence of the displaced Palestinian population poses a permanent threat to stable government.

Nor has Asia produced model democracies, although the Thais began a ricketty experiment in coalition government under a democratic system in 1974, and Malaysia and Singapore are still rubbing along with elected governments, of which Lee Kuan Yew's must, however, be counted a *de facto* one-party regime. In the South Pacific, there remain the Anglo-Saxon outposts, Australia and New Zealand, which appear to be in no more imminent danger of succumbing to non-competitive regimes (despite the fireworks of the Whitlam government in Canberra) than do America and Canada. The rest of the Western hemisphere does not score well: in mainland South America, the only surviving democracies are Venezuela (whose immense oil revenues may be a partial guarantee of institutional stability) and Colombia and Argentina (which are both in danger of succumbing to formidable internal threats).

This is not a complete check-list, but it is sufficiently detailed to make my point that the democratic system is not, as is sometimes imagined in countries whose citizens are habituated to its workings, the *normal* means of regulating political life. The greater part of the world's population, even in this century, has never experienced its workings. This is clearly (but by no means exclusively) related to relative levels of economic and social mobilisation, and specifically, to the emergence or non-emergence of a broad middle class composed of those 'men with a competency' viewed by de Tocqueville as the main props of representative government.

But my concern has been less with what makes democracy possible in a given society than with how it breaks down. I have suggested that the democratic mechanism in itself is secondary to the form of society in which it is applied—and which it may conceivably help to overturn. A totalitarian democracy in which the government is accorded *unlimited* powers to override individual liberties in the name of majority rule may, in certain circumstances, be a less attractive (and certainly far less *liberal*) form of government than a *limited* authoritarian regime of the kind discussed in the next chapter. There may well be situations in which the citizen may reluctantly find himself having to choose between liberty and democracy— although, as I have already argued, representative government subject to fundamental restraints is the best guarantee for individual liberty that has so far been devised. But no existing system of representative government is perfect—far from it—and times of stress demand fundamental adaptation if the system itself is to survive.

It seems to me that the present threat to what remains of the free society in Britain (and many of the points are relevant to other situations) is linked to the following developments:

1   A derangement of the functions of government, which is swollen but not strong, and has progressively narrowed the range of social and economic choice without fulfilling its classic responsibilities to control private monopolies and secure the external defences of the nation.

2   A corresponding growth in private coercion, accentuated in Britain by the legal immunities accorded to trade unions and the undemocratic election procedures in many of them, which has allowed power to fall into the

hands of political extremists.

3   A widespread misunderstanding of the fundamental link between the market economy and political freedom. In the absence of economic pluralism, political pluralism is likely to be minimal or non-existent.

4   The absence of effective checks and balances—through a strong upper house, a supreme court and an entrenched bill of rights—on what can be achieved by a transient majority in a single parliamentary assembly. (The delaying or diversionary tactics of the civil service, described in appetising detail in the Crossman diaries, are not a satisfactory substitute.)

5   A constituency voting system which has—with some notable interludes—helped to ensure the orderly alternation in power of the two major parties, but has left a large part of the electorate unrepresented and has penalised third parties that belong to the mainstream of politics—to the benefit, in recent years, of radical socialists.

6   The failure of elected governments to bring inflation under control, and the general condition of economic stagnation produced by the decapitalisation of private industry, and a doctrinaire, and notoriously inefficient, programme of nationalisation.

7   The presence of disciplined totalitarian groups that are working for the destruction of democracy *through the system itself,* both overtly and covertly.

8   The decline of the public philosophy—a body of shared beliefs about the values of a free society and the rights and obligations of the individual citizen—which is in turn related to the absence of moral leadership.

9   A world situation which poses a more direct strategic threat to the Western democracies than at any stage since 1945, and is characterised by the unbalanced growth of Soviet military power and by increased Soviet support for subversion within Western countries.

The defence of liberty will need to be conducted on all these fronts. It will involve thorough exploration of possible modifications to the constitution which, in the British case, would now seem to be indispensable: the introduction of a bill of rights and a supreme court, the possible uses of the referendum and the case for electoral reform—possibly on the model of West Germany, which combines the principles of constituency and proportional voting. The defence of liberty will involve a determined attempt to curb private coercion, especially through the restrictive practices of trade unions. It will involve the publication and dissemination of all available material on the present dangers to democracy and on the character of totalitarian tactics as well as ideologies.

It will involve, above all, the revival of citizenship in its classical sense through greater participation by the community at large in the decisions that affect everyday life: in schools, trade unions, local government, residents' associations and professional groups. Such participation will often go far beyond party affiliation and, in most of these cases, party affiliation will matter less than the kind of society that the individual is prepared to defend—and the common threats to that society. Governments can help to encourage such participation in some desirable areas—for example, by defraying all or part of the costs of a postal ballot (provided it is conducted according to criteria determined by a responsible supervisory authority) in a trade union election.

Community 'self-help' can accomplish a great deal—although it can never compensate for the absence of strong government and the even-handed enforcement of the law. Take the case of trade union militancy in Britain. An organised minority of Britain's industrial work force is incited by militant leaders to hold the community to ransom by threatening to halt vital services if their demands are not accepted. There is a lawyers' argument that, in the case of some state-controlled service industries, such strike threats could be classed as illegal—despite the condition of legal immunity in which British trade unions bask in the manner described in Chapter 5. According to this argument, the charter of a state corporation such as British Rail provides that it should maintain constant and efficient service. If, as a result of industrial action by its employees, it is unable to do so, it then becomes the responsibility of the chairman of the corporation to go to the government and suggest either (i) that the terms of the charter be altered by a new parliamentary bill or (ii) that he be empowered to end the strike by whatever means are necessary. If this lawyers' argument stands up (which needs to be investigated) certain kinds of strike action in Britain could be handled rather differently than at present under existing law.

But in the meantime, it is open to the community to adopt 'self-help' measures in order to resist some kinds of strike that are damaging the national economy. The organisation of cooperative road transport for commuters in the event of a rail strike—by sharing out motor-cars—is an obvious, and now widely-canvassed, example. (The same principle could be applied to the transport of essential supplies normally carried by rail.) The organisation of civilian volunteers to help to run vital services in the event of a strike that the government ruled to be illegal is a more far-reaching example. Simple survival tactics by local communities—such as the stockpiling of essential supplies—could also conceivably help to reduce the effectiveness of the strike-threat weapon. On a grander scale, it is still more essential to ensure that the means of public communication—above all the press and the broadcasting media—cannot be wholly silenced by union militants on the first day of a major strike.

It is not dishonourable to join the black-legs in a situation where a group of political extremists in the guise of trade union leaders is using its power in an effort to bring about socialist revolution—for example, by organising political strikes, or strikes in support of wage claims well in excess of the rate of inflation. Nor is it dishonourable for a social group that is being ground down by inflation and selective taxation—like small businessmen, the self-employed, and some professional men in Britain—to borrow the tactics of trade union militants. If miners and railwaymen can strike, why shouldn't taxpayers or ratepayers withhold their money? There is surely no *moral* objection to this argument; quite the contrary. There is a legal argument; but if ratepayers' leaders really did reason like trade union militants, they would assert that they could change the law by flexing their economic muscle. The trouble is that Poujadism, like trade union militancy, is based upon sectional interests that may need a vigorous defence but, if pressed too far, will divide society into little pieces. Having said that, I must add that, in a situation like Britain, where government has failed to restrain a peculiarly well-organised social pressure group, the organisation of countervailing pressure groups is not merely unobjectionable, but may be vital to the preservation of a plural society.

But the 'self-help' approach applies *inside* trade unions as well as outside them. There is a great number of desperate men inside British trade unions who are trying to get out from under the present leadership. The visible tip of the iceberg includes groups like the Movement for True Industrial Democracy (Truemid), which produced an initial statement of aims in a pamphlet entitled *The Day of the Ostrich* in April 1975. The organisers of Truemid—who were mainly long-time Labour Party militants—started out with the conviction that effective resistance to the Marxists in British trade unions would hinge on producing a movement that could equal or surpass the organisational ability of the left at the level of shop stewards, and so help to explode the mystique of fear that has induced many moderate men to stay at home and let events take their course. It may take such groups a very long time to catch up with Marxist organisations that have already made enormous headway and are determined not to lose it. Anti-communist trade union leaders are regularly subjected to forms of harassment, intimidation and character blacking that frequently go unreported. In an inflationary environment, they may also find themselves compelled to compete with extremists in calling for spectacular wage increases; what is seen by a Marxist as a means of breaking the capitalist system will be seen by them as a necessity for ensuring their own survival—until the government cuts through the community's inflationary expectations by imposing a rigorous monetary policy, a ceiling on public spending and/or determined wage controls.

'Self-help' should be practised at many other levels. Most individual citizens will be aware of examples of subversion, as defined in this book, in the course of their daily lives. It may be the case of the new local librarian who refuses to authorise the purchase of 'right-wing' literature, but ensures that the shelves are stacked with New Left tracts; it may be the case of the Trotskyist school-teacher who is sending young Willie home with propaganda leaflets attacking the police; it may be the role of a Marxist shop steward in the factory down the road who specialises in organising wildcat strikes on trivial pretexts as part of a systematic campaign to bankrupt his company and introduce workers' self-control with the aid of a government subsidy. It can hardly be stressed enough that there are things that the individual citizen can and should do at all levels to preserve a free society. In the three hypothetical cases mentioned, this might mean bringing pressure to bear on the local council and the school board of governors, writing to MPs and local papers, or even (in the case of the shop steward) organising housewives to practise the 'Lysistrata tactic'; women tend to be more alive to the effects of industrial disruption than men.

Self-help will tend to shade over into 'direct action'— possibly involving the use, or the threatened use, of force—in situations where the government is not seen to apply the law fairly and firmly. I have already mentioned the danger of vigilante counter-violence in a situation where terrorism has gone unchecked. There are lesser, but still serious, dangers where an habitually law-abiding section of the community comes to feel that it is being penalised because it has refused to adopt the militant tactics of other social groups. I have mentioned the possibility of taxpayers' and ratepayers' strikes. Another British example is the case of the squatters—groups of young people who occupied deserted (or temporarily unoccupied) urban property. The scandal of British housing, due more to the restricted market and consequently high commercial prices created by exaggerated government subsidies to council tenants than to the oft-abused property speculators, made the spread of urban squatters entirely predictable in the early 1970s. It was encouraged by a formerly obscure law dating from 1861 that made it impossible for the owners of occupied property to call on the police to evict the squatters in advance of a court order—and prevented them from forcibly entering the premises themselves. The upshot, as Marxist groups opposed to private property on principle organised more and more squattings around the country, was that owners began to resort to hired security guards, muscular friends and, on at least one occasion, a cat-burglar to gain entry, to reclaim their property.

Violence breeds counter-violence; coercion breeds counter-coercion. In this devasting tug-of-war, the initial balance of right and wrong may be forgotten completely as society is torn to shreds. This leads me back to the responsibility of government, which must be to prevent the usurpation of power by a particular social group. It has signally failed to fulfil this duty in Britain, where the Labour government, in its hastily-prepared White Paper (on semi-statutory wage controls) in July 1975 actually saw fit to reprint a large chunk of a policy document of the Trades Union Congress as an appendix— apparently to demonstrate how closely the government had followed it. Whether the social group that is allowed exceptional privileges consists of trade unionists, country landowners or big business, the same principle holds good. So long as an open society survives, other social groups will organise to challenge those privileges. It is the duty of government to mediate. But it can only do that effectively if it is the government of the *nation*, not a sectional oligarchy.

The responsibility of government reaches further. It is to cease from disguising from the electorate the harsh economic options that may be the only key to economic stability, and the power confrontation with the trade unions that may have to be seen through before they are fully possible. It is to accept a self-denying ordinance in some areas where state intervention has been steadily expanding, at an ever-increasing rate, since 1945. It is to accept and to communicate the need to maintain credible national defences at a time of unprecedented national danger, even if this does mean guns before colour television sets in every council flat. It is, finally, to revive those national loyalties and that willingness to work and sacrifice that made of a community of offshore islanders a great imperial and trading nation. Stalin looked at his map and saw Britain as a tiny island, pathetically insignificant by comparison with the vast Eurasian land-mass that he controlled. Britain's record, under inspired leadership, in the war with Hitler may have reminded him that the human qualities of a nation may overshadow everything else. It is precisely those human qualities that foreign visitors to Britain now find to be lacking—whether they attribute this, like the trendy tourists from the Paris office of the Hudson Institute, to the old school tie and Oxbridge accents, or, alternatively, to the demoralising influence of the Welfare State and thirty years' descent into socialism.

It may well be that when a society has passed a certain stage of moral and economic decline, it has to plumb the depths before it can rise again. There is, however, something devastatingly unassuring about the oft-heard British remark, 'Once you have got to 1938, you have to get to 1940 in order to recover.' Two years after Munich, the Royal Air Force was winning the Battle of Britain—but Hitler's troops were in Paris. It is debatable whether Albion today resembles the Third Republic more than Churchill's Britain. I am sure that the basic instincts are still sound. The problem is how to translate them into action if the party system is failing to do so.

There were some heartening signs, at the time when this book was being completed, that there was a spontaneous awakening to the gravity of the threat at a grass roots level throughout Britain. At the same time the Conservative Party, though still bedevilled by internal feuds and backbiting over its past misadventures, was attempting, under Mrs Margaret Thatcher, to restore some of the principles I have defended in this book—the need for private initiative and consumer choice—as popular causes. This return to basic principles appeared to some cynical observers as a curious exercise for the Tories, even in opposition, but it raised the hope that, if the Conservatives were returned to office, they would be intellectually prepared to deal with Britain's economic disorder and constitutional danger—*intellectually* prepared, but *politically* prepared only if they could rediscover the party cohesion and the political nerve required to ride out the confrontation with the left in the trade unions that appeared inevitable. The Conservative reappraisal aroused a good deal of scepticism, not least from the Bismarckian socialists in the midst of the party itself. It was in fact long overdue, but clearly needed to be leavened with a populist appeal, transcending class and occupational divides, that the party was still groping to find.

The divisions in the Tory camp were dwarfed by the gaping schisms in Mr Wilson's party. Here the massed battalions of the Marxist left—in control of the Labour Party's National Executive and its Annual Conference—had steadily encroached on the room for manoeuvre of the precarious social democrat majority in the Parliamentary Labour Party. A new rift was looming, in which the only certainty was that the Prime Minister would take his place on the winning side. Meanwhile, Labour moderates tried to regroup—in bodies such as the parliamentary Manifesto group or the Social Democratic Alliance—to arm themselves more effectively against the left.

Only perennial optimists and soggy thinkers in either of the two major parties seemed to believe that the British crisis would be solved without a fairly momentous social confrontation. It was the extent of that confrontation, and the ground on which it would be fought, that remained to be decided. I have not said much about the British party system—or political parties in general—in this book. Yet Burke once reflected that there are only three sorts of men who are interested in politics but avoid party commitment:

> Those who profess nothing but a pursuit of their own interests, and who avow their resolution of attaching themselves to the present possession of power, in whose-ever hands it is, or however it may be used. The other sort are ambitious men, of light or no principles, who in their turns make use of all parties, and therefore avoid entering into what may be construed an engagement with any. The other sort is hardly worth mentioning, being composed only of four or five Country Gentlemen of little efficiency in public business.[1]

He might have added journalists and academics—at least a few of them—and a further category of people who are either dissatisfied with the workings of the party system or, whatever their own party leanings, have become convinced of the need to seek a national solution to a major crisis. Here we must distinguish between the meaning of a 'national solution' and the possible masquerade of a national coalition. The solution for Britain's present disorders will require more than the discovery of some lowest common denominator between the Labour, Conservative and Liberal Parties—or some cluster of factions from them—which would enable the society to go on living beyond its means for a bit longer in the Micawberish hope that something good will turn up. It will require a series of economic shock measures that are likely to produce a power confrontation with the trade union left. The confrontation will be less jarring, and less likely to imperil Britain's political institutions, if a clear lead and a far-reaching process of political education can be provided by a broad range of national figures from all parties (and from outside them) who are prepared to put the country's interest first and agree to a slate of major economic reforms.

Such proposals may appear, in the routine course of politics, to belong to cloud-cuckoo-land. But, as more people become aware that it is the future of the democratic system itself that is now being placed in jeopardy, they become easier to accept. Electoral politics will not, *by themselves*, decide the outcome of a struggle for power that now involves the whole of society, and which the Marxist left has hitherto been better-armed than anyone else to contest. In this broader and more fundamental battle of ideas and organisations, party differences are relatively unimportant; it is the whole order of society that is at stake. Some of those who understand this best spring from the ranks of trade unionists and Labour Party activists who have lived at close quarters with the Marxists and have had to contend with their techniques—although some of these men may find it hard to accept my view that a society can *evolve* into communism if state intervention in the economy is not confined within clearly specified limits.

It is a common failing to recommend the setting-up of a new committee when a solution is needed for a major problem. At the risk of doing the same thing, I would suggest that the time has come to set up a Society for the Defence of Democracy which would study the existing threats to the free society on a comparative basis and seek to coordinate all the various groups and individuals, regardless of party allegiance, that are at one in opposing unlimited government and the suppression of individual liberties. The urgency of the task should require no further emphasis.

'So long as we can make efficient use of things', wrote a distinguished American historian in criticism of his contemporaries, 'we feel no irresistible need to understand them.'[2] There is nothing like a time of crisis—a period when things no longer respond easily to familiar methods—to induce us to make the effort of understanding. It is rarely a pleasant task, and as we near the end, David Hume's advice that it is safer not to press pessimistic arguments to their conclusion becomes more and more seductive. 'Why rake into those corners of nature, which spread a nuisance all round? . . . Truths which are *pernicious* to society, if any such there be, will yield to errors, which are salutary and *advantageous*.'[3] True to his own counsel, Hume abandoned his philosophical speculations but did not, fortunately for us, leave off the study of history and political economy.

Arnold Toynbee, with the instinct of a poet rather than the eye of a historian, summed up the breakdown of civilisations in three points: 'a failure of creative power in the minority, an answering withdrawal of mimesis on the part of the majority, and a consequent loss of social unity in the society as a whole.'[4] He is talking about more than the absence of strong leaders, of social 'heroes' who offer a model worthy of imitation and who can exact willing effort and sacrifice from a people. But the simple, and frequent, complaint of the man in the pub or the tabac—'We need another Churchill' or 'Il nous faut un autre de Gaulle'—reflects a deep and unsatisfied need that should not be ignored. It is the absence of such human rallying-points in British public life that partly explains the apparent victory of sectional selfishness over loyalty to the community as a whole and the sharpening of the tensions that are inevitable in an open society into bitterly divisive conflicts that society is hard-put to contain. The British public was willing to accept far greater economic sacrifices for the sake of national survival in 1931 or 1945 than in the mid-1970s. For the sake of 'saving the pound', taxpayers queued up to pay the new levies that were imposed in 1931 after receiving their first notices, before payments fell due on 31 December.[5] It was a response that was inconceivable in the mid-1970s. Although it might well be argued that the Depression, like the Second World War, presented a more tangible challenge to the life of a society than incipient hyper-inflation, the doubt remained: would the most awesome challenge elicit the necessary response?

But Toynbee's argument carries us further. He describes the 'nemesis of creativity', the danger of a dynamic and inventive civilisation becoming satiated with its achievements, losing its drive, and finally failing to devise new solutions for new problems. This morbid phase may be characterised by a kind of self-hypnosis, a narcissistic fascination with past glories and obsolete institutions. A whole civilisation may be frozen in the posture of a writer whose inspiration is exhausted, gloating over works he produced a decade before, or a rower complacently resting on his oars while the race is lost. Its presiding feature may be 'the idolisation of some ephemeral self'[6]—of institutions that no longer function, of attributes that belonged to a vanished youth. So we drive forward into the future, our eyes fixed on the rear-vision mirror. The examples that Toynbee chose as cases of the 'idolisation of ephemeral institutions' were the Hellenic world, the Byzantine empire, the late Pharaonic empire in Egypt—and British democracy, with its cult of the 'Mother of Parliaments'. It takes a world-historical vision of a kind that is rarely found among Anglo-Saxons to group such disparate cultures together, but the effort is instructive. Toynbee's most relevant comparison was between the Hellenic devotion to the city-state, the *polis*, as a form of politcal organisation at a time when a federal system was clearly needed to preserve the Greek civilisation from external enemies (and the lengthening shadow of Rome's imperial expansion) and Britain's reluctance in recent times to contemplate a new feat of constitutional innovation that would adapt its model of representative government to an equally urgent challenge. When a civilisation succumbs to spiritual lassitude, when its leaders are content to live off the past rather than add to it, technology and material affluence cannot save it.

15
The Logic of Breakdown

> I readily recognise that the event justified me more
> promptly and more completely than I foresaw (a thing
> which may sometimes have happened to other political
> prophets, better authorised to predict than I was). No, I
> did not expect such a revolution as we were destined to
> have; and who could have predicted it? I did, I believe,
> perceive more clearly than the others the general causes
> which were making for the event; but I did not observe the
> accidents which were to precipitate it.
>
> *Alexis de Tocqueville*[1]

We draw near at last to the painful but inevitable question: if
the democratic system has broken down irretrievably, what
options are left? 'Every good thing', as Thornton Wilder said,
'stands at the razor edge of danger and must be fought for at
every moment.' We have seen how the social consensus that
makes the democratic alternation of governments possible is
imperilled when one set of elected rulers determine to impose
far-reaching and *irreversible* changes on the community in the
name of an ideal. Such an attempt is bound to make broad
sections of the community reconsider whether the values and
interests that are thus put at risk are not more fundamental
than the system of government that makes the assault possible.
We have also seen that the failure of democratic governments to
cope with problems such as inflation or recession, political
terrorism and social coercion will give rise to a widespread
feeling that the country is 'ungovernable' under the existing
system, and to corresponding appeals for Caesarism or
revolution. It should be added that in the rise and fall of
societies, as in the evolution and extinction of species, the
survival of the fittest does not, unhappily, mean the survival of
the *best*, but of those best adjusted to the environment in
which they have to make their way. We cannot afford to ignore
the fact that liberal democracy is a delicate plant, as rare as an
orchid in the jungle of past and present political systems, which

has not been successfully transplanted from its European habitat to the third world and is showing sad signs of blight even in its native environment.

I am not writing as a determinist, and I hope that what has been said in this book had made it plain to the reader that I have no doubt that representative government—so long as it is also *limited* government—is the only *permanent* system of government that is worth defending. The trouble, as we have seen, is that the system is open to abuse. What side should a liberal democrat be on when totalitarians use the system in order to destroy it? The man who said in 1933 that 'Hitler must be stopped' might surely be counted a democrat, yet Hitler was in process of arrogating absolute powers by democratic means. Given the intellectual confusion of our times, it may not be so readily understood that a man who said that 'the communists must be stopped' in Prague in 1948, or in Chile in 1973 (after the Supreme Court had ruled that Allende had systematically violated the constitution) might have been moved by a similar dedication to liberty. These are exceptionally clear-cut examples of situations in which the choice for a society appears less as a choice between the democratic system and some other political system than as a choice between limited and unlimited government—situations in which the *only* viable alternative to totalitarian rule may be limited authoritarian government, where it is not too late even for that.

Our task, in a democracy, is to prevent comparable situations coming to pass. This will require qualities of leadership that have been sadly lacking in many Western countries. One view of tragedy is that it is a condition that arises from 'a disproportion between a man and his destiny'. In this sense, tragedy arises from the disproportion between a great man and a hostile or indifferent environment, but it also arises, as Stefan Zweig observed of Marie Antoinette, 'when a momentous position, a crushing responsibility is thrust upon a mediocrity or a weakling.' Think of Neville Chamberlain at Munich. Think of Louis XVI on 16 July 1789, the day the Bastille was stormed. He wrote the single word *rien* in his diary, signifying that he had not gone hunting or attended a ball, and retired to bed at 10 o'clock. The Duke of Liancourt arrived later and had to wake him up to inform him that the Paris mob was parading the head of the governor of the Bastille on a pike.

There ensued the conversation known to all schoolboys. 'You are bringing me news of a revolt', said the King, in some agitation. 'No, sire,' replied the Duke, 'it is a revolution'. The history of revolutions and *coups d'état* is in some measure the history of rulers who went to bed at 10 o'clock, and of legislators who neglected the mood of the country. De Tocqueville observed of the French assembly on the eve of the revolution of 1848 that 'it was the only place in Paris in which, since the early morning, I had not heard discussed aloud what was then absorbing all France'.

If the politicians fail and a country enters a period of social collapse in which broad sections of the community are disposed to welcome Caesar or communism, if the economy is crumbling and power is in the streets, how is a liberal democrat to choose between paths that seem equally forbidding? In a period of total breakdown, the choice that is made by an individual or a social class is of course more likely to be based on interest (or sheer *survival*) than on principle. But it seems clear to me, as a matter of principle, that—where there is no third choice—an authoritarian solution is preferable to a totalitarian solution. Ghita Ionescu defines a totalitarian regime as having the following characteristics: a compulsory ideology; a monolithic party; a monopoly of communications; a monopoly of all means of armed combat; a centrally directed economy, and a terrorist secret police.[2] But there are many authoritarian regimes that lack many of these features, and it is possible to imagine an authoritarian regime that would lack all of them—except, of course, for the monopoly of force. In a recent work, Brian Crozier defines the basic distinction:

> It is widely assumed that there is little to choose between authoritarian and totalist governments; yet in one important sense, they are mutually antithetical. Authoritarian governments seek to abolish politics; totalist governments seek to involve the whole population in politics.[3]

Franco's Spain—the only remaining European example of an authoritarian regime—is nobody's idea of a free society, and the lot of political dissidents is notoriously severe. Yet there is clearly much greater scope for personal liberty than under the totalitarian systems of Eastern Europe. At least since the

1950s, the average Spaniard is able to travel freely, inside and outside the country, to marry as he likes, to engage in most kinds of business, to read a wide range of foreign literature and a press that (although heavily censored on domestic politics) is often far more radical in its treatment of foreign affairs than the British or American press. He will be scrutinised by the police apparatus and its agents—including the night-porters— but the pattern of his life does not depend on conformity with the doctrines and behaviour-patterns imposed by a totalitarian party. No one interferes with his religious practices. The average Russian (or the average Chinese) is deprived of these liberties together with the political and civic freedoms denied in Spain, which include the right to change the government by peaceful means, the right to join a free trade union, and freedom from arbitrary arrest.

I am not offering Spain as a model for anyone. I am simply using the case of Franco's Spain to assist in clarifying the distinction between an authoritarian and a totalitarian system. We might usefully contrast the situation in Spain with the situation in Albania, another southern European country governed, not by a personal dictator, but by a monolithic party with a (pro-Chinese) communist ideology which is compulsory for Albanians. The press is totally censored, foreign contacts of all kinds are forbidden, and jobs, houses and holidays are dependent on a clean slate with the secret police. The secret police operate a vast network of informers, and small children have been trained to report anything that is overheard which is critical of President Hoxha or Chairman Mao.

The area where the authoritarian and the totalitarian state are most likely to resemble each other is in the existence of a 'terrorist secret police' and the absence of guarantees for individual liberties in relation to the state and its police apparatus. All civilised societies depend upon subordinating the exercise of state power to the rule of law. This can only be secured in a system that allows, *at the very least*, for

1 An independent judiciary to which appeal is allowed from administrative decisions, and of universal laws transcending the aims of governments.
2 Freedom from arbitrary arrest, which should mean that even under martial law or a state of emergency (where the

authorities would be empowered to exercise special powers of arrest and detention) there should be a legal requirement to present prompt and explicit charges, and a right to appeal, within a specified time, to a superior court.

3 The right to proper legal representation before a court or tribunal.

4 Appearance before a magistrate or tribunal within a specified length of time.

5 The right to a medical examination before any formal hearing.

Even these minimal conditions are lacking under totalitarian systems, and under many authoritarian systems. In their absence, the authorities are acting in a legal and moral vacuum, the individual is subjected to an unacceptable intrusion on his basic liberties, and the security forces will be profoundly corrupted by the exercise of total power. We could only be justified in describing a non-democratic government as a *limited* authoritarian regime if it accepted such restraints. A regime that does not formally accept them may still, through the maintenance of institutional discipline within the civil service and the security forces, avoid excesses. But it is in danger of degenerating into a terrorist police state through the process of moral corruption that Solzhenitsyn described in a remarkable passage of *The Gulag Archipelago* in which he reflects on reports that during the early years of the Bolshevik regime, condemned prisoners had been fed alive to animals in the city zoos of Petrograd and Odessa,

Evidently evil-doing has a threshold magnitude. Yes, a human being hesitates and bobs back and forth between good and evil all his life. He slips, falls back, clambers up, repents, things begin to darken again. But just so long as the threshold of evil-doing is not crossed, the possibility of returning remains, and he himself is still within reach of our hope. But when, through the density of evil actions, the result either of their own extreme degree or of the absoluteness of his power, he suddenly crosses that threshold, he has left humanity behind, and without, perhaps, the possiblity to return.[4]

Any student of the Stalinist purges, the cultural revolution in China, the land collectivisation in North Vietnam, or the creation of the SS state in central Europe is aware of how that threshold is crossed: of how terror committed in the name of an ideology or a political order becomes terror for its own sake. Terror in a new revolutionary state may be an entirely rational weapon at the outset: a means of atomising all potential sources of opposition, so that society is broken up into a congeries of mutually suspicious individuals incapable of concerted action against the regime, so numbed to the sense of their own rights as human beings that they may be induced, like Solzhenitsyn at the start of his imprisonment, to lead their bewildered guards to the gates of their jail.

But terror develops a momentum of its own, and the problem for a regime that resorts to it will soon be to control its own professional terrorists. The failure of the colonels' regime in Greece to control Brigadier Ioannides and his security services was one reason why it at last came tumbling down like a house of cards. Communist regimes have been more successful in containing and subordinating the formidable apparatus of the police state within the rigid party hierarchies. But this is an example of ideologically-directed terror which—far from being a *limited* form of terror—has always proved to be the most arbitrary and unbounded kind of all.

Lenin was helpfully candid about the role of coercion in creating and perpetuating a communist state. 'The scientific concept of dictatorship', as he wrote after 1917, 'means nothing else but power based directly on violence, unrestrained by any laws, absolutely unrestricted by any rules.'[5] Trotsky supplemented this statement in a classic work by observing that 'the problem of revolution as of war consists in breaking the will of the foe, forcing him to capitulate and accept the conditions of the conqueror.'[6] But it was long supposed that the Red Terror would be confined to the early stages of the revolution, when it was necessary to sweep away the remnants of the old order. Later, when the Communist Party had fulfilled its task of ideological re-education and the proletariat had 'internalised' the goals of the regime, direct coercion would no longer be necessary. Organised terror is characteristic of the initial stage of any revolutionary takeover, as of many counter-revolutionary coups. The aim is the survival of the regime, through the elimination of those suspected of active hostility, and the deterrent effect that this is presumed to have on those who are not yet committed to the new regime.

But the mass purges carried out under communist regimes usually date from a later stage—the stage that the political scientists now like to call the 'mobilisation' phase, when the regime is trying to achieve a major breakthrough towards one of its social or economic goals: industrialisation, land collectivisation, the elimination of 'bourgeois' elements and ideologies. Here we can draw another clear distinction between the behaviour of totalitarian and authoritarian regimes. Totalitarians are bent on total conformity, on the homogenisation of an entire society. All actual or potentially 'deviant' groups and individuals become targets for physical or psychological coercion. A former inmate of the Soviet labour camps listed some of the major groups from which such targets are selected in Russia:

1 Classes and strata considered to be inimical, either by doctrine or by plausibility.
2 Former members of non-communist parties, and members of oppositionist and deviationist factions within the Communist Party.
3 Persons with foreign contacts, suspect either for 'security' reasons or for fear of contamination of ideas.
4 Ethnic groups.
5 Persons with family ties, or close acquaintance, with other victims on the assumption that they either share the culprits' views or are apt to be guilty of complicity. [7]

At a later stage, the use of physical coercion will tend to decline sharply, and the regime, having laid out a *tabula rasa*, will fall back on *normative* coercion, material incentives, and the use of the secret police to perpetuate a generalised anxiety complex among the population in order to pursue its goals and eliminate opposition.

The use of terror, which Frantz Neumann described as the 'permanent threat against the individual'[8] is characteristic (i) of a regime that has failed to legitimise itself and to win widespread public acceptance; (ii) of a totalitarian regime guided by a chiliastic vision that demands total uniformity; and (iii) of a regime in which the police and security services have been allowed to develop as entirely independent forces, operating outside the bounds of legality, morality and political control. But physical coercion by itself can only serve negative functions, and, in the absence of positive sources of appeal, a regime that relies solely upon it will be no more creative than primitive despotisms like Haiti under Papa-Doc Duvalier* or Gabon under Bokassa and, in an organised society, must eventually be overthrown.

The totalitarian claim to legitimacy is based upon a secular theology and imposed by 'thought reform' and party mobilisation as well as terror. Authoritarian claims to legitimacy may be based on one of the following arguments:

1 *The need for 'temporary' dictatorship.* The argument that the old system has broken down and that the armed forces, or a civilian figure backed by them, are needed to mount a 'holding operation' until the society can safely be returned to its former ways. This position may best be described as 'limited Caesarism', and may or may not be combined with (2) or (3).

2 *The appeal to a charismatic leader.* The politicians have failed, and a man on a white horse (characteristically a military figure like Pilsudski or Louis Napoleon) is needed to 'clean up the mess'.

3 *The appeal to traditional institutions 'transcending' democracy.* Characteristically, an appeal for a return to royal absolutism, as in the monarchist coup in Yugoslavia in the 1920s, or in the propaganda of Charles Maurras and the *Action Française* movement.

4 *The appeal to an alternative model of 'authentic' democracy.* For example, the corporatist claims of the Salazarist regime in Portugal (1927-73) the Vargas dictatorship in Brazil (1937-45) or the Perón dictatorship in Argentina (1946-55).

5 *The need for a 'government of experts'.* The party system has prevented the creation of a government that will take the necessary measures and has encouraged 'demagoguery', 'corruption', and electoral 'bribery'; hence the need for government by 'the best' in the name of the

---

*Even Duvalier's despotism cannot be understood without reference to his use of the voodoo cult to impose supernatural sanctions.

national interest. Appeal is sometimes made to the alleged need for 'technocratic' management of complex modern economies.

Such appeals may all be lodged by an authoritarian group that is bent on assuming power, or has recently acquired it. Its subsequent survival, after immediate enemies have been neutralised, will depend on one of four possible lines of advance. The first I have already defined as limited Caesarism: an honest determination to restore constitutional government once the immediate threats to society have been dispensed with. Two examples of limited Caesarism which did *not* actually result in the creation of authoritarian regimes are de Gaulle's return to power in 1958 (followed by the promulgation of the new constitution of the Fifth Republic) and the recent kingmaking role of the Turkish army. But it is easier still to find examples of military intervention that was initially justified in terms of limited Caesarism but has apparently resulted in indefinite military dictatorship: Brazil and Chile are two notable Latin American examples.

The second strategy involves the 'selective mobilisation' of the population through a new political movement, usually populist or fascist in inspiration. Perón's *Justicialista* movement, the SINAMOS programme in General Velasco's Peru, and plans for 'revolutionary committees' at all levels in Portugal are all symptomatic of this approach.

The third possibility is the attempt to secure the permanent political demobilisation of the bulk of the population. This may be achieved through the combination of material affluence (at least for the politically-conscious sections of the population), appeals to internal (or external) threats as a pretext for authoritarian government, and police repression. Brazil and Indonesia are present-day examples of this model.

Finally, there may be an original attempt to devise a post-disaster system. There are not many examples of constitutional innovation under an authoritarian regime on offer, although Chile may provide one. There are, however, many ideas on this subject in circulation. Brian Crozier has mapped out one possible model for a 'no-party state',[9] and a group of contemporary French thinkers has proposed a kind of latter-day mandarinate, based on the 'examination' (rather than election) of government officers, selected from various qualified groups. Such suggestions, whose pedigree would appear to extend back to Plato's Guardians, will not exercise any compelling appeal to citizens in a functioning liberal democracy. But the necessity to *think* about the consequences of political collapse should not be evaded. The apparent failure of 'limited Caesarism' in some formerly democratic societies—of which Brazil, Uruguay and Chile are perhaps the most relevant examples—is not entirely compensated by the eventual return, after a fairly brutal interlude, to constitutional government in Greece.

It is hardly sufficient to castigate authoritarian governments that have abandoned their original promises to restore democracy without observing the appalling difficulties of carrying them out in a situation where, for example, twenty per cent of the former electorate may have supported a (now illegal) Communist Party whose revolutionary ambitions were themselves a major cause of military intervention, where the 'revenge' factor may have to be borne in mind, or where a legacy of economic chaos may require stringent and unpopular austerity measures over a period of several years. In such situations, a radical reform of the constitution with the aim of fulfilling the need for popular consultation and regular alternation of government *in the absence of the party system* might at any rate be preferable to government without restraints and may provide a solution for the universal problem of non-democratic regimes: how to secure a peaceful transition of power. In short, our analysis of the logic of breakdown in democratic societies will fall very far short of the mark if we do not accept that nostalgia for a system that has collapsed will not resolve the need to find a replacement—at least for an interval. Nor can we begin to resolve that need without recognising the temptation, and the universally corrupting influence, *of power*, especially in the hands of those who have given only cursory thought to how they will exercise it.

The experience of military dictatorship in Brazil, despite its remarkable economic achievements and its equally notable success in suppressing left-wing guerrilla movements, provides some warnings about the risks of exercising authoritarian power within a legal and constitutional vacuum—and the plethora of decree-laws, institutional acts and constitutional amendments issued by the regime are merely an indication of its fundamental, and still unresolved, uncertainty about the appropriate framework for its actions.

Institutional Act No. 1, issued by the Brazilian junta a week after the overthrow of President Goulart in 1964, declared that 'the successful revolution is legitimised by itself. The revolution dismisses the former government and is qualified to set up a new one.' This was a fairly forthright way of saying that might is right. It was acceptable in 1964 to those who had suffered from unchecked inflation, negative growth and a flight of foreign capital, and to a middle class which had been frightened by the appearance of armed revolutionary groups (often with government blessing) and by Goulart's last, semi-alcoholic speech, in which he threatened 'total revolutionary transformation' and issued orders for a new, and far-reaching, nationalisation programme. It was supported by the armed forces, which had seen communist revolution enter the barracks in the shape of the sailors' uprising a few days before—which was left unpunished by the government.

But it provided no clue to the future, no hint of how the armed forces proposed to govern a country with a long constitutional tradition and no experience of sustained military rule. There was the precedent of Getulio Vargas' corporate state (1937-45) but the Brazilian generals—some of whom had fought with the Allies in Italy during the Second World War—were suspicious of this form of 'emotional nationalism'. Furthermore, Marshal Castelo Branco, who became the first military president, seemed to be privately committed to the idea that the role of the armed forces was to 'clean up the mess' and then retire gracefully from the scene, leaving the ring to the civilian politicians. Things did not work out that way, and Brazil today offers one of the primary examples of a military authoritarian regime ruling without a timetable.

Whatever the generals' original aims, the early crises of the regime were resolved in favour of the officers who wanted greater authoritarian powers. The first crisis came with the painful deflationary programme applied under the supervision of Roberto Campos and the gubernatorial elections of October 1965, in which opposition candidates were successful. The outcry from hardliners over the election results persuaded

Castelo Branco to outlaw the existing political parties; the social effects of economic retrenchment supplied the argument that the military were the only force that could guarantee a necessary, but unpopular, return to economic 'sanity'. The second major internal crisis followed in December 1968, at the end of a year of student demonstrations and industrial unrest. It was triggered by the refusal of congress to remove the parliamentary immunity of an opposition deputy, Marcio Moreira Alves, who had called on the people to apply the 'Lysistrata tactic' to the armed forces, by preventing girls from going out with soldiers.[10] The outcome was the introduction of the notorious Institutional Act No. 5—giving the government sweeping emergency powers—and the temporary closure of congress.

The Brazilian regime appears, in some respects, to have been living from hand to mouth, rather than acting according to long-term plans. There have been oscillations back and forth; the trend towards the repressive centralisation of power was reversed during the first year of General Ernesto Geisel's presidency (15 March 1974—) when politicians from the pre-1964 era were brought back into the cabinet and there were renewed promises of a 'gradual but sure' progression back towards democracy. This situation offers hope to the advocates of liberal pluralism in Brazil. To use Juan Linz's terms, the Brazilian regime has shown considerable *staying power,* but it has not fully *institutionalised* itself; it would be more precise to speak of an 'authoritarian situation' rather than an 'authoritarian regime'.[11]

The secret of the regime's staying power is to be detected, first, in the solution that has been found to the familiar problem of how to ensure a peaceful succession. Military dictatorship in Brazil is collective dictatorship. The president is confined to a single four-year term, and is elected by the senior officers, whose succession and retirement is in turn ensured by a strict code of seniority. There has been little scope for *caudillismo,* for the arrogation of power to an individual and the cult of personality. Second, the armed forces have been able to reduce—but not to avoid entirely—the partisan rivalries and identifications that are bound to result from direct participation in government by standing aloof from the ministries that are not directly concerned with national security. The running of the economy is left to civilian technocrats. Third, the regime has been able to manipulate nationalist symbols with considerable success in a sport-obsessed country whose huge expanse and tremendous natural resources are a source of pioneering pride. Fourth, it has presided over the 'economic miracle' of the late 1960s and early 1970s, although the country's dependence on foreign investment leaves it exposed to the effects of world recession and makes the regime vulnerable to populist xenophobia primarily directed against the Americans. The signal achievement of a capitalist model of development in Brazil (as contrasted with the notorious failures of UN prescriptions for redistribution instead of growth elsewhere) has also exposed the regime to criticism based on the obvious persisting economic inequalities—despite the entirely valid response that, if you have increased the size of the national cake, in the end you can give everyone bigger slices. Fifth, the armed forces can still make an effective *negative* appeal to the memory of the situation before 1964 and to the prospect of suppressed communist and guerrilla forces re-emerging from under cover in the event of a 'premature' return to constitutional government. Finally, the regime is supported by a notoriously efficent network of intelligence services, coordinated through the National Intelligence Service (SNI)[12].

Brazil today is one model of a stable but necessarily impermanent authoritarian regime, which has erred severely on the side of police repression and the suppression of individual liberties, but has presided over a period of capitalist expansion that is without parallel outside the European world and Japan. Its stability is impressive; the regime has lasted twelve years (which is not bad going in Latin America) and is probably vulnerable only to internal division, which has been apparent—notably through General Albuquerque Lima's appeals for a populist and anti-capitalist form of authoritarianism—but has so far been successfully contained.

I have used the term 'necessarily impermanent' of Brazil's authoritarian regime because, while the role of the armed forces in controlling and promoting the process of economic modernisation in developing countries is clearly established, that process in itself would seem bound to produce new political forces that will seek and eventually find expression.

The task for the armed forces in this situation is to offer channels for political expression—not necessarily through the vehicles of representative government familiar in the Western democracies.

All ways of ordering society are 'necessarily impermanent'. Representative government based on universal suffrage is still a relative infant among the world's political systems, but it has outlasted communism (at least in the Anglo-Saxon countries) and shows continuing, and encouraging, signs of vitality in at least some of the advanced industrial societies. But the area of the world that appears susceptible to Western concepts of representative government and economic liberalism has been steadily shrinking. You have only to attend a UN debate to see that the Western democracies belong to a club with a dwindling attendance, some of whose members are finding it inconvenient to pay their full subscriptions. The contraction of the West is not an illusion: you have only to glance at the map.

We are told often enough that the 'real' world conflict is not a conflict of ideology, but a conflict between rich and poor, an international class struggle. The battle against hunger and exploitation is an everyday reality over vast areas of the globe, but we should look closely at the motives of those who tell us that because of it, the equally ancient battle between freedom and tyranny is a Western obfuscation. The classical exponents of liberal capitalism, with their dedication to material well-being and their naive optimism that the world would evolve into an economic and social unity, were poorly equipped for this battle of ideologies. It is the materialist and secular elements in their philosophy that endure, not their passionate addiction to liberty or those sometimes deeply-held religious convictions that they were utterly prudish about expressing in public. Yet, as T. S. Eliot observed, 'all our problems turn out ultimately to be a religious problem.'[13] A philosophy founded on nothing more than the promise of material well-being cannot long endure. Cobden and his disciples 'were doing less than justice to themselves when they omitted from their official creed their own personal and traditional beliefs that "Man shall not live by bread alone" and at the same time they were dooming their cause to defeat, for to offer bread alone is almost as uninviting as to offer stones for bread.'[14]

Liberal capitalism had the further drawback of encouraging materialist demands which it could not guarantee to satisfy—although its successes were so great that the rebellion inside Western countries can fairly be described as a rebellion of affluence, or even 'post-scarcity anarchism'.[15] Listen again to Herbert Marcuse: 'At the highest stage of capitalism, the most necessary revolution appears as the most unlikely one . . . Capitalism cannot satisfy the needs which it creates. The rising standard of living itself expresses this dynamic: it enforced the constant creation of needs that could be satisfied without abolishing the capitalist mode of production. It is still true that capitalism grows through growing *impoverishment*, and that impoverishment will be a basic factor of revolution—although in new historical forms.'[16] We are by now familiar with those new forms of revolt, some of which—the critique of economic growth and the campaign for the conservation of natural resources—have helped to make up for the omissions of a materialist culture. We have also seen liberty turned into license, tolerance turned into promiscuity, job security made a base for revolutionary activities or sheer disruption that are justified as an escape from boredom at work, the depressing secularism of the age replaced by totalitarian pseudo-religions and the romantic cult of violence.

We have also found the West in a new predicament which is highly promising for its external enemies: the predicament which lies in 'the disintegration of the moral consensus which has informed the rise and rule of capitalism . . . and a dominant bourgeoisie of mounting self-doubt and distraction.'[17] With so much confusion about the nature of those values—individual freedom, economic progress and rational inquiry—around which the great oak of Western civilisation extends its leaves and branches, it is not surprising that fewer and fewer people seek its shade. There is the legacy of guilt: the inheritance of the former imperial powers that have forgotten how to act but, like an old man remembering the mistresses of his youth, decide to live in penance for what they can no longer do. This is of course too cynical. What had the liberal values to do with slavery or napalm?

But self-doubt is a poor position from which to confront a self-assured mass murderer—you do not pit Hamlet against Lady Macbeth. The struggle for power in the world subscribes to the grim law of the Indian sage Kautilya, that big fish eat little fish, rather than to the sitting-room ethics of *On Liberty*. The means used in the struggle may not always be pleasant, and may even run contrary to the principles that are being defended; but if the struggle is lost, there is nothing left to defend. This argument runs up against the kind of philosophic surrender to which the poet Robert Lowell confessed, during a symposium on the fall of South Vietnam, with a candour that is not often found in company with the cultural guilt complex that he transliterates: 'In our defeat communism is inevitable and cleansing, though tyrannical forever.'[18] While radical intellectuals cheerfully cast themselves in the role of 'white auxiliaries' to the anti-capitalist revolution of the third world, the West contracts and becomes more and more introverted, and the Western public sinks into a morass of confusion about the nature and morality of power. We are assured that if poor countries go communist, that is because 'it's better to be red than underfed' and it's none of our business anyway. In the name of morality, the World Council of Churches and other such estimable bodies support guerrilla revolutionaries who are likely to turn into the next generation of black dictators; but nobody is doing much to propagate the tenets of liberal democracy. On the contrary, we find a popular improvisation on J. S. Mill's theme that 'primitive' peoples need despots; now we are told that liberal democracy is a fig-leaf on capitalist exploitation and that only the decadent Westerners need it.

The Americans (and the Australians) are caught up in a debate about whether intelligence services should be allowed to do more than store newspaper cuttings; the British are in process of dismantling what little remains of their defence commitments outside Europe; the countries of Western Europe were about to ratify, at the time of writing, a document confirming the slavery of their fellow-Europeans on the other side of the Iron Curtain. But the decline of the West, as already noted, is to be measured in psychological and social rather than military or economic terms. Put at its simplest, the decline is the result of a loss of faith in Western values (and doubts about what they have justified in the past) and a consequent reluctance to defend them where they are threatened. After Suez, after Vietnam—both of which were profoundly divisive experiences whose rights and wrongs cannot even now be settled—the creeping consensus appears to be: the outer provinces are lost, but since life is still pleasant enough in Rome, we can forget about which provinces will be next. The Russians (and still less the Chinese) are not *in themselves* the danger. The barbarians—and I use the word 'barbarian' in Lenin's sense, to mean an enemy of the culture, psychology and morality of the West—are always there waiting. But the barbarians only press on to the gates when the empire is dying from within. As Saint Cyprian said to the Romans, 'You complain of the aggression of foreign enemies; yet, if the foreign enemies were to cease from troubling, would Roman really be able to live at peace with Roman?'

Alexander Solzhenitsyn puts it all more clearly than most of the resident critics of the society to which he was unwillingly exiled. He reminds us that we have been engaged in a Third World War since 1945, when it was formally initiated at Yalta by 'the shaky pens of Roosevelt and Churchill, who celebrated the victory by handing out concessions: Estonia, Latvia, Lithuania, Moldavia, Mongolia, millions of Soviet citizens forcibly handed over to face death or the camps; and soon Yugoslavia, Albania, Poland, Bulgaria, Romania, Czechoslovakia, Hungary, East Germany were abandoned to unrestrained violence.' The Third World War came stealthily, 'boring into the flabby body of the world'. Three decades since Yalta have been 'an unbroken descent towards enfeeblement and decadence.' The victors of 1945 transformed themselves into the vanquished, having 'totally ceded more countries and peoples than have ever been ceded in any surrender in any way in human history'. His catalogue of abandoned lands and peoples stretches on: through China (arguably a more important ally to the Western democracies than Russia during Hitler's war) through North Korea, Cuba, North Vietnam, Cambodia, South Vietnam, with Laos and Portugal intended to follow, with South Korea embattled, with Finland and Austria 'resigned to their fate'. And 'there is no room to list all the little countries of Africa and the Middle East that have become puppets of communism, and all the others, even in Europe, that hasten to grovel on their knees in order to survive.'[19]

Not the least of Solzhenitsyn's services to freedom is his readiness to say things that produce a muffled choking sound or an embarrassed turning-away among some of his Western admirers. He has the great gift of vision which consists of being able to look into an extremely simple situation and see what is actually there. As he reminds us,

> The situation as I have described it is clear to any average man in the East, from Poznan to Canton. But Westerners will need a great deal of strength, of resolution, to see and accept the evidence of the implacable tide of violence and bloodshed that has methodically, steadily, triumphantly radiated out from a single centre for nearly sixty years, and to locate the countries already lined up for the next holocaust.

How fortunate we are that Solzhenitsyn is a giant of literature. If his stature had been anything less, he would either have vanished for good into a labour camp or a mental institution in Russia or have been shrugged off by all but a handful among his Western audiences as 'just another of those embittered emigrés' or 'someone who should have stuck to novels'. One final quotation from his article, which goes to the heart of the matter: 'The Third World War', he concludes, 'attacks the West at its most vulnerable point: the side of human nature willing to make any concession for the sake of material well-being.' Do we still need to ask what he means?

ACKNOWLEDGMENTS

Many people helped to kindle this book, often enough without realising it. I was driven to study the conditions for the survival of a free society by the experiences of friends in some of the countries that have learned the cost of revolution in recent years: Portugal, Chile, Cuba, Argentina, Vietnam, Northern Ireland. It became increasingly plain to me that the fate of these 'outer provinces' is bound up with our own, and that the survival of liberal democracy even in Britain (its modern birthplace) cannot be guaranteed in the absence of a renewed awareness of the values of a free society and a more determined resolve to defend them against the totalitarians in our midst. The grim prospect is that the liberties that were lost at the barricades in other places will be lost through a gradual and largely uncomprehended process of evolution in Britain—unless that national renewal takes place.

As I began to wrestle with these problems, in the effort to define the various ways in which democratic institutions break down and the options that are left if the collapse is irretrievable, I gained a great deal from conversations with the following people, many of whom will no doubt disagree with the conclusions I have reached, and none of whom is responsible for any errors of fact or interpretation: José-Mario Armero, Luigi Barzini, Dr Rhodes Boyson, MP, Brigadier Michael Calvert, Lord Chalfont, Dr Richard Clutterbuck, Brian Crozier, Hernán Cubillos, Professor S. E. Finer, Professor Antony Flew, Ralph Harris, Dr Stephen Haseler, Sir Geoffrey Jackson, Josef Josten, Russell Lewis, the Marquess of Linlithgow, Stephen Milligan, James Nadler, John O'Sullivan, Julian Radcliffe, Lord Robbins, Professor Leonard Schapiro, Ariana Stassinopoulos, Professor James Theberge, Sir Robert Thompson, Peter Utley, Professor Alan Walters, Colin Welch and Peregrine Worsthorne. Some of my ideas were strengthened or modified by the many hundreds of people who wrote to me when I began to broach the subject in speeches, articles and broadcasts.

I am also grateful to my publisher, Maurice Temple Smith, for his patience, enthusiasm and a number of valuable suggestions; to the staff of the London Library, that splendid institution that shows that the market economy is still alive and well in St James's Square; to Miss Diana Keigwin, who deciphered the author's hieroglyphs with the eye of an Egyptologist, while maintaining unfailing good humour; to my wife Katrina, who helped to bring order out of chaos; and to my small daughter Pandora, who helped to ensure the kind of insomnia that is useful to authors.

London   *September 1975*

NOTES

Introduction

1 E. F. M. Durbin, *The Politics of Democratic Socialism* (Routledge, 1945) p. 271.
2 J. S. Mill, in his *Considerations on Representative Government* ed. R. B. McCallum (Blackwell, 1946) took issue with both the 'mechanical' and 'organic' conceptions of democracy. My concern is simply to point out that the institutions can be used against the society.
3 Thucydides, *The Peloponnesian War* trans. Rex Warner (Penguin, 1974) p. 569.
4 Walter Lippmann, *The Public Philosophy* (Little, Brown, 1955) pp. 160-1.
5 Brian Crozier develops this argument in his important book, *A Theory of Conflict* (Hamish Hamilton, 1974).
6 John Middleton Murry, *The Necessity of Communism* (Cape, 1932) p. 123.
7 J. S. Mill, *Considerations on Representative Government* p. 112.
8 Thomas Hobbes, *Leviathan*, ed. M. Oakeshott (Collier Books, 1962) Introduction, p. 7.
9 Daniel Moynihan, in *Commentary*, March 1975.
10 R. H. S. Crossman, in the *Evening Standard*, 14 January 1965.
11 Review by S. Golyakov in *Kommunist* (No. 3, 1974) of *The Secret Front* by KGB General S. Tsvigun.

2 From Liberal to Mass Democracy

1 George Orwell, 'Notes on the Way' in *Collected Essays, Journalism and Letters* (Penguin, 1971) vol. 2, p. 30.
2 Ortega y Gasset, *The Revolt of the Masses* (Norton, 1932) p. 134.
3 Robert Kilroy-Silk, 'Labour must not be frightened of making socialism work', in *The Times* 29 April 1975.
4 Edmund Burke, *Reflections on the Revolution in France* (Everyman edition, 1960) p. 153.
5 F. A. Hayek, *The Constitution of Liberty* (Routledge, 1960) p. 103.
6 J. A. Talmon, *The Origins of Totalitarian Democracy* (Secker & Warburg, 1952).
7 This is a summary of *The Republic*, Book VIII. The quotations are

taken from Desmond Lee's translation (Penguin, 1974) pp. 372-91.

8 See M. I. Finley, *Democracy Ancient and Modern* (Chatto & Windus, 1973).

9 Aristotle, *The Politics*, Book V. Quotations from T. A. Sinclair's translation (Penguin, 1972) pp. 200-201.

10 ibid, Book VI. pp. 240-2.

11 Finley, *Democracy*, pp. 8-9.

12 S. M. Lipset, *Political Man* (Mercury Books, 1966) pp. 92-92. Lipset, writing more than a decade ago, was perhaps the most complacent exponent of this viewpoint. He actually felt able to conclude that 'the fundamental political problems of the industrial revolution have been solved: the workers have achieved industrial and political citizenship; the conservatives have accepted the welfare state; and the democratic left has recognised that an increase in overall state power carries with it more dangers to freedom than solutions for economic problems.' ibid, p. 406.

13 Xenophon, *Memorabilia*. Quoted in Finley, *Democracy*, p. 91.

14 Alexis de Tocqueville, *Democracy in America* trans. H. Reeve (Schocken, 1964) vol. 2, p. 351.

15 Quoted in Russell Kirk, *The Conservative Mind* (Faber, 1963) p. 282.

16 Sir Henry Maine, *Popular Government* (London, 1886) p. 106.

17 Ortega y Gasset, *Revolt of the Masses*, p. 18.

18 J. F. Stephen, *Liberty, Equality, Fraternity* (Smith, Elder, 2nd edition, 1874) p. 20.

19 ibid, p. 262.

20 Robert Michels, *Political Parties* trans. E. and C. Paul (Jarrold, 1915).

21 W. H. Mallock, *The Limits of Pure Democracy* (Chapman & Hall, 1918) p. 45.

22 F. A. Hayek, *Law, Legislation and Liberty* (Routledge, 1973) p. 3.

23 A. J. P. Taylor, *English History 1914-1945* (Oxford University Press, 1965) p. 1.

24 For a stimulating critique of the whole trend, see Russell Lewis, *The New Service Society* (Longman, 1973).

25 ibid, p. 103.

26 J. S. Mill, *On Liberty*, p. 3.

27 Herbert Spencer, *The Man versus the State* (Williams & Norgate, 1884) p. 78.

28 ibid, p. 83.

29 Milton Friedman, *Capitalism and Freedom*, p. 24.

30 *Constitution of Liberty*. p. 11.

31 *Law, Legislation and Liberty*, p. 56.

32 R. H. Tawney, *Equality* (Allen & Unwin, 4th edition, 1952) p. 266.

33 Ludwig von Mises, *Socialism* trans. by J. Kahane (Cape, 2nd edition, 1951) p. 17.

34 Sir Leslie Scarman, *English Law—The New Dimension* (Stevens, 1974) p. 29.

3   The Nature of Subversion

1 Curzio Malaparte, *Technique du coup d'état* (Grasset, Paris, 2nd edition, 1948) p. 95.
2 The psychology of this type is beautifully analysed in David Caute, *The Fellow-Travellers* (Weidenfeld, 1973).
3 For an amusing riposte, see Arnold Beichman, *Nine Lies about America* (Alcove Press, 1973).
4 Moscow Radio, 4 March 1975.
5 A. Bovin, writing in *Red Star*, 29 October, 1974.
6 Professor A. I. Sobolev, writing in *The Working Class and the Contemporary World* (January—February 1975).
7 Professor M. Banglay, 'Peaceful Coexistence and the Ideological Struggle in *Trud*, 9 January 1975.
8 For further information, see the pamphlet by Geoffrey Stewart-Smith, *Not to be Trusted* (Foreign Affairs Publishing Co, Richmond, Surrey, 1974).
9 Marx and Engels, *Selected Works*, First published 1948; quotation from vol. 1, p. 50 (Foreign Language Publishing House, Moscow, 1950).
10 *The Tactics of Disruption: Communist Methods Exposed* (TUC, London, 1949).
11 *Trud*, 4 March 1975.

4   The Disease of Money

1 William Rees-Mogg, *The Reigning Error: The Crisis of World Inflation* (Hamish Hamilton, 1974) p. 103.
2 W. H. Hutt, *Politically Impossible..?* (Institute of Economic Affairs, London, 1971).
3 Peter Jay, 'How inflation threatens British democracy with its last chance before extinction' in *The Times*, 1 July 1974.
4 The classic account of the Great Inflation in Germany is Constantino Bresciano-Turroni, *The Economics of Inflation* trans. M. E. Sayers (Allen & Unwin, 1937). A colourful recent account is William Guttmann and Patricia Meehan, *The Great Inflation* (Saxon House, 1975) which is especially interesting on the social consequences of hyper-inflation. For a revisionist and anti-monetarist account, see Karsten Laursen and Torgen Pedersen, *The German Inflation 1918-1923* (North Holland Publishing Company, 1964).
5 Frances Cairncross and Hamish McRae, *The Second Great Crash*

(Methuen, 1975).

6   Emmanuel Beau de Loménie, *Les responsabilités des dynasties é bourgeoises* (Denoel, Paris, 1973) vol. V, p. 93.

7   Lord Robbins *et. al.*, *Inflation: Causes, Consequences, Cures.* (Institute of Economic Affairs, 1974) p. 76.

8   Especially in the publications of the IEA. See, most recently, Ralph Harris and Brendon Sewill, *British Economic Policy 1970-74* (London, 1975).

9   F. A. Hayek, writing in the *Daily Telegraph*, 16 October 1974.

10 John Mackintosh, 'A wages plan for the crisis package' in the *Observer*, 25 May 1975.

11 *Inflation*, op. cit., p. 60.

12 Robert Moss, 'The Moving Frontier: A Survey of Brazil' in the *Economist*, 2 September 1972. For a Brazilian view, see Mario Henrique Simonsen, *Inflação: Gradualismo x Tratamento de Choque* (Apec, Rio, 1970).

5   In Fear of Strikes

1   V. I. Lenin, *Left-Wing Communism, an Infantile Disorder* [1920] (Progress Publishers, Moscow, 1968) p. 34.

2   Ralph Dahrendorf, *Society and Democracy in Germany* (Weidenfeld, 1967) 'In political debate, the ideology of an inner unity of society generally appeared encased in the other ideology of a state of national emergency. Because the nation is surrounded by enemies, it must close its ranks inside and form a "forsworn community".' p. 131.

3   Chie Nakane, *Japanese Society* (Weidenfeld, 1970). See also Brian Beedham, 'A Special Strength: A Survey of Japan' in *The Economist*, 31 March 1973.

4   Roland Huntford, *The New Totalitarians* (Allen Lane, 1972) p. 100.

5   *The United Kingdom in 1980: The Hudson Report* (Associated Business Programmes, London, 1974). This report was widely criticised for its straight-line extrapolations from current trends. A more fundamental criticism, however, is that in calling for more centralised planning and berating private investors for doing the things one would predict in conditions of high inflation and government disincentives to industry they failed to locate the crux of Britain's problem: in the destruction of the market system.

6   ibid, p. 66.

7   John Strachey, *The Coming Struggle for Power* (Gollancz, 1932) pp. 141-3.

8   Gerald Abrahams, *Trade Unions and the Law* (Cassell, 1968) p. 110.

9   ibid., p. 79.

10 See C. Northcote Parkinson (ed.) *Industrial Disruption* (Leviathan House, 1973) pp. 139-40.

11 Stephen Fay, *Measure for Measure: Reforming the Trade Unions* (Chatto & Windus, 1970).

12 There is a very useful account of the life and death of the Industrial Relations Act in Stephen Milligan's valuable (but as yet unpublished) work on *Trade Unions*, to which I am indebted. The left-wing socialist, Eric Heffer, has produced his own account of the 'Kill the Bill' campaign under the revealing title, *The Class Struggle in Parliament* (Gollancz, 1973).

13 Quoted in Hayek, *Constitution of Liberty*, p. 267.

14 V. I. Lenin, *What is to be done?* [1902] trans. S. V. and P. Utechin (Oxford University Press, 1963) p. 132.

15 See, for example, the *Handbook for Strikers* (published by the Claimants' Union, London, 1973).

16 An excellent investigative account of the coup was Eric Jacobs' article, 'Why some Unions are more democratic than others' in the *Sunday Times*, 25 May 1975.

17 Reg Birch, *Guerrilla Struggle and the Working-Class* (published by the Communist Party of Britain—Marxist-Leninist—London, 1973).

18 *The Times*, 8 February 1972.

19 This is based on an article in the *Carworker*, one of the International Socialists' trade publications, which appeared in the October—November issue, 1972. For further thoughts on this tactic, see Tony Cliff, *The Crisis* (Pluto Press, London, 1975).

20 Jack Woddis, *Time to Change Course: What Britain's Communists Stand For* (published by the Communist Party, London, March 1973) pp. 99-100.

21 See Georges Sorel, *Reflections on Violence* trans. T. E. Hulme (Collier, 1972).

22 Ludwig von Mises, *Socialism*, op. cit. p. 483.

23 *Plant Level Bargaining* (TGWU Education and Research pamphlet, 1970, 1st edition).

6   *The Necessity of Property*

1 *Commons' Journals*, 21 May 1604, vol. 1, p. 218.

2 Andrew Shonfield, *Modern Capitalism* (RIIA/Oxford, 1964) p. 239.

3 T. E. Utley, 'Capitalism and Morality' in *The Case for Capitalism*, ed. M. Ivens and R. Dunstan, (Michael Joseph, 1967) p. 21.

4 Ezra Pound, Canto XLV, in *Selected Cantos* (Faber, 1967) pp. 67-8.

5 R. H. Tawney, *Religion and the Rise of Capitalism* (Penguin, 1961) p. 48.

6 Ernest Van den Haag, 'The Political Threat to the Market Economy'

in the *Lugano Review* No. 2, 1975, p. 16.

7   See, for example, John Rawls, *A Theory of Justice*. (Oxford University Press, 1972).

8   Jeremy Bentham, *Utilitarianism* (Everyman edition, 1948) p. 6.

9   Benito Mussolini, 'The Doctrine of Fascism', reprinted in Michael Oakeshott, *The Social and Political Doctrines of Contemporary Europe* (Cambridge University Press, 1939) pp. 175-7.

10 Hilaire Belloc, *The Servile State* (Constable, 3rd edition, 1927) p. 5.

11 ibid, p. 98.

12 ibid, p. 127.

13 Samuel Brittan, *Participation without Politics* (Institute of Economic Affairs, London, 1975) p. 15.

14 Ludwig von Mises, *Socialism*, op. cit., p. 21.

15 For a description of some Californian pilot schemes, see C. B. Cox and Rhodes Boyson (eds) *Black Paper on Education, 1975*. (Dent, 1975).

16 See George Polanyi and John B. Wood, *How Much Inequality?* (Institute of Economic Affairs, London, 1974).

17 Samuel Brittan, *Capitalism and the Permissive Society* (Macmillan, 1973) p. 1.

18 T. E. Utley, 'Why we still need the rich'. *Daily Telegraph* 26 March 1974.

19 Hayek, *Constitution of Liberty*, p. 52.

20 Colin Clark, *The Conditions of Economic Progress* (Macmillan, 1940).

21 H. S. Ferns, 'How socialism broke Argentina', *Daily Telegraph* 3 July 1974.

22 For a useful and stimulating, if strongly partisan, account see Roberto Aizcorbe, *Argentina: The Peronist Myth* (Exposition Press, New York, 1975).

23 ibid. p. 31.

24 Paul Samuelson, 'The Affluent State' in *Sweden Now*, September 1971.

25 Joseph Schumpeter, *Capitalism, Socialism and Democracy*. (4th edition, Allen & Unwin, 1954).

26 c. f. Michael Grant, *The Climax of Rome* (Weidenfeld, 1968) p. 56.

27 Ludwig Erhard, *Prosperity through Competition* (Thames & Hudson, 1958) p. 6.

28 See Glen W. Bradf, 'Study of Beaver Colonies in Michigan' *Journal of Mammalogy* No. 19, 1938. For a popular account see Robert Ardrey, *The Territorial Imperative* (Collins, 1969).

7   *Pseudo-Legality and Revolutions*

1   Friedrich Engels, 'Introduction' to Marx's *Class Struggles in France*,

1848-1850 [1895]in Marx and Engels, *Selected Works* (Foreign Languages Publishing House, Moscow, 1950) vol. I, p. 125.

2   Curzio Malaparte, *La technique du coup d'état* (Grasset, Paris, 2nd edition, 1948) ch. 1.

3   Karl Radek suggested to the Comintern in 1923 that it should organise a special corps to make communist coups throughout Europe. It should rely on technicians, not the local communist parties. For a subsequent post-mortem on the failed insurrections of the early 1920s by Marshal Tukhachevsky and others, see 'A. Neuburg', *Armed Insurrection* (New Left Books, 1971).

4   Edward Luttwak, *Coup d'état: A Practical Handbook* (Allen Lane, 1968) p. 24.

5   ibid, p. 35.

6   A. P. Ryan, *Mutiny at the Curragh* (Macmillan, 1956) p. 142.

7   Diana Spearman, *Modern Dictatorships* (Cape, 1939) pp. 43-4.

8   Lipset, *Political Man*, ch. 3.

9   Sir Henry Maine, *Popular Government* (London, 1885) p. 158.

10 Quoted in S. E. Finer, *The Man on Horseback* (Pall Mall, 1967) p. 81.

11 V. I. Lenin, *'Left-Wing' Communism, an Infantile Disorder*, pp. 79-80.

12 ibid, p. 37.

13 ibid, p. 83.

14 George Orwell, 'London Letter to Partisan Review', January 1941 in *Collected Essays* vol. 2, p. 68.

15 Count Albert Vandal, *L'avènement de Napoleon* 2 vols (Paris, 1905-7). For a full discussion of the literature on Napoleon's rise to power, see Pieter Geyl, *Napoleon: For and Against* trans. Olive Renier (Penguin, 1965).

16 S. E. Finer, *The Man on Horseback* p. 212.

17 c.f. Gaetano Salvemini, *The Fascist Dictatorship in Italy*, vol. 1 Origins and practices (Cape, 1928).

18 Adrian Lyttelton, *The Seizure of Power: Fascism in Italy 1919-1929* (Weidenfeld, 1973) p. 20.

19 ibid, p. 100.

20 Malaparte, op. cit. p. 197.

21 Hermann Rauschning, *Germany's Revolution of Destruction*, trans. E. W. Dickes (Heinemann, 1939) p. 12.

22 ibid, p. 5.

23 c.f. Ralph Dahrendorf, *Society and Democracy in Germany* (Weidenfeld, 1967).

24 H. Rothfels, *German Opposition to Hitler* (Chicago University Press, 1962).

25 Friedrich Meinecke, *Machiavellism: The doctrine of raison d'état and its place in modern history*, trans. D. Scott (Routledge, 1957).

26 John Wheeler-Bennett, *The Nemesis of Power: The German Army in*

Politics (Macmillan, 1953).

27   Karl J. Newman, *European Democracy between the Wars* (Allen & Unwin, 1970) p. 123.

28   Open letter to Chancellor Brüning, 8 December 1931. Quoted in Alan Bullock, *Hitler: A Study in Tyranny* (Odhams, 1964) p. 191.

29   Karl Dietrich Bracher, *The German Dilemma* (Weidenfeld, 1974) p. 286.

30   Frederick M. Watkins, *The Failure of Constitutional Emergency Powers Under the German Republic* (Harvard University Press, 1939) p. 10.

31   ibid, p. 35.

32   Konrad Heiden, *A History of National Socialism* (New York, 1935) p. 134.

33   Franz von Papen, *Memoirs* (André Deutsch, 1952) p. 210.

34   Robert Manvell and Heinrich Fraenkel, *The Hundred Days to Hitler* (Dent, 1974).

35   c.f. Erich Eyck, *A History of the Weimar Republic* trans. P. Hanson and R. G. L. Waite (Harvard University Press, 1964) vol. 2, pp. 281-2.

36   Watkins, op. cit. p. 64.

37   André François-Poncet, *The Fateful Years* (Gollancz, 1948).

38   Quoted in Joachim C. Fest, *The Face of the Third Reich* trans. M. Bullock (Penguin, 1972) p. 244.

39   Papen's own version, naturally, is substantially different. One of the most readable accounts is Manvell and Fraenkel, op. cit. Rauschning's judgement on the failure and self-deception of German conservatives is particularly relevant. He observed that Papen, Schleicher and their friends, differed fundamentally from genuine conservatives in their 'complete scepticism as to the relevance of spiritual and moral forces to practical politics'.

40   There is a useful brief account in Karl J. Newman, *European Democracy* pp. 256-68.

41   Philip Selznick, *The Organizational Weapon*, p. 308.

42   See Ernst Fraenkel, *The Dual State: a contribution to the theory of dictatorship* (Oxford University Press, 1941).

8   The Prague Model

1   Leon Trotsky, *History of the Russian Revolution* (Simon & Schuster, 1932) vol. 1, pp. 206-7.

2   These terms are used by the Czech communist ideologist, Jan Kozak, in his notorious essay 'How Parliament can play a revolutionary part in the transition to socialism and the role of the popular masses'. The 14th edition, with an introduction by Robert Moss, was published by the Independent Information Centre, London, in 1975, under the title *Without a shot being fired*.

3   Josef Josten, *Oh My Country* (Latimer House, 1949) p. 32. Josef Frolik, *The Frolik Defection* (Leo Cooper, 1975) contains some further details.
4   Hubert Ripka, *Le coup de Prague* (Plon, Paris, 1949) p. 38.
5   Kozak, op. cit., p. 11.
6   Kurt Glaser, *Czechoslovakia: A Critical History* (Caxton Press, Caldwell, Idaho, 1961) p. 145.
7   *Rude Pravo*, 4 October 1947, quoted in Kozak, op. cit., p. 39.
8   Josef Korbel, *The Communist Subversion of Cezechoslovakia 1938-1948* (Princeton University Press, 1959) p. 64.
9   Ripka, *Le coup de Prague* pp. 162-5.
10 Kozak, *Without a shot being fired*, p. 22.
11 Marx and Engels, *Selected Works.*

9   Lessons from Chile

1   The private sector contributed only twenty-eight per cent of new investment in the year before Allende took office.
2   For a fuller discussion on this theme, see my article, 'The Cloak-and-Dagger Controversy' in *International Review* No. 3, Winter 1974.
3   See, in particular, *Chile's Marxist Experiment*, (David & Charles, Newton Abbot, 1973), and 'Chile's Coup and After' in *Encounter* March 1974.
4   See A. Sobolev's article in *The Working Class and the Contemporary World* (Moscow) No. 2, 1974.
5   Pedro Vuskovic, quoted in Alain Labrousse, *L'Expérience chilienne* (Seuil, Paris, 1972) p. 262.
6   This document is reprinted as an appendix to Pablo Rodríguez Grez, *Entre la democracia y la tiranía* (Printer Ltda, Santiago, 1972).
7   By the then finance minister, Orlando Millas; c.f. *Chile's Marxist Experiment* pp. 75-9 for more details of the cost of nationalisation.
8   *La Nación* (Santiago) 2 February, 1973.
9   *Tarea Urgente* (Santiago) July 1973. For more information on 'workers' control', Santiago-style, from a Marxist viewpoint, see Michel Raptis, *Revolution and Counter-Revolution in Chile* (Allison & Busby, 1974).
10 *Noticias de Ultima Hora* (Santiago) 10 September 1973. For a useful account of Altamirano's role, see Genaro Arriagada Herrera, *De La Via Chilena a la Via Insurreccional* (Editorial del Pacifico, Santiago, 1974).

10   The Portuguese Way

1   For more detail on these early meetings, see Pierre Audibert and

Daniel Brigon, *Portugal: les nouveaux centurions* (Belford, Paris, 1974).

2   Arcadia, Lisbon, 1974.

3   For some of Otelo's subsequent thoughts on Spínola, see Brigadier Otelo Saraiva de Carvalho, *Cinco meses mudarão Portugal* (Portugalia Editora, Lisbon, 1975).

4   Published in *O Seculo* 22 April 1975.

5   Captain Salgueiro Maia, a key conspirator in April 1974, was apparently expected to bring the Escola Practica de Cavalharia out behind Spínola in March. When the moment came he declined to move. See the article 'Quem armou a mão de Spínola? in *Expresso* 15 March 1975.

6   *La Settimanale* (Rome) 12 April 1975. This article contains some interesting claims of KGB involvement in Portugal. It alleges that the AFM was subsidised by the Russians to the tune of 38 million dollars in 1974; the money was derived from capital taken out of the country after 23 April 1974. Its catalogue of Soviet agents and associates in Lisbon includes a number of naval officers, among whom Commander Correia Jesuino, 'social communications' minister, Commander Arbantes Serra (considered particularly in league with the Cuban DGI), Captain Costa Martins and Commander Martins Guerrero of the Supreme Revolutionary Council are mentioned.

7   See Brian Crozier, *Soviet Pressures in the Caribbean* (Conflict Studies No. 35, 1973).

11   The Limits of Tolerance

1   Herbert Marcuse, quoted in Maurice Cranston, *The New Left* (Bodley Head, 1971) pp. 87-8.

2   J. S. Mill, *On Liberty* ed. R. B. McCallum (Blackwell, 1946).

3   ibid, p. 33.

4   J. F. Stephen, *Liberty, Equality, Fraternity*, p. 63.

5   See F. A. Hermens, *Demokratie oder Anarchie* (Frankfurt, 1951).

6   Alexis de Tocqueville, *Democracy in America*, op. cit., vol. 2, p. 19.

7   John Milton, *Areopagitica* (Oxford University Press, 1949) pp. 18-19.

12   Violence and the State

1   Paul Wilkinson, *Political Terrorism* (Macmillan, 1974).

2   See the 'Minimanual of the Urban Guerrilla', reprinted as an appendix to Robert Moss, *Urban Guerrilla Warfare* (IISS, London, 1971).

3   See, for example, '700 spie sovietiche operano in Italia' in *Il*

Settimanale, 18 June 1975.

4 See 'The Companies in the guerrillas' sights' in the *Economist*, 1 June 1974.

5 For a full description, see Roberto Aizcorbe, op. cit.

6 Dotson Rader, quoted in Arnold Beichman, 'An Angry Fancy: The Politics of Terror' in *Lugano Review* No. 2, 1975.

7 See, for instance, John McGuffin, *The Guinea Pigs* (Penguin, 1974).

8 T. A. Critchley, *The Conquest of Violence* (Constable, 1970).

9 For further recommendations, see my booklet *Counter-Terrorism* (Economist Brief Books, 1973) and 'The Anti-Terrorists' in the *Economist* 16 September 1972.

13 The Need for the People's Veto

1 Philip Goodhart, *Referendum* (Tom Stacey, 1971).

2 In a symposium in the *National Review*.

3 The remainder of this chapter is largely based on an article which I published in *International Review* No. 5, Summer 1975.

4 A. V. Dicey, *Introduction to the Study of the Law of the Constitution* (9th edition, Macmillan, 1948) p. 200.

5 Sir Leslie Scarman, *English Law—The New Dimension* (Stevens, 1975).

6 F. A. Hayek, *Law, Legislation and Liberty* (Routledge, 1973).

7 Frank Stacey, *A New Bill of Rights for Britain* (David & Charles, 1973).

8 Ralph Harris and Brendon Sewill, *British Economic Policy 1970-74* (Institute of Economic Affairs, London, 1975).

9 Ludwig von Mises, *Socialism* trans. J. Kahane (2nd edition, London, 1951) p. 484.

14 In Defence of Liberty

1 Burke to Richard Shackleton, 25 May 1779; *Correspondence* vol. 4, ed. J. A. Woods (Cambridge University Press, 1963) p. 79.

2 Carl L. Becker, *The Heavenly City of the Eighteenth-Century Philosophers* (Yale University Press, 1963) p. 28.

3 David Hume, *Essays* (London, 1767) vol. 2, pp. 35213.

4 Arnold Toynbee, *A Study of History*, vol. 4 (Oxford University Press, 1939) p. 6.

5 c.f. Paul Einzig, *Decline and Fall?* (Macmillan, 1969) ch. 1.

6 Toynbee, op. cit. p. 197.

15 The Logic of Breakdown

1 Alexis de Tocqueville, *Recollections* ed. J. P. Mayer, (Harvill Press,

1948) p. 16.

2   Ghita Ionescu, *The Politics of the European Communist States* (Praeger, 1968).

3   Brian Crozier, *A Theory of Conflict* (Scribner, 1974) p. 85.

4   Alexander Solzhenitsyn, *The Gulag Archipelago*, trans. Thomas P. Whitney (Collins, 1974) p. 175.

5   Quoted in Alexander Dallin and George W. Breslaver, *Political Terror in Communist Systems* (Stanford University Press, 1970) p. 10.

6   Leon Trotsky, *Terrorism and Communism* (University of Michigan, 1963) p. 23.

7   J. Gliksman, 'Social Prophylaxis as a form of Soviet Terror' in Carl J. Friedrich (ed.) *Totalitarianism* (Harvard University Press, 1954) pp. 68-9.

8   Frantz Neumann, *The Democratic and the Authoritarian State* (Free Press, 1957).

9   See Brian Crozier, 'Post-Disaster Systems' in *International Review* No. 4, Spring 1975.

10 Mario Moreira Alves has since published a book on the revolutionary possibilities in Brazil. See *A Grain of Mustard Seed: The Awakening of the Brazilian Revolution* (Doubleday, 1973).

11 See Juan J. Linz, 'The Future of an Authoritarian Situation' in Alfred Stepan (ed.) *Authoritarian Brazil* (Yale University Press, 1973).

12 For further discussions of the Brazilian model, see R. Roett (ed.) *Brazil in the Sixties* (Vanderbilt University Press, 1972); Philippe C. Schmitter, *Interest Conflict and Political Change in Brazil* (Stanford University Press, 1971) and Alfred Stepan, *The Military in Politics: Changing Patterns in Brazil* (Princeton University Press, 1971).

13 T. S. Eliot, 'Christianity and Communism' in the *Listener,* 16 March 1932.

14 Arnold Toynbee, *A Study of History,* IV, p. 184.

15 c.f. Murray Bookchin, *Post-scarcity anarchism* (Wildwood House, 1974).

16 Herbert Marcuse, *Counter-Revolution and Revolt* (Allen Lane, 1972) pp. 7, 16.

17 Ronald Segal, *The Struggle against History* (Weidenfeld, 1971) p. 15.

18 *New York Review of Books,* 12 June 1975.

19 *Le Monde,* 31 May 1975.

INDEX

Abrahams, Professor (quoted), 101
activation (subversion), 73, 75
Acton, Lord (quoted), 51
agency shop, 104
Albania, 265
Allende, Salvador, 175-91 *passim*
Altamirano, Carlos, 184
Alves, Major Vitor, 204
anarchist groups, 229
Antunes, Major Melo, 203, 204, 210
Argentina, 92, 130-2, 227, 230
Aristotle, 42
armed forces, communist infiltration of, 192
Armed Forces Movement (AFM), 192-211 *passim*
Asquith, Herbert, 102
Athens, ancient, 8, 29, 43, 242-3
Attlee, Clement, 238
AUCCTU (Soviet trade union federation), 59, 70, 71
AUEW (engineers' union), 109-11
Austria, Dollfuss regime in, 161
authoritarian rule, 10, 269-75
totalitarian rule contrasted, 10-11, 250, 264-9
Averyanov, Boris, 69-70

Balfour, Arthur (quoted), 242
ballot-rigging, in trade unions, 109-10
Banglay, Professor M., 63-4
barbarians, 278
Baudelaire, Charles (quoted), 72
Bauer, Otto, 161
BBC television, 73
Belloc, Hilaire, 124-5

Benes, Edward, 163, 165, 171, 172; quoted, 162
Benn, Anthony Wedgwood, 109, 221, 238-9
Bentham, Jeremy (quoted), 120
Berlinguer, Enrico, 73-4
Betteshanger colliery dispute, 103
'big' government, expansion of government, 47-50, 53-4; *see also*
limits of politics; state intervention
Bill of Rights, 12-13, 242, 243-5, 251
Birch, Reg, 111
Bismarck, Otto von (quoted), 150
'Black Wednesday', 112
Blum, Léon, 73
Bolingbroke, Lord (quoted), 43
Bolshevik coup (1917), 138
Born, Max (quoted), 122
Botvinov, Anatoli, 70
Boyd, John, 110
Bracher, Karl Dietrich (quoted), 153
Branco, Marshal Castelo, 272-3
Brazil, 93-4, 271-4
Bremen university, 10
Brigate Rossi, 228
Britain:
communism in, likelihood of, 13-14, 46, 100
as example of democratic breakdown, 11
failings and weaknesses of, 19-20
functions of government deranged, 47-8, 250
mass democracy in, approach

of, 36-40
parliament *see* House of
Commons; House of Lords
threat to free society in, 250-1
trade unions *see* trade unions,
British
two special features of, 12
Brittan, Samuel, 37, 125; quoted,
129
broadcasting, 73, 253
Brüning, Chancellor, 152, 153,
156, 157, 157-8
Bruno, Colonel Almeida, 196
Burke, Edmund (quoted), 39, 77,
258

Calvin, Jean, 122
capitalism, market system,
118-36, 275-6
demise of, forecast, 61-2, 101,
122-3
democracy may conflict with,
132
Carson, Sir Edward, 101
Carvalho, Otelo Saraiva de, 194*n*.,
194-5, 196, 198, 200, 202,
207-8
Castro, Fidel, 136
CDS *see* Social Democratic Centre
Central Intelligence Agency
(CIA), 75
in Britain, 59-60
in Chile, 176-7, 202, 208
Centre Point, 88
Chapple, Frank, 111
Charais, Manuel, 203, 210
Cherednichenko, Evgeny, 69
Chile, 84, 175-91
Churchill, Winston, 40, 81
CIA *see* Central Intelligence
Agency
citizenship *see* participation
civil service, 48
Clark, Colin, 130
class war, 97-8, 117
Clause IV, 66
Clementis, Dr Vladimir, 164
closed shop, 104, 106
coalition, 258

Coke, Sir Edward, 54, 242
cold war, 61
Coleridge, Samuel Taylor
(quoted), 236
collectivism, 14-15, 39, 124-5
common ownership, 66; *see also*
public ownership
communications, public, 253
communism, Marxism:
appeal of, 18, 53
in Britain, likelihood of, 13-14,
46, 100
in British trade unions, 12, 67,
107, 108, 143
democratic pretensions of, 56,
57
European expansion of, 18-19
Labour Party and, 64-5
tactics and methods of *see*
revolution; subversion
Western Communist Parties,
Soviet view of, 62
world danger of, 17
see also Soviet Union
Conservative Party, 257
conspiracy theories, 72-3, 177
constitution, British, 12-13,
242-5, 251-2
construction workers' strike
(1972), 112
Continental Operations Command
(Copcon) 196
corporatism, 116
Correia Jesuino, Commander, 205
Correia, Brigadier Pezarat, 211
Costa, Brigadier Orlando, 203
Costa Gomes, General Francisco
da, 195, 198, 204, 210
Costa Martins, Captain, 194
coups d'état, 137-61; *see also*
Chile; Czechoslovakia; Portugal
Coutinho, Admiral Rosa, 199
Crespo, Admiral, 204
Critchley, T.A., 233
Cromwell, Oliver (quoted), 242
Crossman, Richard, 17; his diaries,
251
Crozier, Brian, 10; quoted, 11,
264

Cunhal, Alvaro, 194, 196, 202
Curragh mutiny, 139
Curzon, Lord (quoted), 238
Czechoslovakia, 70, 71, 162-74

Dahrendorf, Rolf (quoted), 97
defence, 15
deficit financing, 82, 86, 87
democracy, 7-8
  alternatives to, after collapse,
    10-11
  ancient Greek views of, 41-2
  capitalism may conflict with,
    132
  destroyed by its own
    institutions, 8, 12-14
  economic, 9
  elitist theory of, 42-3
  liberal democracy and mass
    democracy distinguished, 36
  liberalism distinguished from,
    40
  and oligarchy, 46
  pluralist, 15, 118, 133, 135,
    251
  social basis of, 8-9
  subversion of, 9-10
  survey of democracies today,
    248-50
  tolerance of opposition by,
    limits to, 212-24
DGB (West German trade union
  federation), 70
Dicey, A. V. (quoted), 236, 244,
  245
dictatorship, military, 270, 274-5
  in Brazil, 271-4
'direct action', 255
diversion (subversion), 73, 74-5
Dollfuss, Engelbert, 160-1
Donovan Report, 107
dual power, 162, 184
Duvalier, Papa-Doc, 269

Ebert, Friedrich, 151, 153
economic democracy, 9
education 54, 127, 219-22
electioneering, 79-80
electoral reform, 251, 252

electricians' union, 111
Eliot, T. S. (quoted), 275
elitism, elitist theory of
  democracy, 42-3
Engels, Friedrich, 61; quoted, 137
envy, politics of, 43-4, 52, 53,
  167
equality, egalitarianism, 12, 37,
  52-3, 128
  equality of opportunity, 50,
    52, 134
  liberty contrasted with, 37,
    51-2
  oligarchy re-created by, 45-6
Erhard, Dr Ludwig, 135; quoted,
  134
European Trade Union
  Confederation (ETUC), 68
excellence, and mediocrity, 44-5

fascism, 58-9; *see also* Hitler;
  Mussolini
Fay, Stephen, 103
Feather, Vic, 71
Feltermeier, Hans, 70
Fierlinger, Zdenek, 164, 170, 172
Finley, Professor M.I., 42
FitzGibbon, Constantine, 19-20
France, 97, 99, 217-18
Freitas do Amaral, Professor
  Diogo, 205
Friedman, Milton, 127; quoted,
  50-1, 86, 90n., 94
Friedrich, Carl J. (quoted), 150-1
Frolik, Josef, 66
Fucik, Josef, 167

Galbraith, Professor, 126
Galvão de Melo, General, 198
Gaulle, General de, 152, 237
general strike:
  in Chile, 188
  of 1926, 102
  revolution and, 114-15, 188
Gensous, Pierre, 69
George-Brown, Lord, 76
Germany *see* Weimar Republic;
  West Germany
gold standard, 94-5

Gomes, Colonel Varela, 194
Gonçalves, Vasco, 193, 194, 194-5, 196, 210-11
Goodhart, Philip, 237-8
Gormley, Joe, 112
Gottwald, Klement, 164, 166, 171
government:
expansion of, *see* 'big' government
functions and responsibilities of, 47-8, 250, 255-6
limits to powers of, *see* limits of politics
Greissig, Paul Bidegain, 185
Guardian, The, 59-60, 76
Guerra, Dr Miller, 196
Guillaume, Guenther, 70

Hailsham, Lord (quoted), 247
Hart, Judith, 212
Hattersley, Roy, 65
Havenstein, Rudolf, 82
Hayek, Friedrich, 37; quoted, 40, 46-7, 51, 76, 91
Heath government (1970-4), 12, 92
Henry, Emile (quoted), 225
Hindenburg, President, 151, 157-8
Hitler, Adolf, 85-6, 148-9, 151-2, 155-6, 237; quoted, 51, 152, 152n., 155
Hobbes, Thomas, 15
Hoffmann, Karel, 72
Holland Park Comprehensive School, 219-22
House of Commons, 12-13, 239
House of Lords, 139, 242
Hume, David (quoted), 259
Hutt, Professor W. H., 79

incomes policy, 92-3
indexation, 93-4
individualism, 14-15
Industrial Relations Act (1971), 103-5
inflation, 77-8, 81-96
in Argentina, 131-2
in Chile, 182-4

in Portugal, 209
in the Weimar Republic, 81-2, 84-9
institutions, conservative, 139-40
International Communist Movement, The (Zagladin), 61
International Confederation of Free Trade Unions (ICFTU), 68, 71
inverted patriots, 56-7
Ionescu, Ghita (quoted), 264
IRA, 218, 232-4
Italy, Communist Party in, 73-4, 218

Japan, 98, 99
Jay, Peter, 80
Jenkins, Clive, 67, 99
Jenkins, Roy, 110
Jones, Jack, 108

Kapp putsch, 151, 154
Keynes, Keynesian economics, 78, 79, 81, 99
KGB, 70-1
Kilroy-Silk, Robert, 38-40
Klimov, Igor Konstantinovich, 70
Korean War, 90n.
Kozak, Jan (quoted), 164-5, 169-70, 173
Krajina, Professor Vladimir, 167-8, 168

La Rochefoucauld (quoted), 80
labour camps, Soviet, 268
labour monopolies, 100, 101, 116
Labour Party, 257
Clause IV, 66
and communist front groups, 64-5
and trade unions, 107
Laidler, Professor David (quoted), 92
law:
natural, customary, 54-5
rule of, 13, 227, 244, 265-6
trade unions and, 100, 101-6, 245-6
see also constitution

Law and Order (school discussion
pamphlet), 219-22
'Leeds United' (BBC TV
programme), 73
legitimacy, 137, 140-1
authoritarian claims to, 269-70
Lenin, 142-4; quoted:
on coercion, 267
on currency, 84
on revolutionary tactics, 142-3,
144
on trade unions, 72, 97, 107
liberal democracy, 40
collectivist threat to, 39-40
market system the precondition
for, 118
mass democracy distinguished
from, 36
survey of democracies today,
248-50
see also democracy
liberalism, 40, 214-15
liberty, 37, 46, 51-2
limits of politics, limited
government, 9, 40, 46, 48-50,
78-9, 242-5
Linz, Juan (quoted), 273
Lippmann, Walter (quoted), 9
Lipset, S.M., 140
Livy (quoted), 175
Locke, John (quoted), 95, 213
Louis XVI, 263-4
Louis Napoleon, 237
Lowell, Robert (quoted), 277
Luttwak, Edward (quoted), 138
Lüttwitz, General von, 151

Macmillan, Harold, 103
McWhirter, Ross, 76
Maine, Sir Henry (quoted), 44,
140-1
Major, Vaclav (quoted), 165
majority rule, tyranny evolved
from, 37
Malaparte, Curzio (quoted), 56,
138, 148
Mallock, W.H., 45, 46
Marchais, Georges, 56
Marcuse, Herbert, 213; quoted,

213, 276
Marighella, Carlos, 228
market system *see* capitalism
Marx, Karl, 61-2, 120, 123;
quoted, 123
Marxism *see* communism
Masaryk, Jan, 164, 172
Masetti, Albertino, 69
mass democracy, 36, 44-5, 46; *see
also* democracy
Matus, Carlos, 183
Meany, George, 68
medicine, 54
medievalism, 119-22
mediocrity, and excellence, 44-5
Meinecke, Friedrich, 150
Michels, Robert, 45
middle classes, 84-5
Mill, John Stuart, 214-15; quoted,
14, 48, 214
Milton, John (quoted), 223
miners' strike (1972), 112
minorities, disciplined, power of,
9, 46
Mises, Ludwig von, 37; quoted,
53, 116, 126, 246
monarchy, 139-40
monetarism, 90-1
money, *see* inflation
monopolies, 100; *see also* labour
monopolies
Moraes, Sergio de, 185
Movement for True Industrial
Democracy (Truemid), 254
Moynihan, Daniel, 16n.
multinational corporations, 133
Murray, Len, 85
Murry, John Middleton, 13
Mussolini, 56, 58n., 120-1, 146-8;
quoted, 121, 148

Napoleon, 145-6, 237
National Council for Civil
Liberties, 232
National Industrial Relations
Court, 104
nationalisation:
in Argentina, 131
in Britain *see* public ownership

in Chile, 180-2
Nazi party, _see_ Hitler
Neto, General Diogo, 198
Neumann, Frantz (quoted), 268
New Left, 121
Newman, Karl (quoted), 151
Northern Ireland, 232-4
Novoa, Eduardo, 181

Observer, The (quoted), 37
oligarchy, 45-6
opposition, political, need for, 8
Ortega y Gasset, José (quoted), 37, 40, 44, 248
Orwell, George, 144-5; quoted, 36, 144
Owen, Robert, 52

Paget, Sir Arthur, 139
Papen, Franz von, 157, 158, 159
parliament, British _see_ House of Commons; House of Lords
participation, public involvement in politics, 14, 252
party system, 258; _see also_ Conservative Party; Labour Party
past, the, reverence for, 77
Pastorino, Enrique, 69
peaceful coexistence, 61, 63
penetration (subversion), 73, 75
Penkovsky, 70
Pericles, 29
Perón, Juan Domingo, 130-2
Peru, 58
picketing, 112-13
Pilsudski, Marshal, 141
Pisander, 8
Plato, 41; quoted, 192
pluralism, pluralist democracy, 15, 118, 133, 135, 251
police state, 266
politics, limits to _see_ limits of politics
politics, public involvement in _see_ participation
Ponomarev, Boris, 60, 178
Portugal, 17, 18-19, 192-212
postal ballot, in trade unions, 106,

110-11
post-disaster systems, 11, 270-1
Pound, Ezra (quoted), 119
power:
    dispersal of, in democracy, 8-9, 49, 133; _see also_ limits of politics
    dual, 162, 184
    foci of, in Britain, 12
    legitimacy as source of, 137
    of trade unions, 12, 115-17
Prague _see_ Czechoslovakia
Prats, General Carlos, 187
press freedom, 9, 253
    in Chile, 184
Primo de Rivera, General, 141-2
private sphere, need for, 50-1; _see also_ property
propaganda mediation, 56-7
property, 43-4, 51, 118-36
pseudo-legality, 137-61
public interest, appeals to, 128
public involvement in politics _see_ participation
public ownership (public/state sector, state ownership), 66, 124, 129, 133-4
public philosophy _see_ values

rates, ratepayers, 247, 253
Rauschning, Hermann (quoted), 149
redistribution of wealth, 11-12, 43-4, 52, 130
Rees-Mogg, William, 77-8, 95
referendum, 236-47, 252
Reichstag fire, 160
revolution:
    general strike and, 114-15
    pseudo-legality and, 137-61
    see also Chile; Czechoslovakia; Portugal
Robbins, Lionel, 37
Russia _see_ Soviet Union

Salmon, Lord Justice, 245
Samuelson, Paul, 132
Sanches Osorio, Major, 205_n_.
Scanlon, Hugh, 108, 110-11

Scarman, Lord Justice (quoted), 55

Schleicher, General von, 151, 157, 159

Schumpeter, Joseph, 132

secessionist movements, 228-9

sedation (subversion), 73-4

'self-help' 252-5

Selznick, Philip (quoted), 161

Sen, Mahendra, 69

Sewill, Brendon, 245-6

Sharp, Clifford, 238

Shelepin, Alexander, 59, 67, 70, 71

shop stewards, 107, 107-8

Silveiro Marques, General, 198

Simons, Henry C., 105

sit-ins, 113-14

Soares, Mario, 210

Sobolev, Professor A., 62, 178

Social Democratic Centre (CDS), 204-6

social justice, 37

social services, 48

socialism, egalitarian, 12, 38-40

SOGAT, 76

Solzhenitsyn, Alexander, 278-9; quoted, 266, 278, 279

Soviet Union (Russia, USSR):
British trade with, 74
labour camps, 268
and Portugal, 197, 208-9
strategic parity with America, 15
technology of, 17-18, 129
threat to Western Europe from, 18, 59-64, 74
see also communism

Spain, 141-2, 264-5

Spartakists, 151, 153

Spencer, Herbert, 49

Spínola, Antonio de, 195-6, 198, 199, 200-3

squatters, 255

stability, precariousness of, 77

state intervention, 15, 125, 127, 128-9, 133-4; *see also* 'big' government; limits of politics

Statutory Regulation and Order 1305 (1940), 102-3

Stephen, James Fitzjames, 44-5, 214-15; quoted, 214-15

Stinnes, Hugo, 84

Strachey, John (quoted), 100-1

strikes, 97-117, 246, 252-3

subversion, 9-10, 56-76
definition, 56
'self-help' and, 254-5
Soviet classification of, 73
and violence, 226
see also pseudo-legality

supreme court, need for, 12-13, 243, 245, 251

Sutton, Anthony, 17

Sweden, 98-9

Swoboda, General Ludwig, 164, 169, 172

Tacitus (quoted), 247

Taff Vale affair, 102

Tawney, R.H. (quoted), 120

taxation, 135

Taylor, A.J.P. (quoted), 47-8

Teheran agreement, 163

territory, animals' need to establish, 136

terror, terrorism, 226, 228-35
in a police state, 266-9

Thatcher, Mrs Margaret, 257

Time Out 59-60

Tocqueville, Alexis de (quoted), 43, 223, 250, 262, 264

tolerance, limits of, 212-24

totalitarianism, 9-10
authoritarian rule contrasted, 10-11, 250, 264-9
see also communism; Soviet Union; tolerance, limits of

Toynbee, Arnold, 47, 260-1

trade, Anglo-Soviet, 74

Trade Disputes Act (1906), 101-2, 245

trade unions, British, 12, 13, 97, 99-117
ballot-rigging in, 109-10
communists in, 12, 67, 107, 108, 143, 254

east-west contacts, 64, 67-72
free society and, 106
and inflation, 90-1, 95
and Labour Party, 107
and the law, 100, 101-6, 245-6
militancy of, 108, 252-3
occupation of factories
('sit-ins'), 113-14
picketing, 112-13
postal ballots, 106, 110-11
power of, 12, 115-17
shop stewards, 107, 107-8
and violence, 111
trade unions, East European, 72
trade unions, West German, 70
Trades Union Congress, 67, 71
Trotsky, Leon (quoted), 148,
162, 267
Truemid
(Movement for True Industrial
Democracy), 254

unearned income, 135
unemployment, 79, 81, 83, 91
United States, 17, 97
USSR *see* Soviet Union
Utley, Peter (quoted), 119, 129

values, social (public philosophy),
9, 76, 277
socialist, imposition of, 38-40
Van de Haag, Ernest (quoted),
120

Vetter, Heinz, 70
Victor Emmanuel, King, 148
Vietnam, 8, 16-17, 277
violence:
political, 225-35, 255
trade unions and, 111
voucher system, in education and
medicine, 54, 127

wages prices freeze, 92-3
Watkins, Frederick M. (quoted),
157
wealth, redistribution of, 11-12,
43-4, 52, 130
Weimar Republic, 81-2, 84-9, 146,
149-60, 216-17
Welfare State, 48, 52, 54
West Germany (Federal Republic
of Germany), 10, 70, 97, 99,
134-5
Wheeler-Bennett, John, 151
Wilder, Thornton (quoted), 262
Wilkinson, Paul (quoted), 226
Woddis, Jack (quoted), 114-15
Wordsworth, William, 41
Worker's Press 59-60
World Federation of Trade Unions
(WFTU), 67, 68-72

Yugoslavia, 18, 140n.

Zagladin, V.V., 61
Zweig, Stefan (quoted), 87